Youth and the Condition of Britain

CONFLICT AND CHANGE IN BRITAIN SERIES
– A NEW AUDIT

Series Editors Paul Rock and David Downes (London School of Economics)

The series will provide reports on areas of British life conventionally conceived to be conflict-laden. It will assess the scale and character of the conflict in those areas, considering new or little heeded evidence, balancing the claims of different commentators and placing such conflict in its historical and social context, allowing intelligent judgements to be made. It will provide prognoses about the likely development of that conflict; and ascertain what measures have been taken to manage it and what success they have met with; drawing on international experience where helpful.

Later volumes will include
Nigel Fielding **The Police and Social Conflict** (1990)
Brendan O'Leary **The Politics of Antagonism: Explaining Northern Ireland** (1990)
Christopher Husbands **Race in Britain** (1990)
Frances Heidensohn **The Position of Women** (1991)
Nicholas Buck **Urban Change** (1991)
John Carrier **Health and the National Health Service** (1992)
Roy Wallis **Religious Conflict and Change** (1993)

CONFLICT AND CHANGE IN BRITAIN SERIES
– A NEW AUDIT

1
Youth and the Condition of Britain
Images of Adolescent Conflict

JOHN DAVIS

THE ATHLONE PRESS
London and Atlantic Highlands, NJ

First published 1990 by The Athlone Press Ltd
1 Park Drive, London NW11 7SG
and 171 First Avenue, Atlantic Highlands, NJ 07716

© John Davis 1990

British Library Cataloguing in Publication Data
Davis, John *1950-*
    Youth and the condition of Britain: images of adolescent conflict. –
    (Conflict and change in Britain – a new audit)
    1. Great Britain. Adolescents. Social conditions
    I. Title   II. Series
    305.2'35'0941

    ISBN 0-485-80001-2
    ISBN 0-485-80101-9 pbk

Library of Congress Cataloguing in Publication Data
Davis, John, 1950-
    Youth and the condition of Britain: images of adolescent conflict
    /John Davis.
        p. cm. – (Conflict and change in Britain: 1)
    Includes bibliographical references.
    ISBN 0-485-80001-2. – ISBN 0-485-80101-9 (pbk.)
    1. Youth – Great Britain – Social conditions.   2. Great Britain – Social
    conditions – 20th century.   I. Title.   II. Series.
    HQ799.G7D39   1990
    305.23'5'0941 – dc20

Typeset by Scarborough Typesetting Services
Printed in Great Britain by Billings, Worcester

For Bob and Lila

Contents

Acknowledgements

The history of this project has itself been a long and convoluted one and a number of debts of gratitude have been incurred along the way.

Thanks are due to Michael Lane and Stan Cohen for early inspiration and suggestions. Jon Stratton was a valued colleague. Paul Thompson made salutary comments on an earlier draft. My special thanks must go however to David Downes, not only for his extensive and invaluable editorial comment but also for his continuing belief in the viability of this work.

Finally I would like to put on record my gratitude to Teresa Tinsley for all her support, of which typing and re-typing has been only a part.

Preface

Britain is evidently undergoing rapid social change, and the language of crisis and conflict is widely used, not least by sociologists, to describe what is afoot. It is clear that crises and dissensions do exist. But it is also clear that it is often difficult to gain a sensible appreciation of their character and significance. There are fashions in reporting which over-simplify and by-pass problems of interpretation and analysis; observers sometimes have a political or journalistic stake in writing in a dramatic, exciting and perturbing way; and the uneventful does not often receive attention merely because it is unremarkable. The outcome has been surprisingly few dispassionate and systematic attempts to ascertain what exactly is meant by conflict in particular social regions, how it may be gauged, how recent or unusual it is, and how it may be set against countervailing and conciliatory processes.

'A New Audit' will be a series of reports about areas of British life conceived conventionally to be conflict-laden. It will assess the scale and character of the conflict in those areas, considering new or little heeded evidence, balancing the claims of different commentators and, placing such conflict in its historical and social context, allowing intelligent judgements to be made. It will provide prognoses about the likely development of that conflict; ascertain what measures have been taken to manage it and with what success; and draw on international experience where appropriate.

The 'youth question' continues to be a fertile source for imagery of a turbulent and at times apocalyptic character, though in the 1980's, perhaps because more major problems have intervened, levels of concern have abated somewhat. Such respite is likely to be temporary. From the 1950's to the late 1970's, youthful deviance and dissent tended to be viewed as novel portents of increasingly serious eruptions of inter-generational conflict. Yet, at the same time, studies that tended to be little regarded indicated mass adolescent conformity to core values and beliefs; and a handful of works explored the long genealogy of chronic adult dis-ease concerning youthful misconduct.

Efforts to resolve these seeming inconsistencies have been remarkable by their absence and John Davis's book – the first in our series – is a pioneering attempt to do so. It opens up the question, long apparent but little addressed in the social sciences, of how we might best pursue ways of differentiating conflict, continuity and change. Sociology is in the main locked into a cycle where the thesis that things are changing, usually for the worse but occasionally for the better, is pitted against its antithesis, the assumption of constancy, that things are *really* no different. A principal hope for this series is that its contributions stimulate a better grasp of the problems involved in either reconstituting or transcending this impasse.

David Downes
Paul Rock
London School of Economics

1
Social change and images of youth

A major theme in the popular and academic discourse on the condition and direction of post-war Britain has been provided by what, in the broadest terms, could be characterized as the 'youth question'. Academics, journalists, politicians, churchmen, social workers, members of the police force and judiciary and plain 'concerned adults' alike have all been much preoccupied with the various manifestations and imputed deeds of contemporary youth. On the face of it there has indeed been much to be preoccupied with. From the 1950s onwards British society has witnessed an explosion of youth subcultures, styles and movements and a wide range of social and cultural phenomena and 'social problems' that have been centrally associated, in one way or another, with youth.[1]

The mass media and the mechanisms of serious professional scrutiny alike – and sometimes in concert – have responded with the creation and dissemination of a wide array of images of youth and youthfulness, which have then in turn provided further material for the never-ending but constantly shifting youth question debate. (And as we now know the mass media in particular have often played a large part in the actual creation of the very phenomena and 'problems' that they have supposedly merely reported.)[2] Such images have been sometimes contradictory, sometimes entirely negative and hostile in tone and sometimes considerably more ambivalent. They have all, however, been highly spectacular and have all portrayed contemporary youth, in its various guises, as a 'new force' – for better or for worse – on the social, cultural and political scene.

Thus a range of subcultural stereotypes from Teddy boys to punks, via mods, rockers and hippies (to name but a few) has figured large at one time or another in the post-war public – and professional – imagination, as has the image of a disparate assortment of youth-related phenomena and problems such as juvenile delinquency, drug-taking, pop culture, football hooliganism, mugging and mass unemployment. The very idea of youthfulness itself has also frequently come to be detached from its original point of reference in the chronologically young and has acted as a kind of unconsciously applied shorthand for all that was (and is) seen as most wrong or right, dangerous or desirable, in modern British society. Indeed it does not seem too far-fetched to speak of a 'cult of youth' when we consider our period's excessive fascination with the idea – and reality – of youth at all of these levels and in all of these senses.

As suggested above, the highly charged and often hyperbolic presentation of the youth question to be found in the period's popular discourse is also inherent, if in a somewhat more subtle manner, in a good deal of the professional and academic literature. (And for this reason this body of literature is as much a topic for analysis as it is a resource to be drawn upon in the formulation of analyses.) The question of why, in the specific context of post-war Britain, such images of youth should be endemic will provide one of the underlying themes for this study. It may be of value at the outset, however, to review some of the recent empirical psychological and sociological work on 'normal' adolescence and youth in order to highlight the contrast between the somewhat mundane lives and attitudes of the majority of contemporary young people in actuality and the range of considerably heightened images of youth that is to be found in much of the popular and professional social theorizing of recent years. The findings of such studies point to an often considerable gap between 'image' and 'reality' in the area of the youth question: ultimately this gap is itself a phenomenon in need of explanation, and what follows below can in one sense be seen as an attempt to account for its existence and persistence.

The academic scrutiny of specific youth-related phenomena and problems has in turn often drawn upon, or at least taken for granted, a more general theoretical model – or range of models – in terms of which adolescence/youth is seen as a particularly problematic stage of the life-cycle at both individual-developmental and social levels. Theoretical work in psychology and psychoanalysis has from at least the start of the twentieth century onwards tended to portray adolescence as a period of innate and inevitable developmental 'storm and stress', while more sociological theories of adolescence and youth have laid great emphasis on the identity crisis, role confusion and contradictory socialization that are seen as typifying this stage of the life-cycle in advanced societies.[3] Each of these theoretical perspectives has been highly influential for the formation of conventional wisdom in relation to the 'problems of adolescence' and together these perspectives converge on a generalized image of the adolescent or young person as psychologically troubled or overtly delinquent, invariably in pronounced conflict with his or her elders and particularly susceptible to the generally undesirable influence of peer group and youth culture. Writ large, the prevalence of this same image contributes a great deal towards the current tendency to view 'youth' as somehow automatically constituting a 'social problem'.

Since the 1950s however, while hyperbolic images of adolescence/youth have flourished elsewhere, there has been steadily accumulating a body of survey-based and ethnographic data that calls into doubt much of the general validity of such images at both individual and social levels. The first study to consider in this respect is Douvan and Adelson's (1966) in-depth interview-based national survey of *The Adolescent Experience* amongst 3,500 American high school students in the mid-1950s. Drawing on a psychoanalytic framework and therefore still theoretically committed to a view of adolescence as an innately fraught period for psycho-sexual development, the authors nonetheless had this to say in their concluding remarks:

> The adolescent at the extremes [of the psychological and behavioural spectrum] responds to the instinctual and psycho-social upheaval of puberty by disorder, by failures of ego-synthesis and by a tendency to abandon earlier values and object attachments. In the normative [i.e. general] response to adolescence, however, we more commonly find an avoidance of inner and outer conflict, premature identity consolidation, ego and ideological constriction, and a general unwillingness to take psychic risks.
>
>   . . . The normative adolescent tends to avoid overt conflict with his family.
>
>   . . . American adolescents are on the whole not deeply involved in ideology, nor are they prepared to do much individual thinking on value issues of any generality. (Douvan and Adelson, 1966: 351–5)

From the perspective of the current study these concluding remarks should clearly be treated with a measure of caution since – to anticipate a major argument developed throughout this work – they too can be viewed in terms of the common tendency for the discussion of youth to become entangled with broader, if often submerged and implicit, issues of social commentary and critique.[4] Also there are the obvious problems of extrapolation from the case of American high school students of around thirty years ago to any more general consideration of contemporary British youth. Notwithstanding this, Douvan and Adelson's survey represents an initial step towards the challenging of the kind of theoretical over-generalization in psychology and sociology that tends, at least by implication, towards the idea that *all* or *most* young people are actually 'troubled' – or trouble – and in a state of serious conflict with adults.

A later psychoanalytically grounded survey of the psychological development of young people in the USA by Daniel Offer rejected the evaluative aspect of Douvan and Adelson's concluding remarks (and therefore their implicit social critique) whilst confirming their overall findings as to the psycho-social 'normality' of the majority of contemporary American youth:

> Certain investigators who have also observed the low level of turmoil in a large number of adolescents have interpreted their findings somewhat differently than we have. . . . Implicitly these investigators have adopted the position that lack of turmoil is a bad prognostic sign and must necessarily prevent the adolescent from developing into a mature adult. All our data, including the psychological testing, point in the opposite direction. The adolescents not only adjusted well; they were also in touch with their feelings and developed meaningful relationships with significant others.   (Offer, 1969: 184)

Offer's empirical findings on normal adolescent psychology are such as seriously to call into question, at least for the population sampled, the general validity of the psychological notion of the 'generation gap'. Thus it was found that adolescent rebellion and rebelliousness, when present at all, were generally mild only, and still occurred within the broader framework defined by parental values. Adolescent mood swings, which should, according to the storm and stress model, have been pronounced and violent, were only small. At the more directly sociological level there was a distinct *lack* of intergenerational conflict and hostility of an either latent or overt kind between adolescents and parents. In the area of values in particular, those of Offer's sample adolescents showed a marked congruence with those of parents, and this was taken by the author as a partial refutation of the then-current sociological orthodoxy, deriving from James S. Coleman's *The Adolescent Society* (1962) that there was coming into existence a distinct youth culture whose norms and values diverged in many key respects from those of 'adult society'. Finally Offer found 'gradualisn.' rather than the theoretically predicted 'volcanic eruptions' to be characteristic of adolescent psychological and social development as a whole (Offer, 1969: 185–224).

In the British context, early studies into adolescent values and intergenerational attitudes were carried out by E. M. and M. Eppel (1966) and Frank Musgrove (1964), again using questionnaire surveys and projective techniques. The general drift of this work was once more to underline the psycho-social integration and conventionality of the majority of contemporary youth – in this case in the Britain of the early 1960s – and thus to call into question much of the essentially theoretical received wisdom concerning the problematic nature of adolescence. Both studies, however, drew upon small and probably unrepresentative samples, and both suffered further from very low adult response rates.[5] The methodological shortcomings of these two works are sufficient to call into doubt their general validity, but nonetheless it is interesting to note that both the Eppels and Musgrove found that the adults they surveyed (or rather the self-selected group of concerned individuals who chose to respond) manifested a significantly greater degree of animosity towards the young than vice versa. Some twenty years later a detailed ethnographic study of an older group of working-class 'young adults' (aged between 16 and 28) growing up in the depressed north-east of England reveals the same phenomenon:

At various points in our project we examined the attitudes of our sample towards older adults: were they becoming increasingly critical of their treatment by older adults? Were they filled with anger against adult society? Were they on the point of rioting? Had they abandoned the will to work? Were they withdrawing into alternative lifestyles? What we found were non-political, pragmatic young adults who were still eager for employment even on modest wages, who were conservative on most social issues, and who had turned their frustration not against their elders but against themselves. As our study progressed, what became worthy of notice was not hostility to or a retreat from the world of older adults by our sample, but the abuse of power and position by many adults who belittled, humiliated and derided young people. (Coffield *et al.*, 1986: 209)

However, such conclusions are perhaps not as surprising as they might initially appear: if, as this study will seek to demonstrate, there is a common tendency for adults to *project* fears – and sometimes hopes – about the state of contemporary society on to the screen (as it were) that is provided by the youth question, then one would indeed expect many adults to subscribe to a somewhat heightened and often negative image of 'contemporary youth' and perhaps act accordingly. If, furthermore, 'contemporary youth' is in fact considerably more conventional and conformist in its attitudes than is often supposed, then one might also expect this heightening of image and negativity of sentiment to be largely unreciprocated in the adolescent view of adult society.

Since the early work of Musgrove and the Eppels on the psychology, attitudes and values of 'normal' young people, a number of methodologically sounder pieces of research have all tended to further underscore the essential conformity and conventionality of the mass of contemporary British youth. One of the most extensive surveys in this area was conducted in the mid-1970s as the third follow-up of the National Child Development Study (Fogelman, 1976), itself a long-term project based on the periodic surveying of a cohort of children made up of all those born in Great Britain (approximately 17,000 in number) in one week in 1958. This cohort had reached the age of 16 in 1974, when it was re-surveyed not merely to gather data of a purely descriptive nature (family size and structure, material standards in the home, schooling, leisure activities, health, etc.) but also for quality of relationships within, and attitudes towards, the family and the school. The picture that emerged here was not only one of 'conventional youth' but also of the existence of a high degree of intergenerational accord, at least *within the family unit*.

As a measure of the state of relationships within the family, cohort parents were presented with a list of issues on which it is commonly thought parents and 16-year-olds might disagree and asked to report how often they argued with their 'study child' on these issues. Dress or hairstyle and time of coming in at night or going to bed proved to be the most common sources of intergenerational stress, but even on these questions 54 per cent and 66 per cent respectively of the 11,531 respondent parents 'never or hardly ever disagreed' with their children. On what one might expect to be such contentious issues as choice of friends of the same sex, choice of friends of the opposite sex, places visited in own time, smoking and drinking, the overwhelming majority of parents reported 'never or hardly ever disagreeing' with their adolescent offspring (81 per cent, 89 per cent, 85 per cent and 94 per cent respectively).

The 'study children' themselves were also asked to indicate how true or untrue they found a number of statements concerning their relationship with their parents; again over 80 per cent (N = 11,045) thought it either 'very true' or 'true' that they got on well with both parents (Fogelman, 1976: 35). As far as family relationships were concerned, then, the authors of this survey summed up their conclusions thus:

> The concept of the 'generation gap' is part of popular mythology. However there is little evidence for its widespread existence among our figures. The great majority of both parents and children reported harmonious family relationships. The latter's physical appearance was the most commonly reported cause of friction.
>
> The young people's intentions regarding their own future family life were remarkably conventional. Just three to four per cent did not want children, over half having two children as their preferred family size.   (Fogelman, 1976: 60)

The attitude of the study group towards school – and it is worth noting that it formed part of the first-year group required to remain in full-time education until the age of 16 – was on the whole rather less positive than that expressed towards parents and family relationships.

Thirty per cent say they do not like school and thirteen per cent that they do not take schoolwork seriously. As many as eleven per cent said they felt school to be largely a waste of time, although there was strong disagreement with this from a majority. Homework is clearly not at all popular, with 54% thinking that 'it's a bore'. (Fogelman 1976: 51)

However, as its authors point out, this study still revealed disaffectedness with school to be an essentially minority phenomenon:

The figures taken overall [do not] present too discouraging a picture. A majority of these young people do not feel that school is a waste of time, say that they get on with their work in the classroom and take work seriously, like school and are willing to help their teacher. (Fogelman, 1976: 52)

The conclusions of the National Child Development Study follow-up are clearly subject, in as far as they purport to tell us about attitudes and actual behaviour, to all of the usual problems associated with the use of surveys based on subjects' self-reports. Nonetheless this research still remains as a valuable corrective to the wilder flights of speculation concerning the 'unconventional', 'radical', 'oppositional' and/or 'problematic' nature of British youth that were widely current in the 1970s, as in every other decade of the post-war period.

More recently John Nicholson's survey of the subjective experience of the various stages of the human life-cycle from cradle to grave has added further weight to many of the points already made above as to the 'normality' of most young people as revealed by empirical research.[6] Indeed Nicholson locates his own findings on the experience of adolescence and youth in contemporary Britain, and on adolescent values and attitudes, in the wider context provided by the kind of empirical study so far considered:

Many large scale surveys of adolescents' attitudes have been carried out in Europe and America over the last 20 years and their results show a remarkable degree of uniformity. Whatever parents may think – and two thirds of the adults we interviewed in Colchester were convinced that the younger generation had an approach to life very different from their own – adolescents are more worried about incurring their parents' disapproval than about falling out with their friends. Moreover, on the big issues

like moral or political beliefs, adolescents are more in tune with
their parents than with their peers.   (Nicholson, 1980: 78)

Nicholson's research revealed very little evidence in support of
the theoretical conceptions – quite fundamental in this area – of the
existence of a generation gap and the prevalence of adolescent
rebellion[7]:

> When children are questioned, almost 90% of 16 year olds say
> that they get on well with their mothers, and three quarters of
> them say the same about their fathers. . . . When college
> students are asked to look back over their adolescence, only a
> quarter of them describe it as a period of rebelliousness.
> (Nicholson, 1980: 81)

Nicholson argues that it is the mass media and professional
psychology and psychiatry that are chiefly responsible for the
propagation of what he regards as the myth of the problematic
nature of adolescence, and even goes so far as to suggest that a fair
deal of actual adolescent 'awkwardness' might be attributable to
adult expectations:

> Many [adolescents] spontaneously say that they are very aware
> that adults expect them to be difficult, and some even admit that
> they occasionally make a conscious effort to fall in with these
> expectations, behaving badly not because they want to but simply
> because they feel it is expected of them.   (pp. 81–5)
>   . . . In short one important reason why some adolescents have
> problems is simply that their parents and teachers expect them to
> have problems.   (pp. 83–4)

Two other more-or-less contemporary in-depth social psychological investigations bear further witness to the overwhelming
normality of the vast majority of contemporary British youth, and
therefore to the often considerable gulf between image and reality
in this area. In the first of these Tom Kitwood and his assistants
conducted open-ended interviews with a broadly representative
sample of 153 male and female 14–17-year-olds from both urban
and rural areas of England, with the general objective of research-
ing into adolescent values (Kitwood, 1980). The picture revealed by

this research is once again at substantial variance with many of the central tenets of the theoretical psychology and sociology of adolescence and indeed with a good deal of conventional wisdom. Thus it was found that TV and pop music, far from being all-pervasive influences, could only be viewed as 'background noise' in adolescent life and that the adolescents interviewed, contrary to the predictions of much developmental psychology, were in fact little concerned with abstract ideals and ideas. Similarly the research sample manifested a relatively low level of preoccupation with sex and little evidence could be found of the much-vaunted adolescent 'quest for identity' (Kitwood, 1980: 112–18). Once again intergenerational relations within the family emerge as more harmonious than is commonly supposed: on the basis of his findings Kitwood argues that 'any stereotype of contemporary adolescents as being typically in revolt against their parents is incorrect' (p. 124). Overall, the conclusion is that:

> The participants in this inquiry did not show much resemblance to the adolescent of the popular stereotype: they were not mindless consumers, practitioners of violence and sensuality, rebels against all authority, degenerate, feckless or lazy.   (p. 280)

Finally John C. Coleman's interview-based investigation into *The Nature of Adolescence* (1980) provides yet more corroboration – if any should now be needed – for the 'conventional' image of adolescence that emerges out of survey research.[8] This review of what would seem to be the perennial findings of such research can perhaps appropriately be concluded with some of Coleman's own concluding remarks:

> . . . research provides little support for current theories [of adolescence] and fails to substantiate much of what both psychoanalysts and sociologists appear to believe. To take some examples, while there is certainly some change in the self-concept, there is no evidence to show that any but a small minority experience a serious identity crisis. In most cases relationships with parents are positive and constructive, and young people, by and large, do not reject adult values in favour of those espoused by the peer group. In fact, in most situations peer group values appear to be consistent with those of important

adults, rather than in conflict with them. Fears of promiscuity among the young are not borne out by research findings, nor do studies support the belief that the peer group encourages anti-social behaviour, unless other factors are also present. Lastly, there is no evidence to suggest that during the adolescent years there is a higher level of psychopathology than at other times . . . the great majority of teenagers seem to cope well and to show no undue signs of turmoil or stress. (p. 178)

It should be abundantly clear by now that the generally mundane picture of normal adolescence as revealed by empirical work is a long way from the 'problematic' view of this stage of the life-cycle to be found in a great deal of psychological and sociological theorizing. As Coleman again states:

There would appear to be a sharp divergence of opinion therefore between what have been called the 'classical' and 'empirical' points of view. . . . Beliefs about adolescence which stem from theory (the 'classical' view) do not in general accord with the results of research (the 'empirical' view). (p. 178)

By the same token the various highly spectacular *images* of adolescence and youth that have permeated both professional and popular analyses of post-war British society are now also revealed as, at the very least, highly unrepresentative of the vast majority of contemporary young people in reality. The question now arises as to why this gap between theoretical and empirical points of view and between 'image' and 'reality' should be so widespread and pervasive a feature of the academic and popular discourse on the youth question. A number of distinct but nonetheless closely interrelated factors would seem to be involved here; for clarity's sake these can be considered under three general headings:

Over-theorization

As has already been pointed out, the 'problematic' view of adolescence and youth to be found in much of the academic discourse derives at base from certain theoretical assumptions concerning the 'developmental tasks' of this stage of the life-cycle, the 'given' nature of adolescent storm and stress, adolescent identity quest, the generation gap, etc. Such assumptions have enjoyed currency for at least as long as social scientists have identified this period of the life-cycle as a distinct object of study, and indeed have come to constitute a generally taken-for-granted orthodoxy for both professional and – by diffusion – popular theorizing alike. They have moreover – and this may be one reason for their power – tended to be accorded the special prestige and prominence associated with social scientific work of an essentially speculative and theoretical, as opposed to applied and empirical, nature. The parallel tradition of empirical study into the life and values of contemporary youth – whether 'normal' or 'problem' – that has existed alongside the theoretical tradition has tended, perhaps simply because of the generally unspectacular nature of its findings, to occupy a far less prominent position in the popular – and perhaps professional – imagination.

It is interesting to note that, in the British context at least, much of the close ethnographic work that has been carried out among deviant or problem youth still produces an essentially mundane and unspectacular picture. Such studies as Parker's *View from the Boys* (1974) reveal 'juvenile delinquents' as mere 'dead-end kids' trying to get by and 'make things happen' under extremely constricting circumstances, and engaged in only intermittent and often petty deviant activity: a long way indeed from the colourful and thoroughgoing outlaws and rebels or the dangerous and mindless hooligans of myth.[9] The ethnographic aspect of the work of Paul Corrigan (1979) and Paul Willis (1978) on working-class 'near delinquent' youth reveals what is in many respects a similarly unspectacular picture, which sits, however, somewhat uneasily with the more grandiose objectives of these authors at the social-critical and theoretical levels.

The obvious point to make, then, is quite simply that many of the major and fundamental theoretical assumptions concerning the problematic nature of adolescence in contemporary society are just that: a set of interrelated hypotheses deriving from more general theoretical models dealing with the socialization process, developmental stages, the social-psychological problems of advanced industrial/late capitalist society, etc. Such hypotheses have by and large come to be derived from theory, with in the first instance little by way of empirical interrogation. For a variety of reasons, however, some of which have already been mentioned and some of which will be explored more fully below, they have come to be widely accepted as though they were statements about the reality of contemporary adolescence and youth as commonly lived out and experienced. As noted above, when these various hypotheses on the problematic nature of this period of the life-cycle are put to the empirical test then they fail to hold for the majority of contemporary British youth.

At another level it is possible to see a similar over-commitment to a particular theoretical stance and a consequent neglect or glossing over of inconvenient aspects of the empirical domain in much of the recent British sociology of youth, especially the 'new subcultural theory' of the Birmingham Centre for Contemporary Cultural Studies and associates.[10]

Thus despite their avowed and commendable objective of locating each specific subculture in socio-historical context, theorists in this tradition often seem in fact to impose an 'external' – and often highly convoluted – line of theoretical explanation upon the empirical phenomena that they set out to analyse. The fundamentally neo-Marxist and semiological perspectives of the 'new subcultural theory' too often seem to lead to a situation in which its proponents *start out* with certain theoretical assumptions – most notably and centrally the 'resistance through rituals' thesis that (all) working-class youth subcultural phenomena, whether in the realm of style (mods' scooters, punks' safety pins . . .) or of action (riots, hooliganism . . .) can be read as 'symbolic', 'displaced' (. . . etc.) manifestations of the class struggle and the contradictions of capitalism – and *work back* from this to the empirical domain, when it is by no means always clear that the latter can in fact sustain the theoretical demands that are being made of it.[11] (My general point here is not to deny the absolute indispensability of theory as such to the sociological enterprise: it should rather be seen as a plea for theory and empirical investigation to be brought into closer and more mutually beneficial interrelationship.)

This problem of over-theorization perhaps emerges most acutely in those solidly empirically based examples of the new subcultural theory that take as their starting point the ethnographic study of the life of groups of working-class youth and their relations with authority, e.g. Robbins and Cohen (1978), Corrigan (1979), Willis (1978) and Humphries (1981). Here the ethnography itself is generally sensitively handled and highly revealing; the trouble arises, however, when its 'findings' are all too readily and too exclusively located within the explanatory framework provided by the 'resistance through rituals' thesis. Is it really always necessary – or sufficient – for example, to explain the conflict between working-class school kids and their teachers, in all of its many and varied forms, through the invocation of an elaborate theory of historical class struggle or the contradictions of capitalism?[12]

In short, it would seem that the extent to which (any given) youth subcultural phenomenon can be interpreted as 'resistance through rituals' – and therefore as somehow ultimately *political* – is essentially a question to be resolved empirically rather than assumed at the outset. This would involve a more detailed scrutiny of subcultural members' own individual and collective attitudes *and* behaviour than has been attempted to date. It is likely that whereas subcultural formation, affiliation and behaviour can in fact be seen as 'symbolic' and/or 'political' in some cases (and for some individuals and groups), in others it will prove to be far more a simple question of fashion, imitation and commercial exploitation. The following remarks from a 14-year-old girl in Nicholson's (1980) Colchester study say a great deal about the limitations of the applicability of the idea of 'resistance through rituals' to the explanation of spectacular subcultures in the Great Britain of the late 1970s at least:

> I became a mod because Mum wanted me to, really. She'd seen mods in the street and thought they looked smart. And she said 'Why don't you turn mod?' So I said Yeah, if you'll buy me the clothes. So she bought me them. I'm glad I'm a mod.   (p. 87)

Over-emphasis on the problematic and spectacular

As a number of commentators have noted, the theoretical conception of adolescence as a period of psychological turmoil has depended in some large measure for its empirical validation upon the clinical experience of psychiatrists and psychoanalysts. Yet the task of such professionals is by definition the processing of those deemed psychologically disturbed, and as such it is hardly surprising that a picture of adolescent storm and stress should emerge from the clinical data (see Offer, 1969: 174–92; J. C. Coleman, 1980: 179). By focusing its – and our – attention on *problem adolescents*, psychiatry – and to a lesser extent academic psychology as a whole – has tended to produce a one-sided 'problematic' view of *adolescence*; a view which has moreover often, and quite falsely, come to be taken as typical for the adolescent population as a whole.

What is in many respects a similar process has also been at work in sociology. Traditionally the discipline has tended to take for granted the general idea of 'youth as a social problem' and has largely concerned itself at an empirical level with the investigation of specific, undoubtedly genuinely (social) problematic aspects of the youth question, until recently largely within the framework of the sociology of education and the sociology of deviance and delinquency.[13] As Coffield, Borrill and Marshall remark in the introduction to their ethnography of conventional working-class youth in the north-east of England in the early 1980s:

> . . . the standard approach of the mass media and professional conferences on adolescence . . . tend[s] to sensationalize the scabrous deeds of a few rampant or exotic adolescents. Too often discussions of young people are confined to a catalogue of 'teenage problems' such as glue sniffing, schoolgirl pregnancies, vandalism, aggro and delinquency. In contrast our fieldwork constantly underlined the essential normality and conformity of most young adults. (Coffield *et al.*, 1986: 1–2)

Here again can be discerned the same broad tendency to focus attention on the 'problematic' at the expense of the 'normal'; a tendency which is perfectly understandable, and which may even be necessary or inescapable if social scientific investigation is seen as going in tandem with the formulation of social policy. Nonetheless it remains a tendency that has often contributed towards the generalization of an unwarrantedly 'purple' image for youth as a whole.

Even those more recent schools of sociological thought that quite explicitly reject the moral absolutism and adult middle-class bias inherent in much of the traditional 'social problems' approach to the study of youth – consider the application of labelling or transactional perspectives in this area and, in the British context in particular, the attempts of the new subcultural theorists to combine these with a rigorous Marxist political economy – still tend, however, to promote a similar over-generalization.[14] In this case this is a result not so much of an overriding concern for the (supposedly) socially problematic aspects of the youth question, as a concentration of analysis, and therefore of the professional imagination, upon the working-class youth subcultures that have been so visible a feature of the post-war British scene.

For this latter approach, then, concern for youth as a *social* problem has been to some considerable extent displaced by interest in youth as a *sociological* problem: the seemingly unprecedented proliferation of youth subcultures in contemporary Britain and the intensity of social reaction to these has undoubtedly posed major problems of explanation which the new subcultural theorists and others have attempted to meet.

The imputed doings of such groupings of contemporary youth have also, almost from the beginning of the post-war era, provided a great deal of 'ideal copy' for the mass media. In this way spectacular subcultures have come to loom even larger in the discourse surrounding the youth question as a whole, and the sheer normality of post-war British youth in general has been yet further obscured. Theorizing on the topic of youth has, in short, come to be over-fascinated with and over-reliant upon the idea of *youth subculture*, where this is in fact a concept of only limited utility and applicability. As Kitwood has written concerning the relationship between his study of 'normal' adolescence (see above) and the analysis of youth subculture:

> The observations made in this research . . . do not contradict those of specific subcultural studies though two qualifying comments must be made. First since most boys and girls do not belong to clearly defined subcultures, subcultural phenomena cannot be used as major keys to the interpretation of normal adolescent life. Second, for those who do belong to a subculture, it can be misleading to characterize their existence solely on that basis.   (Kitwood, 1980: 278)

The second point above is particularly important in that it raises the issue of what could be characterized as the 'over-committed image' of subcultural affiliation – and the consequent reification of the concept of subculture – that is at least implicit in much of the contemporary sociology of youth. The new wave of subcultural theory has not been so naive as to assume that, for the majority of those who are involved in youth subculture, 'membership' is anything other than marginal and transitory (Hall and Jefferson, 1976: 16). Such a disclaimer, however, still rests on the assumption that there is, for every spectacular subculture, a 'hard core' of individuals for whom over an extended period subcultural membership constitutes a core identity or master status (and for whom such membership may therefore transcend a mere leisure-time activity). This may or may not be the case but once again it would seem to be a topic in need of empirical investigation. (Certainly for perhaps the majority – as has been argued above – in this era of youth subcultural revivalism and diversity, subcultural affiliation would seem to be as much a matter of passing fashion as anything else.) The whole area of the way in which youth subcultural affiliation 'fits' into biographical and existential time has yet to be explored, as has the closely related topic of its role in the construction, (re)negotiation and possibly transformation of individual and collective identity.[15]

Projection

Finally, and most fundamentally of all, the considerable hyperbole so often associated with images of youth at all levels and in both popular and professional discourse can be explained, along with the sheer *volume* of concern over youth in our society, through the idea of *projection* or *youth-as-metaphor*. Thus it has been argued by A. C. H. Smith *et al.* in their (1975) study of the news coverage of the *Daily Express* and the *Daily Mirror* in the post-war period up until 1965 that:

> Youth was in both papers, and, perhaps in the whole press of the period (continuing right into the 1970s) a powerful but concealed *metaphor* for social change: the compressed image of a society which had crucially changed in terms of basic life styles and values – changed in ways calculated to upset the official political framework, but ways not yet calculable in traditional political terms.

In more general terms, in their theoretical introduction to *Resistance Through Rituals*, John Clark, Stuart Hall, Tony Jefferson and

Brian Roberts have described the growth in significance of the category of 'youth' in post-war Britain thus:

> Youth appeared as an emergent category in post-war Britain, one of the most striking and visible manifestations of social change in the period. 'Youth' provided the focus for official reports, pieces of legislation, official interventions. It was signified as a social problem by the moral guardians of society – 'something we ought to do something about'. Above all youth played an important role as a cornerstone in the construction of understandings, interpretations, and quasi-explanations of the period. (Hall and Jefferson, 1976: 9)

This is an invaluable theoretical lead and one whose implications have yet to be thoroughly explored. The starting point for much of the sociological and historical analysis in the chapters that follow is that the youth question – since at least the turn of the century but especially in the post-war period – has served as a kind of 'screen' upon which social commentators and analysts of all ideological and theoretical persuasions have 'projected' far more general hopes and fears concerning the condition and future of our society as a whole. The particular power and persistence of exaggerated and unrepresentative images of youth – with widely differing *content* and specific points of reference – can only be fully understood with reference to the central, but essentially indirect or metaphorical role that such images have generally played in the more extensive project of making sense of a seemingly rapidly and fundamentally changing social order.[16] To this extent the often hidden projective dimension in the youth question discourse can be said to underlie the tendencies to over-theorization and over-generalization in analyses in this area as discussed above: over-theorized, over-generalized and generally exaggerated images of youth have been *so* prolific and *so* widely and uncritically accepted in some large part because of their 'metaphorical fit' with more far-ranging perceptions of the period's major trends and transformations.

Objectively speaking there have certainly been youth-related social problems aplenty in modern British society. It is also an objective fact that the post-war period has witnessed the emergence on an unprecedented scale of 'youth' in all its manifestations and sub-groupings, as a distinct, highly visible and much remarked-upon social entity. Nonetheless it is also undeniable that the voluminous body of popular and professional theorizing that has appeared post war on the topics of 'youth', 'the younger gener-ation', 'the generation gap', etc., is on the whole characterized by a quite marked degree of over-generalization, over-simplification, exaggeration, paranoia and sometimes blind admiration. This gulf between the often fairly mundane objective realities of 'youth in post-war British society' and the often highly coloured images projected on to youth by adult society, especially when amplified by the mass media, is in itself both indicative of and also explicable in terms of the way in which statements about youth have (often unconsciously) fed into the formulation of broader social diagnoses during what has often seemed to be a particularly perplexing period.

It is this utility of statements about youth for the making of disguised and more general points concerning the projected future of society (for good or for ill, dependent roughly upon the author's radicalism or conservatism) that renders the discussion of the younger generation, with all of its associated hyperbole, such a staple form for social critics and analysts. As such, the use of the discussion of youth as a technique for conservative social criticism and the expression of more generalized social anxieties may well have a lengthy history. The following passage, possibly apocryphal but attributed to a thirteenth-century German monk, can perhaps be taken as one example of this perennial phenomenon:

> The world is passing through troublesome times. The young people of today think of nothing but themselves. They have no reverence for parents or old age. They are impatient of all restraint. They talk as if they alone know everything. (Booker, 1970: 144)

Such statements still have a very contemporary ring to them.

The major analyst of this phenomenon of the minority stereotyp-ing *en masse* of the younger generation has been Edgar Z. Friedenberg. Speaking of the USA of the 1950s Friedenberg argued that the concept of the 'teenager' had come for adult society to represent a 'hot blooded minority stereotype' (of which another better-known example would be 'the negro') which, 'though affected by the actual characteristics of the minority group develops to fit the purposes and express the anxieties of the dominant group', i.e. of middle-class adults (Friedenberg, 1963: 149). As with the imputed characteristics of 'the negro', those of Friedenberg's stereotypical teenager represented an inversion and subversion of bourgeois convention:

> Here is a people that are usually carefree, exuberant, long of limb and fleet of foot. Noted for athletic and (it is whispered) sexual prowess, they are nonetheless essentially childlike, irresponsible and given to outbursts of unrestrained violence.   (Friedenberg, 1959: 131)

This minority stereotyping of the teenager/adolescent which as Friedenberg pointed out was remarkable indeed, considering that the group thus identified was in part made up of the sons and daughters of the *dominant* adult group, became intelligible on consideration of the supposed alienation of 1950s middle-class society.

> I do believe that the growth of hostility toward the adolescent is one more index of the rootlessness of modern life; of the intense need for status in a society which provides few stable guarantees of respect on which a sense of personal wealth can be based.
>   . . . The role of the adolescent in adult imagery and feeling is [therefore] to remind us what might have been expected of adult life.   (Friedenberg, 1959: 131)

In the USA of the 1950s and 60s, and to a lesser extent in Great Britain over the same period, the widespread minority stereotyping of the young led on occasion to the formation of a generic image of youth in which the categories of 'teenager' and 'juvenile delinquent' were collapsed and merged into one. *All youth* was seen as at least potentially delinquent – writing in the early 60s Friedenberg noted that, 'in my experience it is just not possible to discuss adolescence with a group of American adults without being forced onto the topic of juvenile delinquency', and this in turn was perceived as another symptom of a fundamentally disturbed social order (Friedenberg, 1963: 151). In Friedenberg's view, and this is an insight which can be applied in a more general and sociological sense to a whole range of images of youth, the prevalence of social concern over juvenile delinquency at this time had to be viewed as the product not only of objective but also of subjective factors:

> Young people today find themselves very often used as something between a charade and a Thematic Apperception Test. Adults read their own hopes and fears into the actions of adolescents, and project onto them their own conflicts, values and anxieties. . . . The youngsters in their turn respond to the mistrust with even more vigour than could reasonably have been expected, living up to adult expectations with really impressive viciousness.
>
> It is not that adult fears are groundless, or without substantial foundation. The adolescent behaviour that disturbs them really occurs and is really disturbing. However, the adult response to the way adolescents act seems often to be influenced more by the adult's own unconscious needs and tensions than by what the adolescents are actually doing. The most obvious example is the popular outcry about juvenile delinquency. (Friedenberg, 1959: 114)[17]

Against the possibility of such blanket condemnation and perhaps also fear of the young it is necessary, however, to set an opposite tendency, also seemingly to a degree inherent in the discussion and 'stereotyping' of youth: that of adult idealization, admiration and even emulation. This is the *cult of youth* in its purest and most positive form, which has in various manifestations been a notable feature of post-war British culture.

Thus the concept of youth can also present the image – if not the reality – of the 'pre-corrupted', i.e. pre-socialized, pre-acculturated individual, and radical-progressive social critique has often used the portrayal of contemporary youth and its 'potential' to point the way towards a better future.[18] This process represents in many ways the *inverse* of the minority stereotyping of youth outlined above (which, of course, embodies an essentially pessimistic and dystopian view of 'where society is going to'). The way in which this highly positive image of youth came to assume a position of particular prominence and significance in the period from the late 1950s till the early 1970s will be explored in due course. In practice, however – and this has certainly been the case in post-war Britain – the totality of attitudes towards and images of youth will often embrace elements of 'love' and 'hate' simultaneously with one pole or the other tending to gain ascendancy at certain moments.

It is important to remember, then, that the exact nature of the metaphorical relationship between given images of youth and the process of making sense of social change is open to a considerable degree of variability. (And that not all images of youth have simply reflected a negative view of the condition of the nation.) Thus, in the contemporary British context, youth has been variously seen not merely as the *product* of social change but also as its *epitome*, a portent now of how things will soon be for the whole of society. Sometimes this line of thinking has been taken even further and youth has been seen as the *active vanguard*, shaping through its efforts the future of society (see introduction to Hall and Jefferson, 1976). (This phenomenon is of course in part an objective one, at least at the level of *cultural innovation*. Certain sectors of post-war British youth have enjoyed an unprecedented degree of emancipation from adult constraint, both economically and otherwise, and have therefore been able to fashion – within limits – their own mode of existence. It is also at least arguable that cultural changes originating with youth have in time found their way into 'mainstream' adult culture. The much-vaunted role of youth as an active and significant *political* force in recent years is however a far more debatable question.)

Irrespective of the objective realities of what may actually be happening to youth or what youth may be doing, images *projected on to* youth are often closely connected with what seems most uniquely new about the present – and therefore what is regarded as being most wrong or right (or both) with contemporary society – and what seems to have changed the most, for worse or for better, since the bad or good old days when the adult generation was itself young. Specific images of youth will then vary in the metaphorical relationships that they bear to wider currents of (perceived) change in society at any given historical moment. More than this, however, it should be also borne in mind that most images of youth, or constellations of images of youth with a common point of focus, will tend to reflect a social response that is, overall, *ambivalent*. If images of youth, and constellations of images, are linked to broader perceptions of social change, it is perhaps not surprising that they should embody many of the contradictions that are present in adult society in attitudes towards social change itself.[19]

As will be explored in detail in the following chapters, the very ambivalence and contradictoriness of the totality of images of youth in post-war British society – or at least in the period from around 1955 to 1975 – can be seen in part as a product of a more generalized sense of ambivalence concerning where society was going. The 'boom years', spanning the late 1950s and most of the 1960s, were in particular a time when it was commonly held that the old social order was in many ways *changing for the better*: it is in this period that there can be found the high concentration of positive and 'progressive' images of youth that constitutes the peak of the post-war cult of youth. At the same time, however, although all agreed that society was changing as perhaps never before, by no means everyone saw this in so favourable a light: hence at the height of the positive cult of youth there can nonetheless be found some very negative images and evaluations indeed. Such images in fact stood out in even sharper relief at this time as youthful deviance became less readily explicable in material terms: if, as many believed, society was improving in so many ways, why was youth refusing to be grateful and conform?

In part the ratio of positive to negative in any given image or constellation of images will be determined in relation to the wider ideological set and value-system of its author(s), but in part it will also vary according to the general 'mood of the times'; in part the embodiment of contradiction may be innate to images of youth in any complex and rapidly changing society. Indeed this very ability to embrace many levels of ambiguity, ambivalence and even contradiction is probably one of the sources of the metaphorical strength and flexibility of the concept of youth, and of the high degree of prominence that is currently accorded by our society to the youth question at all its levels.

Since the Second World War what can be termed the *youth spectacle* has come to occupy a prominent position in the overall output of the mass media. At the same time the youth question in its various manifestations has much preoccupied the thoughts of professional social analysts. When we examine the specific phenomena that have attracted this attention however, e.g. the Teddy boys, rock 'n' roll, angry young men, CND, teenagers, mods and rockers, 'Swinging London', hippies, students, counter culture, skinheads, football hooligans, unemployed school leavers, punks, yuppies etc., what becomes apparent is not merely the sheer disproportion of volume of media output devoted to such images – when there were and are in most cases far more important things going on in the life of the nation – but also the general degree of overstatement almost invariably associated with them.[20] Nor has much of the 'serious' academic and professional scrutiny of youth been immune from similar tendencies to over-fascination, simplification and generalization.

The way should now be clear to commence an explanation of the special prominence and significance that has come to be occupied in our society by the emergent concepts and categories of adolescence and youth. This can be understood as the product of an ongoing interaction between objective and subjective factors. *Objectively*, as will be traced in subsequent chapters, a process has been in motion since at least the nineteenth century whereby adolescence/ youth has increasingly come to be separated out as a distinct phase of the human life-cycle. This process has been given additional impetus in the post-war period through such factors as the rise of the teenage consumer and the spread of secondary and higher education. *Subjectively*, again since at least the previous century but perhaps finding special impetus from the 1950s onwards, images of youth have been variously and widely employed in the projective manner discussed above as an expression of more generalized diagnoses of the state of the nation. The discussion will now proceed to a detailed examination of the interplay of objective and subjective factors in the emergence and rise to prominence of adolescence and youth.

2
The history of pre-adulthood

All societies seem to possess some kind of model of (and therefore set of taken-for-granted assumptions about) the 'ages of man', whereby the basic biological given of human progression from birth to death is subdivided and structured overall, and thus used as a principle for social differentiation and organization. Everywhere the human life-cycle has come, in various ways and to varying degrees, to be subdivided into a number of 'ages', the distinctive nature of each of which is continually objectified through the processes of social interaction, and which may furthermore come to be formally organized and institutionalized. In the anthropological literature the convention is that such 'ages' be referred to as *age-grades*, a term that was first suggested by A. R. Radcliffe-Brown in a letter to *Man* in 1929:

> This term should be kept for the recognised division of the life of an individual as he passes from infancy to old age. Thus each person passes successively into one grade after another, and, if he lives long enough, through the whole series – infant, boy, youth, young married man, elder, or whatever it may be.   (Radcliffe-Brown, 1929: 21)

Considered cross-culturally and historically, age-grading systems are subject to a marked degree of variability. The number and nature of age grades and the social roles thus demarcated, the relation of any given age grade to others, the mode of transition from one age grade to the next, these and many other age-grading arrangements exist in unique configuration in each society.[1] Similarly there is considerable variability in the nature of the *mesh* of age-grading systems with other aspects of social structure and in the extent to which, for any given society, age grading can be regarded as a particularly significant criterion for social organization.[2]

In our own society the most fundamental age-grading division of all is that between childhood and adulthood. Since the seminal arguments of Philippe Aries we have become aware that the crystallization of this division is itself a historically and socially relative phenomenon, the outcome of the rise of the modern family and the rise of the modern educational system, trends which from around the seventeenth century onwards have served progressively to remove the child from the life of adult society at large. 'Family and school together removed the child from adult society', according to Aries (1973: 397)[3]

Indeed the central argument of what has come to be known as 'the Aries thesis' is that in the Middle Ages what we know as childhood *simply did not exist*, at least at the conceptual level. Thus Aries has written:

> In medieval society the idea of childhood did not exist, this is not to suggest that children were neglected, forsaken or despised. The idea of childhood is not to be confused with affection for children, it corresponds to an awareness of the particular nature that distinguished the child from the adult, even the young adult. In medieval society this idea was lacking.   (Ibid., p. 125)[4]

Recent detailed historical work has tended to cast doubt on the assertion that the pre-modern period lacked *any* kind of conceptual awareness of the distinct nature of childhood.[5] What seems certain, however, is that while childhood remained relatively undifferentiated in terms of *formal institutionalization*, so too the specifically modern 'scientific' awareness of childhood as an object for special professional scrutiny – and intervention – remained little developed. This situation was to change dramatically in the period from the seventeenth to the twentieth centuries. As Pinchbeck and Hewitt (1969) have written in their history of childhood in English society:

> Just as the institutional development and acceptance of formal education in schools with the consequent isolation of the child from adult society was a pre-requisite of the emergence of modern sociological and psychological concepts of childhood, so

also the gradual isolation of the family as a social and psychological entity ultimately contributed to the same ends.   (p. 306)

With the opening up of an ever more sharply defined – and socially objectified – division between childhood and adulthood the possibility also arises of the entry of a mediating phase into the ambiguous space between these two primary categories. It is this process that underlies the history of the categories of adolescence and youth. In as far as it occupies an intermediate space between childhood and full adulthood, adolescence can be seen as partaking of features of both of the primary age grades (and this in its own right is often cited by theorists as a source of 'adolescent role confusion': the adolescent is never fully boy nor man, girl nor woman, but rather the one thing in one respect, context and time and the other in another; often he or she is simultaneously an uneasy mixture of the two). Although childhood is now at least fairly clearly defined and institutionalized versus adulthood, the transition between the two in advanced industrial societies is far from instantaneous. The twentieth century has indeed seen a considerable chronological expansion of the institutional space occupied by adolescence (or youth), as a whole range of benchmarks between childhood and adulthood – the age of leaving school or college, commencing full-time work, joining a youth organization, being permitted to vote, drive, drink, engage in sexual activity, marry etc. – have been continually negotiated, formalized and re-negotiated across almost the full span of the teenage years, and, in the case of the central education–work transition, often beyond. It is in this extensive and highly ambiguous space that there has emerged, largely in the present century and in particular since the Second World War, a fully fledged and quite distinct 'world of adolescence' which is now universally the domain of each successive younger generation.

Thus although the conceptually separate nature of adolescence as this term is now understood had its initial and classical definition in the eighteenth century, and although there have existed at various times from at least the Middle Ages onwards groups which appear from a late-twentieth-century vantage point to possess many of the characteristics of youth groups or subcultures, it is only from the mid-nineteenth century onwards that it is possible to see the

beginnings of our contemporary pattern for the universal institutionalization of this age grade as a major subdivision of the human
life-cycle. These processes came to fruition in the twentieth century
and it was furthermore at this time, despite foreshadowings in
previous eras, that adolescence/youth began to establish itself as the
age grade around which there was centred the greatest degree of
general social scrutiny, interest and concern.[6] A quotation from
Aries is highly suggestive here and could indeed be taken as
providing in a general sense the central theme of the whole of this
study:

> Thus our society has passed from a period which was ignorant of
> adolescence to a period in which adolescence is the favourite
> age. . . . It is as if, to every period in history, there corresponded
> a privileged age and a particular division of the human life:
> 'youth' [i.e. early adulthood, or the 'prime of life' in contempor-
> ary terms] is the privileged age of the seventeenth century,
> childhood of the nineteenth and adolescence of the
> twentieth.   (Aries, 1973: 28–9)

As has been suggested above, it is possible to identify something
akin to an adolescent age grade at certain periods and in certain
socio-cultural milieux *before* the nineteenth century. From a
contemporary point of view, (although not necessarily from any
point of view current at the time) it could furthermore be argued
that the incumbents of such age-graded positions manifested forms
of behaviour which are associated with adolescents in present-day
society, and indeed the members of the 'adolescent groups' thus
defined could be regarded as sometimes having constituted distinct
adolescent or youth subcultures. Certainly it has been argued that
there have occurred 'cycles of anxiety' in the parent culture around
the issue of what we would term 'juvenile delinquency' from at least
the sixteenth century onwards, and as has already been discussed in
Chapter 1 it is probable that there has always existed a more
generalized and diffuse tendency for the 'older generation' to
express concern about, and/or disapproval of, the deeds of the
'younger generation', although this may well be more pronounced
in certain periods and contexts than in others (Gillis, 1975: 96–126;
Pearson, 1983).
    All in all, then, the tendency of some commentators to regard the

emergence of adolescence as a concept, as an institutionalized position in the age-grading system, and also as a way of life with its own particular characteristics and problems as a *uniquely* nineteenth-century phenomenon, must be regarded, historically speaking, as an over-simplification.[7] At the same time, however, and this incidentally may explain why the significance of the nineteenth century has perhaps been over-stressed in this respect, it is certainly true to say that it is from this latter period that there can be dated the consolidation of the current – essentially 'psychological' – and commonsensically taken-for-granted definition of the (universal) characteristics, problems, etc., of this period of life, and therefore one component of its status as a truly separate age grade. The other component was the establishment, for all of the population, of the objective and institutionalized social reality of adolescence in terms of the life-cycle as lived out. In terms of our contemporary social institutional matrix of home and school, work and non-work, this again must be regarded as having its roots in the nineteenth century with its full flowering not occurring until this century. While it undoubtedly has real historical antecedents, the full crystallization of the idea and reality of adolescence as a distinct age grade is still a relatively recent occurrence.

To turn now to some of the 'historical antecedents' of adolescence and youth as currently understood and objectified, it firstly needs to be stressed that medieval and early modern European society was, in terms of crude demographic structure, an extremely *youthful* one. A low average of life expectancy coupled with a relatively high rate of fertility combined together to produce a situation in which the majority of the population fell into the age ranges that would be described today as childhood, adolescence and young adulthood (and/or youth). In England in 1640 the overall expectancy of life at birth has been estimated at only 32 years, and at around this time between 40 and 50 per cent of the population would have been below the age of 20.[8] However, high 'proportional representation' in the demographic structure – especially if this is coupled with a high rate of mortality – does not necessarily mean that the age range thus defined will in any sense come to be recognized as a separate, let alone special and privileged *age grade*.

Thus in medieval and early modern European society the basic age-grading system consisted of a simple division between a brief period of dependency ('infancy') on the one hand, and a period lasting for the rest of the life span of 'proto-adulthood' merging into adulthood on the other. From the age of about seven upwards 'children' and 'adolescents' were already more or less fully *in* the world at large in a kind of 'trainee adult' capacity, and thus the passage of the individual into adulthood proper was gradual and *continuous* (see Aries, 1973; Pinchbeck and Hewitt, 1969; 1973; Shorter, 1977; Stone, 1977). The years of childhood and adolescence were not passed in a state of institutionalized separation and possibly protection, and in this sense hardly existed as distinct age grades at all. While medieval and early modern society was demographically young it was also therefore largely structurally undifferentiated along the dimension of age. However, rather more than is the case with childhood, it is possible at a secondary level to make out a case for there having existed *some* institutional differentiation of what would today be regarded as the years of adolescence and youth, and for there also having been some generalized awareness of the (real and imagined) 'problems' for society that could be posed by this age group.

Although in medieval and early modern society the age of entry into the full-time workforce was generally very low – anything from about seven upwards – the age of marriage was generally late, the late twenties being the modal period, as was the age of setting up an independent household. In this sense the age span of 'youth', which could encompass what would now be regarded as childhood, adolescence and young adulthood, shared a common, inferior and exploited position in society, and was potentially, therefore, the basis for the formation, within any given community, of a sense of group identity and solidarity. It must be borne in mind that in so far as 'the youth' was already proto-adult it was also by the same token, in theory at least, partially 'free to make its own history', in John Gillis's phrase. A community's youth could potentially represent a considerable force for social disorder, or else for the promotion of social order. This has led Gillis to argue, and in one sense the point seems inescapable, that traditional and early modern society was faced with the considerable 'problem' of the social containment of the energies and potential dissatisfactions of the young unmarrieds who formed so numerically significant a proportion of the entire population (Gillis, 1974).

A good deal of youthful energy and potential rebelliousness seems to have been channelled into the institutions of the *charivari* and the 'traditions of misrule'. The *charivari* was basically a 'noisy public demonstration to subject wayward individuals to humiliation in the eyes of the community' (Shorter, 1977: 216). It was found throughout the rural (and sometimes urban) areas of Europe and North America, persisting in England until well into the nineteenth century and perhaps beyond.[9] The *charivari* functioned as a powerful mechanism for social control in an era and in areas that were largely lacking in more formal constraints, and was directed at anyone who departed from more significant social, economic and sexual norms of the community at large. Such categories of deviants as cuckolded husbands, unmarried mothers, wife-beaters, battered husbands, those who failed to hand out gifts on traditional occasions, and men who did 'women's work', were all at one time and one place or another brought back into line through the 'rough music' of the *charivari*. Just as the targets for *charivari* could vary, so too could the composition of the group that carried it out, but the local youth was generally fairly centrally involved, and often this activity was exclusively the domain of young male unmarrieds. Here, then, can be seen an early example of the frustrations of youth being directed into the function of the maintenance of the status quo.

There are examples of attempts to politicize the *charivari* and traditions of misrule to a revolutionary end.[10] Nonetheless in traditional society the characteristic role of 'the youth' – in so far as such a group was recognized – must be regarded as having been a doubly conservative one. Through the *charivari*, youth's own possibly disruptive potential was defused, while at the same time and by the same token a more general policing of society was accomplished. A similar role to the *charivari* proper was also played by the traditional and institutionalized 'days of misrule' such as May Day (in practice the two institutions were, and indeed to a lesser extent still are, inseparable) (Gillis, 1974: 27). On such occasions[11] the generally tightly hierarchical structure of society was momentarily relaxed, and widespread, but still contained, role-reversal and disruption permitted to erupt between young and old, servant and master, and for that matter between rival groups of 'the youth'. Often youth groups were organized especially for such occasions and took a leading role in the proceedings. In various modified forms, such as town–gown riots and mods versus rockers Bank Holiday confrontations, such days of youthful misrule have remained with us right down to the modern era.

The widespread custom in medieval and early modern society of sending out quite young children into service or apprenticeship can also be viewed from this perspective as having performed the latent function of the 'containment' of youth. Throughout this period at almost all levels of English society it was common practice to send out one's children from a very early age (around 10 in the case of the landed, upper bourgeois and professional classes, and anything from 7 to 14 lower down the social ladder) either to attend boarding school, or else more commonly in the medieval and early modern periods, into another household as apprentices proper or as mere servants. At the same time all but the humblest of households would receive other people's (often neighbours') children into their midst. In this manner the whole of society was covered by a network of exchange established through the system of fostering out (Stone, 1977: 107).[12]

The major implication of this practice is that many young people at this time spent much of the pre-adult phase of their lives away from the parental home in a position of subservience in another household. Perhaps even the majority of those who would now be regarded as being in their adolescent years were in this position. As Stone has pointed out, out of the four major benchmarks in the process of attaining full adulthood, two – leaving home and entering full-time employment – occurred very early in life, say 10 to 12 years of age on average, whereas the other two – marriage and the setting up of an independent household – occurred quite a lot later, in the late twenties, and actually often quite late in life, if one considers the generally low level of life expectancy at this time (Stone, 1977: 108–9). In this manner medieval and early modern society must be regarded as having institutionalized a lengthy period of social dependency and (supposed) sexual moratorium – both now regarded as prime characteristics of adolescence – through which the individual had to pass before reaching the destination of full adulthood.

In a number of important ways, however, the medieval and early modern proto-adulthood outlined above fails to correspond with 'adolescence proper' as contemporarily conceptualized and institutionalized. Firstly a period of the life-cycle similar to (although more extensive than) modern adolescence may have been institutionalized for many, if not all of the pre-adult population, through the system of fostering out and servanthood; but this is not the same thing as the contemporary *universal* institutionalization of ado-lescence as the period encompassing the last years of schooling and the first years of work, when full adult rights and obligations are formally denied. We have now come to institutionalize adolescence as a distinct age grade in a fundamentally different and more thoroughgoing manner. Secondly, medieval society at least seems to have had little explicit awareness of the special nature of adolescence as a distinct period of the life-cycle, as we would now understand this in psycho-social terms, or of adolescents as a distinct and possibly particularly problematic group within the social structure. By the same token, any group self-awareness amongst medieval proto-adults seems to have been relatively undeveloped. For these reasons it is arguable that although it is possible in retrospect to establish similarities between medieval proto-adulthood and contemporary adolescence, this is not to say that the comparison can be pushed so far as to imply that these can somehow be seen as essentially the same thing.

In England the phenomenon of fostering out took on a special significance with regard to the city apprentices and especially those of the great City of London. (It should be borne in mind that the English case is unique here in comparison with the other nations of western Europe by virtue of the sheer size of medieval and early modern London, and the extent to which it dominated the life of the nation as a whole, being responsible amongst other things for a constantly high level of geographical mobility of population not to be found elsewhere.) So far the discussion of the role of youth, of the *charivari* and the traditions of misrule, and of the system of exchange of young servants and apprentices, has been confined to a largely *rural* and for want of a better word what could be termed *traditional* society. In this context there would appear to have existed a kind of partial age grading of the years leading up to full adulthood that resembles in some ways and provides a kind of historical antecedent for the modern concept and reality of adolescence/youth.[13]

When the focus of attention is shifted to the urban and decidedly early modern example of seventeenth-century London, there can be perceived amongst the craft and trade apprentices of the City not only a common age-graded social structural position, but also a collective response to the problems and possibilities of life-as-lived thus marked out that foreshadows far more closely in many

aspects the realities and experience of twentieth-century adolescence and youth, especially with reference to the development of
distinct youth subcultures or movements. Basically, all City apprentices shared the same exploited and inferior situation – that of being
removed from the parental home and bound to the master of
another household for a period of seven years, often under harsh
conditions and always with a high degree of formal restriction of
personal liberty. There were many regulations – oft broken no
doubt – dictating hours kept, places out of bounds, non-permissible
leisure activities, correct haircut and dress, etc. Also of course the
apprentices were relatively numerous and concentrated into a
geographically (and socially) limited space. Just as was the case with
the historically rather later institution of the (boarding) school, the
institution of trade and craft apprenticeship provided then the
classic pre-conditions for the development of a strong sense of peer
group identity and solidarity, and the possible emergence of
age-specific subcultures.

This is exactly what seems to have occurred: by the seventeenth
century the London apprentices had acquired their own traditions
and organizations, their own heroes and literature, and regarded
themselves and were thought of as a 'separate order' within the
social structure of the City as a whole (S. R. Smith, 1973: 149–61).
Various value systems coexisted uneasily within the world of the
apprentices, and often also within the various individual apprentice
biographies that we know about – in both cases the basic tension
seems to have been between the tradition of riotous living on the
one hand, and that of high Puritan moral fervour on the other. By
the same token, although the impact of the action of the apprentices
– individually, in groups and as a collectivity – on the life of the City
as a whole seems never to have been negligible, its exact significance, and to a lesser extent form, was also capable of considerable
variation. Relatively insignificant riotousness was, on occasion,
transformed into socially and politically significant group action
which could be either essentially conservative or else radical in its
import. Here, more strongly than before, there can be glimpsed the
potential for youth – in the sense of the immediately pre-adult sector
of the population – to be a significant social force in any society that
institutionalizes and concentrates it as a separate group, whilst
simultaneously relegating it to a markedly inferior social status.[14]

What conclusions can be drawn, then, concerning the existence or non-existence of adolescence as a distinct age grade in traditional and early modern society? 'The youth' was in some respects and especially on some occasions a recognizable group in rural society, but at the same time it was still fully integrated into the life of the community as a whole, and its activities if anything tended to function in such a way as to reinforce the community's most deep-seated norms and values. Beyond the practices associated with the *charivari*, adolescence as such was largely non-institutionalized, and certainly any definition of this time of life as an autonomous age grade that may have existed seems to have had very little practical significance.

However, as set out above, a stronger argument can be made out for the apprentices of early modern London as 'seventeenth-century adolescents'. It does seem to be the case that these apprentices formed a clearly demarcated *age set* by virtue of their occupancy of a common (pre-adult) age-graded position in the social structure as a whole.[15] Out of this situation there also arose, furthermore, specific apprentice subcultures of an at least potentially oppositional nature, and a generalized awareness of this group as an entity in its own right posing its own particular problems. Thus the City apprentices must be regarded as passing through a period of life which was *structured* and also *experienced* (both by the apprentices themselves and also by the wider society) in a manner that is similar in some respects to the contemporary age grade of adolescence/youth. Similarly, although on the whole individually rather than collectively, young aristocrats and some members of the upper-middle classes can also be regarded as having passed through something akin to adolescence/youth in so far as 'service' (perhaps at court) coupled with the Grand Tour also had the effect of institutionalizing a lengthy period before the assumption of full adult status and responsibilities.[16]

Caution, however, must be exercised when making such comparisons: apart from the obvious fact that City apprentices – and young aristocrats – would only have been a minority within any given generation, and that any adolescent age grade that might be regarded as having existed would therefore have been far from universal, we must also beware of 'projecting back' our own taken-for-granted assumptions concerning the ('universal') nature of adolescence and its social institutionalization on to a period for which these may have very little validity. The problems posed by 'riotous apprentices', and the existence of a sense of solidarity amongst apprentices as a group, cannot be taken as evidence that the seventeenth century possessed any awareness of *adolescence* as a social phenomenon, even if the formal and informal groupings of the City apprentices of this time can with hindsight be regarded as an early example of the tendency towards the emergence of distinct ('problem') adolescent or youth subcultures, groups and movements which has increasingly come to be a feature of contemporary societies.[17]

Furthermore, even if one accepts the questionable contemporary theoretical wisdom concerning adolescence as a period of role moratorium, identity quest and crisis, it is still possible to question the general applicability of these typifications before the modern period.[18] The highly ascriptive nature of status allocation in traditional society, the sense of existential certainty thus engendered and the very *continuity* of the human life-cycle would together tend to rule such possibilities out, even in theory. Again, significantly, the seventeenth-century apprentices provide an interesting 'cross-over' example. Here a high density of peer group interaction, plus the wide range of possibility for role experimentation that London at this time provided, plus a status that was in any case highly ambiguous, together combined – perhaps for the first time on any major scale – to form a social context within which a distinctively *adolescent* psychology could emerge along with a view of this time of life as 'problematic', both for the individual apprentice and also for society as a whole (S. R. Smith, 1973: 159–61). In conclusion it is probably fair to say that the emergence of the 'problem adolescent', along with an awareness of adolescence, was an epiphenomenon of the rise of bourgeois urban-industrial society. In this case the seventeenth-century London apprentices may well have been at least partially 'early adolescents'.

However, for the final emergence of adolescence as an autonomous, socially universalized and *formally institutionalized* age grade it is necessary to wait until the nineteenth century, and the various social interventions – especially in the fields of education and social welfare – that were to accompany the rise of the modern state. The same is broadly true at the theoretical, conceptual or psychological level. It is possible to see the *idea* of adolescence (and of stage psychology in general) foreshadowed in medieval and early modern society, but it was not until the Enlightenment that there were to emerge secularized and scientific theories of adolescence, ascribing to this stage its autonomous status and special significance for the developmental process as a whole. This is not to say that the idea of the 'seven ages of man' (or however many ages it might be) was not an important one for the thought of the Middle Ages. In Aries's words it formed part of an 'attempt to render the essential unity of Nature and God', whereby it was held that 'a single rigorous law governs at one and the same time the movement of the planets, the vegetative cycle of the seasons, the connections between the elements, the human body and its humours and the destiny of man' (Aries, 1973: 17–18). Nonetheless, relatively little attention was paid to the actual and distinctive attributes of each age. On this point Joseph Kett has written that:

> In the Middle Ages speculations about the 'ages of man' had usually included a stage of youth or adolescence and at times two separate stages. Such speculation had often centred more on the exact number of the ages than on their moral or psychological content, however. Indeed the fascination with dividing the life cycle by whole or magical numbers survived into the early 1800s.   (Kett, 1971: 283–4)

More significant than this, though, any such *schema* for the division of the ages of man remained largely hypothetical rather than being of practical consequence in the ordering and institutionalization of social reality. Speculation as to how to divide up the human life-cycle so as to make it fit in with a general and cosmic system of correspondences seems to have had very little impact in terms of objectified age grading and, as has been noted, any institutional differentiation of childhood and youth was largely lacking.

Once again it is possible to see the beginnings of something akin to the contemporary concept of adolescence in the urban, bourgeois and largely Puritan context provided by seventeenth-century London, and this was later echoed in Puritan New England (Kett, 1971: 285).[19] Steven Smith has argued that any conception of adolescence/youth as a distinct period of life with its own particular attributes and problems would at this time and in this context have been expressed primarily in *religious* terms (rather than 'scientifically'), citing as evidence the published sermons and books of moral and spiritual advice of the period.[20] Here he finds a theoretical recognition of an autonomous, and from a moral and spiritual point of view particularly critical, period of life between childhood and adulthood, which at an objective and social institutional level corresponded in large part with the status of apprenticeship (see above). The existence of this institutionalized and age-graded role seems to have lent particular force to the emergence of a belief in the moral significance of adolescence/youth (roughly the period from 15 to 24 years of age) and the puritan 'moral entrepreneurs' of the seventeenth century were consequently much concerned with youth as a 'special period of life and one which somehow found favour with God despite [its] great sinfulness'. (S. R. Smith, 1975: 511.)

Sermons and 'guidebooks' aimed at the newly identified (urban) age grade depicted youth as fickle and prone to sin – pride, sensuality, susceptibility to peer group pressure, etc. – but at the same time full of strength and vigour, and therefore with the potential to bring about great changes in God's name. For these reasons a good deal of stress came to be laid in Puritan circles on the importance of the individual's undergoing an often difficult and deeply troubling experience of religious conversion in his youth (S. R. Smith, 1975: 497–513). It should now be readily apparent that many contemporary characterizations of adolescence as a psycho-social state – along with social interventions informed by these – represent the secularized continuation of strands of thought and programmes of action that have their origins with the Reformation.

However, despite precursors in this field (humanists and philosophers such as Elyot and Ascham in the sixteenth century and Comenius in the seventeenth have been cited as placing some stress on the importance of the moral as well as physical changes that occur with puberty), it was Rousseau who was responsible for the classical definition of the separate and special nature of adolescence (Kett, 1971: 284).[21] *Émile* (1762) marked the crystallization of a clear distinction between adolescence and childhood, and at the same time adolescence now came to be defined as something separate from, if still in transition to, adulthood. It is also from *Émile* that it is possible to trace the emergence of an inventory of the characteristics and qualities of adolescence as a psycho-social stage which has now come to form the basis of our taken-for-granted assumptions concerning the 'innate' nature and problems of this particular time of life.

From this time onwards the age grade of adolescence was established as a *theoretical* entity: in the nineteenth and twentieth centuries this was to become objectified for an increasingly all-embracing cross-section of society. As Frank Musgrove has written, 'the position of youth in contemporary society is only intelligible in terms of the rise since the late eighteenth century of a psychology of adolescence which has helped to create what it describes' (Musgrove, 1964: 2). In one sense the 'problems of adolescence', both for the individual and also for society as a whole, stem initially from this process of first the conceptual and then the social institutional separation out of this age grade, and in particular from the latter's establishment and chronological prolongation as the time of moving towards, but not yet attaining, full adult status.

> The adolescent was invented at the same time as the steam engine. The principal architect of the latter was Watt in 1765, of the former Rousseau in 1762. Having invented the adolescent, society has been faced with two major problems: how to accommodate him in the social structure, and how to make his behaviour accord with the specification.   (Musgrove, 1964: 33)

For what reasons can this degree of significance be attached to Rousseau and to *Émile*? Firstly, it was *Émile* that laid the foundation for the distinctively modern version of the idea of the human life-cycle as divided into a number of discrete and autonomous *stages*, each with its own particular psychology, problems, and requirements for healthy development. This rigorous conceptual division of the life-cycle can be viewed as one aspect of the basis upon which rests our differential institutional – especially educational – response to the pre-adult years. Secondly it is in *Émile*, with its view of the child almost as a 'noble savage', that there is foreshadowed the view (later to be even more influential) that each individual in his or her passage from infancy to maturity *recapitulates* the progress of humankind from savagery to civilization.

These strands of thought have been of great importance in the shaping of our contemporary conceptualization – and *realization* – of the general outline of the age grading of the human life-cycle. However, it is Rousseau's conceptualization of adolescence (in this case, as so often, seen in specifically male terms) that is of particular interest for the purposes of the current study. Book IV of *Émile* deals with this stage specifically, which for Rousseau, as for most subsequent writers on developmental and educational psychology, not only has its beginning marked by the onset of puberty (in Émile's particular case at what by modern standards would be the rather late age of 15) but which also has its essential characteristics determined by the major physiological and psychological changes which now occur:

> But, speaking generally, man is not meant to remain a child. He leaves childhood behind him at the time ordained by nature; and this critical moment, short enough in itself, has far reaching consequences.
>
> As the roaring of the waves precedes the tempest, so the murmur of rising passions announces this tumultuous change . . . a change of temper, frequent outbreaks of anger, a perpetual stirring of the mind, make the child almost ungovernable. He becomes deaf to the voice he used to obey; he is a lion in a fever; he distrusts his keeper and refuses to be controlled.
>
> With the moral symptoms of a changing temper there are perceptive changes in appearance. His countenance develops and takes the stamp of his character. . . . He is neither a child nor a man and cannot speak like either of them . . . he is beginning to learn to lower his eyes and blush, he is becoming sensitive, though he does not know what it is that he feels; he is uneasy without knowing why.
>
> This is the second birth I spoke of; then it is that man really enters upon life; henceforth no human passion is a stranger to him. Our efforts so far have been child's play, now they are of the greatest importance.   (Rousseau, 1974: 172–3)

In the work of Rousseau the physical and psychological changes ushered in by puberty took on tremendous significance: 'We are born, so to speak, twice over', he wrote, 'born into existence and born into life; born a human being, and born a man' (p. 172). By virtue of this formulation the stage of adolescence was elevated to a position of key importance for the development of the individual; Rousseau argued that it was only at this time that the faculty of reason emerged, and that therefore this was the appropriate moment at which to commence the programme of education proper. Also by implication adolescence now became a stage that needed to be nurtured and correctly handled in order to ensure the smooth development of the individual and the continuity of society as a whole.

Rousseau portrayed the stage of adolescence as one that was *innately and inevitably* troublesome and 'stormy' for Émile (and his tutor alike). Émile now was 'neither fish nor fowl' and suddenly he became highly volatile and unpredictable in the extreme. This is of course a characterization of the nature of adolescence which has become deeply embedded in our commonsense assumptions, and which has come to shape a good deal of the contemporary response to young people, both individually and collectively. It is also a basis for regarding the state of *being adolescent* as something that cuts across other social divisions. If the psycho-social properties of adolescence as defined above are innate and therefore universal, then an adolescent will first and foremost *be an adolescent* and should be treated and is explicable as such, irrespective of his or her social background and circumstances.

Some of the partial historical antecedents of contemporary adolescence and youth have been sketched above.[22] Nonetheless it was Rousseau, with his emphasis on the significance of physiological puberty and his conceptualization of the years of adolescence as a distinct and crucial period at both developmental and social levels, who first formulated the specifically modern idea of the special nature of this age grade. It is therefore from Rousseau onwards that there can be traced the process of dialectical interplay between theorization on the one hand, and professional and popular response on the other, that has led to the establishment of the universal reality of adolescence as an age grade *sui generis*, and its subsequent rise to prominence as an object of concern. In the nineteenth and twentieth centuries this concern with the recently identified and increasingly socially objectified adolescent age grade was to come to be ever more entangled with the very question of the condition and direction of British society overall.

3
The youth question at the turn of the century

The concept of adolescence as we know it may have been invented by Rousseau but throughout the nineteenth century, while demand for the labour of the young remained high, this had little objective realization for the majority of the population. The 1833 Factory Act was the first piece of legislation to limit the working hours of 'young persons' but more or less full-time child and adolescent labour remained the norm amongst the urban working class and the rural poor right up until the introduction of compulsory universal elementary education in the closing decades of the nineteenth century.[1] Even when this principle was established, however, half-time attendance on the grounds of 'family necessity' was common until the early years of the twentieth century and, in any case, the minimum age of school-leaving remained low. (This was raised in 1893 to 11 and in 1899 to 12, with the statutory minimum of 14 years not being universally established until the Education Act of 1918.) Whether they were officially 'half-timers' or not, most working-class children still performed a great variety of jobs around the home and many also earned vital extra coppers doing work for others. (P. Thompson, 1979: 59–60, 66–7; Vigne, 1975: 10–12; E. Roberts, 1975: 14–19) In some cases this resulted in an early emancipation, either partial or total, from parental control: certainly the self-supporting 'street arab'. was a common enough sight in late Victorian and Edwardian cities (P. Thompson, 1975: 29). For the majority of the young then it was still hardly possible to speak of *adolescence* as a formally institutionalized, distinct and possibly privileged period of the life-cycle.

Nonetheless important developments in these respects were occurring around this time amongst the middle and upper classes. As the nineteenth century progressed the anarchy and riotousness that had previously characterized the public schools now came to be replaced under the great early nineteenth-century wave of moral reform by the culture and cult of 'muscular Christianity'. The ethic of 'team spirit' replaced that of 'boy freedom' and in the reformed public school upper- and middle-class youth was made to abandon the more outward and visible aspects of its previous traditions of misrule. The image of adolescence – and this can perhaps be taken as a factor that distinguishes adolescence proper from youth – shifted in this context from that of *troublemaker* to *troubled* (Gillis, 1974: 95–131).

Following on from the theoretical model first defined by Rousseau, the 'problems of adolescence' now increasingly came, in upper- and middle-class circles, to be defined as individual, innate and psychological, rather than social in character. At the same time it now came to be felt that, given the correct sort of treatment and environment, these problems could be overcome and what was seen as the tremendous energy of this period channelled in the right direction: basically, in the context of late nineteenth-century Britain, the service of Queen and Country. Out of the mid-Victorian public schools then there emerged a *model* – in both descriptive and normative senses of the word – of adolescence, which in subsequent decades came to be spread, albeit with ever-lessening real success as it passed down the social scale, throughout the whole of society. Amongst the 'adolescent qualities' emphasized by the public schools and taken up with perhaps even more enthusism by the burgeoning educational establishments of the lower middle classes were peer-group loyalty, militarism, manliness, anti-intellectualism, and implicitly a dislike of women and a strong element of homo-eroticism.

At the same time as this official model of adolescence was coming to be developed in the public and grammar schools, urban working-class young people were developing what we can perhaps regard as the first true, modern youth subcultures. As the nineteenth century advanced the attention and anxiety focused upon these groups served to promote a new awareness of 'the youth problem' as an important issue for contemporary society. In the early stages of industrialization many of the young people of the new manufacturing towns were already enjoying a considerable degree of social and economic independence (Anderson, 1971: ch. 9; Musgrove, 1964: ch. 2). Adult concern at this state of affairs, especially amongst the middle and upper classes, seems in turn to have been tied up with a more generalized anxiety over the newly emerging urban-industrial order and the potential threat to the status quo posed by the urban proletariat. By the early Victorian period the perceived need for the 'right' sort of educational provision for urban working-class youth, in the face of a supposed collapse of the traditional authority of the working-class family, had become a major issue of educational and social policy (Johnson, 1970: 96–119).

Richard Johnson has noted how in the eyes of the educational inspectorate of the 1840s adolescence was coming to be seen as a period of particular moral, social and political peril. One such inspector commenting upon the adolescent subculture of West Riding towns, 'pointed to the early financial independence of children, their tendency to take their values from 'bigger, rougher and more lawless' boys and a general failure of parental control' (Johnson, 1970: 108). The same inspector then went on to draw a connection between lack of respect for parents and lack of respect for social superiors, remarking that:

> I have often passed with a clergyman through a knot of young people, either of long-haired idling youths, or of flaunting giggling girls, and seen no other notice taken of the minister of religion than an independent nod or a half-impudent recognition.[2]

By the latter part of the nineteenth century, then, the distinctive styles and subcultures of working-class youth were well established as a highly visible, much remarked upon and often disapproved of feature – or 'problem' – of the urban scene. Writing of his own childhood in Edwardian Salford Robert Roberts has recalled:

> The groups of young men and youths who gathered at the end of most slum streets on fine evenings earned the condemnation of all respectable citizens. They were damned every summer by city magistrates and unceasingly harried by the police. In the late nineteenth century the Northern scuttler and his moll had achieved a notoriety as widespread as that of any gangs in modern times. He too had his own style of dress – the union shirt, bell-bottomed trousers, the heavy leather belt, pricked out in fancy designs with a large steel buckle and thick, iron-shod clogs.

His girl friend commonly wore clogs and shawl and a skirt with vertical stripes. . . . In many industrial cities of the late Victorian era and after, such groups became a minor menace. Deprived of all decent ways of spending their leisure time they sought escape from tedium in bloody battles with belt and clog – street against street. The spectacle of two mobs rushing with wild howls into contact added still another horror to the ways of slumdom. Scuttlers appeared in droves before the courts, often to receive savage sentences. In the new century this mass brutality diminished somewhat, but street battles on a smaller scale continued to recur spasmodically in our district and in others similar until the early days of the First World War.   (R. Roberts, 1977: 155–6)

The latter part of this account – that dealing with gangfights and the official response to these – may very well be somewhat overdrawn, as is the tendency with statements on the topic of 'problem youth'. Nonetheless spectacular or highly visible working-class youth subcultures such as the 'scuttlers', 'ikeys' and 'peaky blinders' were a real enough phenomenon at this time, and the mere existence of such groups was probably enough to provoke a good deal of adult anxiety.[3] At the far more generalized level of intergenerational conflict and hostility over teenage fashion, Paul Thompson has pointed out that adult criticisms in this area have in fact 'echoed down the generations': as early as 1888 the *Oxford Times* was asking 'what would our grandmothers have thought of girls, sixteen or eighteen, parading the fair alone, dressed in jockey-caps . . . [with] imitation open jackets and waistcoats, and smoking cigars or cigarettes . . .?'.[4] Another highly visible manifestation of the already well-established youth culture of the period was the local 'monkey parade' a kind of communal working-class courtship ritual (P. Thompson, 1979: 75–6).

These (sub)cultural developments were thrown into particular relief in the period around the turn of the century through certain factors of an essentially social structural nature. Firstly the leisure time available to 'working youth' was expanding, and was increasingly coming to be commercially exploited through an emergent mass fashion industry (see the remarks on distinctive youth style and clothing above) and also through such cultural institutions as the music hall, the new improved public house of the period and, a little later, the cinema.[5] Secondly, following the establishment of universal elementary education from the 1870s onwards working-class children now came for the first time to be institutionally contained within the school. As a consequence of this, youth (or adolescence) was now more clearly demarcated as a distinct age grade, and the discipline of post-school young people began to be perceived as a social problem in its own right, especially within an urban context. C. E. B. Russell, a pioneer of the Boys' Club movement, itself one major middle-class adult response to this newly identified 'youth problem' of the late nineteenth and early twentieth centuries, wrote that:

> It is at this age, when the organized control of the school has ceased, and parental authority, slight as it often is, has lost most of its cogency, that the boy . . . is most susceptible to influence good and bad, that his character may be formed and his career determined. The years between fourteen and twenty will decide whether each individual is to become a valuable asset to his country, a negligible quantity possessed at best of the value of a machine, or a worthless parasite and a drag on its prosperity. Multiplied by hundreds of thousands it is the decision on which the future of England rests (Russell, 1932: 3).[6]

Finally, and perhaps most significantly of all, demographic factors combined with the recent establishment of universal elementary education to produce, in the Edwardian period, a situation under which in informal, if not in formal institutional terms, pre-adulthood came to be extended into a very lengthy period indeed. For whatever reasons, the average age of marriage in early twentieth-century Britain was at its highest level ever: 25 for women and 27 for men (as opposed to 22 and 24 respectively today); at the same time the most frequent age of school-leaving was 14. Thus the typical male Edwardian lived through a period of up to thirteen years between leaving school and the attainment, through marriage and leaving the parental home, of full adult status and independence. In these informal terms early twentieth-century youth could be up to twice as long as its typical contemporary duration (P. Thompson, 1979: 71 and 292). In a period when sexual abstinence before marriage was a firmly enforced norm – if not always a reality – and when parental authority was seen as absolute, there was a great deal of *potential*, at least, for intergenerational conflict in this lengthy phase of semi-independence (P. Thompson, 1975: 35).

Much adult concern over working-class youth at around the turn of the century was given focus through the highly prevalent theme of 'hooliganism'. This term acted as a useful shorthand in the social discourse and analysis of the period to cover a wide range of (supposed) phenomena from thoroughgoing youthful criminality or juvenile delinquency as portrayed in Clarence Rook's *The Hooligan Nights* (1899),[7] through the near-delinquent youth subcultures described above, to generalized youthful disrespectfulness and unruliness. Robert Roberts has descreibed the official reaction to the male working-class street gang in early twentieth-century Salford thus:

> The gang bursts into a scatter of flying figures. From nowhere gallop a couple of 'rozzers', cuffing, hacking, punching, sweeping youngsters into the wall with a swing of heavy folded capes. The street empties, doors bang. Breathing heavily the Law retires, bearing off perhaps a 'hooligan' or two to be made an example of.   (R. Roberts, 1977: 162)

The theme of hooliganism was made much of in the press: writing of turn-of-the-century London Charles Booth argued that whilst the 'problem' may well have been exaggerated there was nonetheless real cause for concern and a real need for action:

> 'Hooliganism has been exaggerated by the press' but still 'there is real ground for complaint' and need for stronger action on the part of both magistrates and police. So say our witnesses. Undoubtedly the checking of this evil lies in repression, but agencies are needed to keep loafing boys out of the street, and turn their energies in some better direction.   (Booth, 1902: 139)

Discussion of hooliganism is also to be found occupying an important place in the period's more scholarly literature on contemporary social problems and the state of the nation. C. F. G. Masterman's *The Heart of Empire* (1901) was a collection of pieces by young Liberal intellectuals and activists of the day on the 'problems of modern city life' and – more or less explicitly – the relation of these to the current state and future of the British

Empire (Masterman, 1973). A number of the essays in this volume made direct connections between the physically and morally unwholesome nature of prevalent urban conditions and anxieties concerning what was seen as the 'degenerate' character of contemporary urban working-class youth. Masterman himself speculated thus as to the physical and psychological impact of city life upon the younger generation:

> The result is the production of a characteristic *physical* type of town dweller: stunted, narrow-chested, easily wearied; yet voluble, excitable with little ballast, stamina or endurance – seeking stimulus in drink, in betting, in any unaccustomed conflicts at home or abroad.   (Masterman, 1973: 8)

This new urban physical type was also characterized by new and dangerous attitudes and forms of behaviour, not least of which was hooliganism.

> Throughout the century the population of England has exhibited a continuous drift into the great cities; and now, at the opening of a new era, it is necessary to recognise that we are face to face with a phenomenon unique in the world's history. Turbulent rioting over military successes, Hooliganism, and a certain type of fickle excitability has revealed to observers during the past few months that a new race, hitherto unreckoned and of incalculable action, is entering the sphere of practical importance – the 'city type' of the coming years; the 'street bred' people of the twentieth century; the 'new generation knocking at our doors'   (Masterman, 1973: 7).

In the same volume Reginald A. Bray further spelled out the part-real, part-metaphorical connection that was widely coming to be drawn between the perceived problem of hooliganism and a far more generalized social and national anxiety, one major feature of which was concern over the (real and imagined) problem of the impact upon the mass of the population – and especially the young – of a predominantly urban mode of life:

> Intercourse with Nature in excess tends to create an inactive dreaminess or the stolid stupidity of the rustic; the human

element [which predominates in an urban existence] in excess
gives the town child that restless temperament which appears in
its most accentuated form as Hooliganism. (Masterman,
1973: 115)

Finally, in what again has become a perennial theme in discussions of the youth problem, F. W. Head suggested that
hooliganism might simply be the product of a lack of legitimate
outlets for the abundant physical energies of urban youth. The
solution, soon to be taken up with renewed vigour by the various
boys' clubs and the schools, was the provision of adequate sports
facilities for the 'ordinary' boy:

Now in any normal development of youth there must be two
influences at work, and it is precisely the absence of these two
influences which makes the youth of the lower classes abnormal.
The first of these is athletics. The body must have exercise. A
favoured minority, under the auspices of philanthropic clubs, do
often manage to have some sort of exercise on a Saturday
afternoon . . . [but] for the generality there are only left the
streets and their own strong muscles. And the combination of
these two into a violent form of recreation is called Hooliganism.
Of course this is an evil, but it is after all only the abuse of a good
. . . the second influence . . . may be called the want of ideal in
love. (Masterman, 1973: 267)

The idea that contemporary urban conditions were contributing
towards a physical, mental and possibly moral deterioration of 'the
race', as expressed in the social criticism of Masterman and his
colleagues, was given a very considerable extra emphasis, shortly
after the publication of *The Heart of Empire*, through the growing
controversy over Britain's startling lack of success in the Boer War,
and the revelation of the extremely poor condition of most potential
army recruits at this time. In South Africa the might of the British
Empire was being outflanked by a small colony of farmers, and in
the crisis of national identity that ensued much attention came to be
directed at the condition and inadequacy of provision for the
nation's youth -- a group which was now increasingly coming to be
thought of *en masse* as representing the future of the Empire.
   The problem of 'national physical deterioration' as it was styled,

within the context of military recruitment and the wider debate on 'national efficiency', was first drawn to public attention in the spring of 1901 with the publication of Arnold White's polemical *Efficiency and Empire*. As part of his case for the 'racial decay' of the British, White revealed that between the outbreak of the war in October 1899 and July 1900 the reports from the Inspector General of Recruiting showed that two out of three potential recruits at the Manchester depot had to be rejected as physically unfit, even by the lower standards of wartime (White, 1972: 102–3).[8] The controversy really took off, however, in January 1902 when a pseudonymous article in *Contemporary Review* again stressed the appalling physical condition of most recruits, and underscored the idea that this was not only a contributory factor towards Britain's poor showing in the war, but that it also represented a far wider problem and danger for the nation's continuing status as the leading imperial power ('Miles', 1902: 78–80). By the following year general concern over this topic was running so high that the Government set up a fully fledged Inter-Departmental Committee on Physical Deterioration to investigate exhaustively the nation's state of health and living conditions. The report of this body was published in 1904, and demonstrated fairly conclusively that previous accounts of the poor physical condition of the mass of the population, and especially of working-class youth, had been far from exaggerated (excerpts in Van Der Eyken, 1973: 33–55).

As well as calling to general attention the issue of the simple physical condition of youth, the Boer War also highlighted the wider topic of the education of youth at large, and the inadequacy of existing educational provision. By the beginning of the twentieth century Germany was seen as Britain's major foreign rival, and many unfavourable comparisons now came to be made, not merely between the British military and the German military, but also between the British educational system as a whole and that of Germany. After making just such comparisons, one contemporary commentator went on to remark that:

The first step in finding a cure for those defects which the present campaign in South Africa has brought into such sharp relief is to recognise the fact that the real root of the evil does not lie in the condition of what is called military education, but in a general deficiency in the mental training of the young at large. (Perry, 1901: 900)

Imperial anxieties at this time were as closely connected with the possibility of Britain's decline as a first-rank manufacturing and trading nation as they were with military setbacks. The Boer War motif appeared again in this call for improved scientific and technical education at the higher levels, to put Great Britain back on a par with industrial competitors such as Germany:

We are spending a hundred millions to save our Empire in South Africa. . . . Our educational war is also waged to save the Empire. It requires no sacrifice of life, and its cost is a trifle compared with that called for month by month by the Commander-in-Chief in South Africa. Moreover, if all this is true, if England by her supineness and blindness is running even a remote risk of losing her trade and her imperial position, surely we are not asking too great a boon . . . when we say help us combat the enemy not by shooting him down, but by proving to him in peaceful contest that the Englishman is the better man. (Roscoe, 1901: 87)

The idea that the youth of the nation represented a valuable national asset (see C. E. B. Russell's equation of 'youth' with the future of England, above) that was being wantonly squandered through insufficient educational and post-educational provision, thereby endangering Britain's position in the world, also surfaced in the debate surrounding another major social issue of the period – the so-called 'boy-labour problem'. From at least the mid-nineteenth century onwards it had been remarked upon that there existed a strong tendency for employers of all kinds to take on relatively low-paid juvenile labour in preference to that of adults for the performance of unskilled tasks.[9] When – if not before – young workers reached an age at which they would by law command adult wages they were then commonly fired, to be replaced by a new generation of 'cheap' juveniles. This practice was cause for concern on a number of grounds since it not only deprived unskilled and sometimes skilled adults of employment (or so it was widely thought) but it also ensured that a large sector of working youth received no training, and therefore had diminished employment prospects on attainment of majority.[10] Robert Roberts has provided us with this first-hand account of youth employment – and of the prospects of youth on attaining manhood – in the period before the First World War:

> Many skilled workers used boys, not as apprentices, to assist them. There were the printers' devils, the feeders, the piercers, and those in boot factories who placed the tacks ready for the soldering machines. There were our local lads in the glassworks, on twelve hour night shifts taking bottles to the blowers. . . .
>
> In the modern, Americanized factories mass producers had quickly seen the advantages to be gained from the use of juvenile labour. Some shops ran almost entirely on young teenage workers; one notorious sewing machine factory managed to turn out its wares with only four or five skilled adult workers to every hundred adolescents, all of whom were sacked before they reached twenty. There were innumerable other jobs besides in foundry, ironworks and shipyard, all of which led youth nowhere except to dismissal on approaching manhood and a place among the mass of unskilled labourers fighting for jobs of any sort in the industrial maelstrom.   (R. Roberts, 1977: 158)

At the start of the present century the use of boy labour in lieu of that of adults was widely regarded as a major social problem, the economic, political and educational implications of which were coming to be widely discussed and analysed.[11] In the period from 1900 to 1914 over sixty books and articles were published on this topic (Springhall, 1986: 95). One major contribution to this debate was that of R. H. Tawney in the *Economic Journal* of 1909. Tawney introduced his article by noting the high level of scrutiny that had come to be focused upon the boy-labour problem in recent years:

> There has been in the last few years a remarkable concentration of attention upon the circumstances surrounding the entry of youth into industrial life, and a disposition to see in them one of the causes of the prevalence of adult unemployment.   (Tawney, 1909: 517)

Tawney then reported the results of a study of his own, carried out in Glasgow, which bore out that there was indeed seemingly a connection between the use of adolescent labour and high adult unemployment. More recently the general validity of the idea of a direct link between the widespread use of boy labour and adult unemployment at this time has been called into question and it has been suggested that the latter phenomenon is, rather, explicable in strictly *structural* terms. What is of significance here is the chain of connection that was coming to be established between the boy-labour problem and more general concerns over the condition or control of working-class youth and ultimately the issue of 'national efficiency'. (Springhall, 1986: 106–8)

Thus Tawney argued for a link between juvenile unemployment (after relatively short periods of work in 'blind alley' jobs), demoralization of the young and even juvenile delinquency:

> It would appear to be the case: (i) that among large sections of boys the character of the work done is such as to make it difficult for them to find employment when displaced at manhood, and in some cases such as to actually demoralise them; (ii) that as a matter of fact the influence of these tendencies is visible in the records of juvenile crime and unemployment. (Tawney, 1909: 535)

(It was also widely argued around this time that boy labour might 'cause' juvenile delinquency, or at least indiscipline, through providing young casual workers with a relatively high level of disposable income and thus a measure of financial independence (Springhall, 1986: 95–108) – a line of argument oft-repeated in the more recent past.)

In his final remarks Tawney also made explicit the (waste of) youth-as-national-asset theme, itself a major strand of the debate over national efficiency, which was prevalent in so much of the period's discussion of youth, including that of the boy-labour problem:

> It is quite possible for a town or a country, by using boys to satisfy its passion for evening papers and cheap cartage, to court a shortage of (say) steel workers or bricklayers or good citizens in the future. (Tawney, 1909: 536)

Tawney's remarks raise once more the topic of juvenile delinquency, already a well-established issue in the social discourse of the early Victorian period. As with the nineteenth and early twentieth-century youth problems discussed above, that of juvenile delinquency was associated with the growth of the industrial cities, the changes in class structure thus occasioned, and the living conditions of the urban poor. Matthew Davenport Hill, the Recorder of Birmingham, had ennumerated the following leading causes of juvenile crime to the 1852 Select Committee on the 'Criminal and Destitute Juveniles' of the nation:

> The growth of towns, which had destroyed the 'natural police' operating upon the conduct of each individual . . . the gradual separation of classes which takes place in towns . . . [whereas] previously 'rich and poor lived in proximity and the superior classes exercised [a] species of silent but very efficient control over their neighbours . . .' the state of the dwellings of the poor; the unnecessary exposure of property for the attention of customers.[12]

By the turn of the century, following the publication (in 1895) of William Douglas Morrison's influential *Juvenile Offenders*, the problem of juvenile delinquency had been a topic of official and academic investigation for some time.[13] The question now arises as to the extent to which juvenile delinquency 'really' was on the increase in late nineteenth and early twentieth-century Britain. This was certainly widely *felt* to be the case – much of the widespread anxiety over hooliganism at this time had as its basis the belief that young people, especially working-class young people, were more lawless and more disposed to criminality than they were at some undefined period in the past. The question of whether, in objective terms, crime is on the increase or decrease over a given period is of course always an extremely difficult one to answer, since official criminal statistics tell only part of the story and may, notoriously, reflect changes in the law and its enforcement as much as actual shifts in the level of crime committed. In the case of overall trends in the incidence of juvenile delinquency at around the turn of the century, the problem is further compounded by the fact that before the Children's Act of 1908, and the subsequent establishment of a system of juvenile courts for the under-sixteens, national judicial statistics did not adequately differentiate juveniles from adults. (The first decade of the century also saw the beginnings of the borstal system for the special institutionalization and supposed rehabilitation of post-juvenile offenders – 16–21-year-olds until 1932 and 17–21-year-olds subsequently.)

However, a study of the more detailed *local* statistics of juvenile delinquency in Oxford over the period of 1890 to 1914 does reveal a marked upward trend: from a decennial average of 32.8 offences per year in the 1880s, the rate rose to 72.7 in the 1890s and 99.2 in the first decade of the twentieth century (Gillis, 1975: 99). These figures are thrown into relief by the fact that the 10 to 19 age group as a proportion of the total population actually declined slightly over the period 1891 to 1911, and they also represent a rate of increase well in advance of the city's rate of population growth over the same period. Furthermore, adult crime rates actually declined in Oxford around the turn of the century, from an overall average of 704.2 offences per year in the last half of the 1890s to one of 644 per year in the first decade of the twentieth century.

Similarly and significantly, the *national* statistics for adult criminal activity were also in decline at around the same period. On all major statistical indicators – numbers and ratios of offences known to the police, arrests for indictable and non-indictable offences, committals to trial and convictions – the level of adult criminality declined markedly in the period from 1869 onwards, especially in London but also in the country as a whole, reaching in the case of the capital at least its lowest ebb of modern times in the mid-1920s.[14] For England and Wales, the number of indictable offences known to the police per 100,000 of population stood at approximately 365 in 1880, 300 in 1890, 240 in 1900, 275 in 1910, 220 in 1915, 270 in 1920 and 300 in 1925.[15] In the case of London the overall downward trend in the various crime indicators over the period from 1869 to the late 1920s was more pronounced: total arrests fell by an average of 11 per cent per decade, convictions by 12 per cent, indictable offences known by 10 per cent, arrests for indictable offences by 14 per cent and convictions by trial for indictable offences by 14 per cent.[16]

The upturn in recorded levels of juvenile delinquency in Oxford, and possibly more generally, from the 1870s to the 1900s was therefore an even more remarkable phenomenon since it occurred against a backdrop of a general downward trend in police and court activity as directed against adults. At first sight such an upturn might indeed seem 'to substantiate contemporary fears of juvenile immorality' (Gillis, 1975: 99). However, it is more probably the case that, rather than providing evidence for any 'real' increase in the levels of juvenile law-breaking, the Oxford figures reveal a new willingness on the part of police and courts to prosecute and convict working-class youth for offences of a predominantly non-indictable nature that had previously been tolerated as part of the traditions of youth, or else dealt with informally by the community itself (Gillis, 1975: 99–101). Such a shift in attitude was in its own right in part a product of the period's increasing differentiation of the juvenile offender in legal terms (the establishment of juvenile courts, remand homes, probation orders etc.) that was to culminate with the Children's Act of 1908.[17] In part it was also an expression of more generalized concern over the perceived indiscipline of urban working-class youth, as discussed above. Indeed *all* working-class youth was now coming to be perceived as problematic and at least potentially deviant. Hence the emergence from the late nineteenth century onwards of a breed of middle-class youth workers who sought to bring the disciplined public school model of adolescence to an often unwilling working-class population.[18]

Central to what has come to be known as the 'child saving' project was the idea of *rehabilitation*: the conviction that with correct handling potentially or actually deviant working-class youth could be taught new and socially or nationally useful ways. In England as in America much of the debate that surrounded the establishment of special juvenile courts and institutions for young offenders was from the outset couched in terms of *treatment and cure* rather than *punishment*. Writing in 1910 in support of the newly established borstal system, C. E. B. Russell noted that:

As might be expected the large majority of youthful criminals are drawn from the ranks of youths who spend idle and vicious days in the least reputable districts of great centres of population, and these youths again have commonly been reared by feckless parents in the very poorest circumstances.

but

The hopeful thing is that there are many – the great number in fact – who with wise and careful and sympathetic supervision, and above all with removal from their early surroundings, are capable of becoming useful men. (Russell, 1910: viii–ix)[19]

And again, echoing the physical degeneration theme:

The starved, stunted, round shouldered, pigeon breasted, mentally underdeveloped young criminal would in many cases gain health for mind and body during a course of from one to three years' training with good food, wholesome living, moral and religious influences and labour adapted to develop without overstraining his powers. (Russell, 1910: 226)

Nor, as has been previously noted, was the urge to 'improve' working-class youth confined to those officially defined as deviant. One further manifestation of the upsurge of generalized middle-class adult intervention into the domain of working-class youth in the late nineteenth and early twentieth centuries was an explosive growth of independent militaristic youth organizations, again with the explicit aim of providing working-class boys with the public school code: 'Trying to teach some of the public school spirit to the elementary schoolboy', in the words of Baden-Powell (Springhall, 1977: 54).

The pioneer organization in this field was the Boys' Brigade, which was founded in Glasgow in 1883, had a membership of 35,148 in England, Wales and Scotland by 1899, and reached its peak in 1934 with a total membership of 96,762 (Springhall, 1977: ch. 1, pp. 22–36). This was soon outstripped, however, by the most famous of all such organizations, the Boy Scouts, which was founded with the publication of Baden-Powell's *Scouting for Boys* in 1908, and which attained its peak in 1933 in the UK with a total of 461,740 members and many more throughout the rest of the world.[20] Other similar youth organizations that flourished in the late nineteenth and early twentieth centuries were the Church Lads Brigade, the Jewish Lads Brigade, the Catholic Boys' Brigade and the various armed service cadet forces (Springhall, 1977: ch. 2, pp. 37–52). It was also from the 1880s onwards that the 'doyen of youth organizations', the YMCA, founded in 1844, began to make a mass impact amongst the older youth of the urban working and lower-middle classes. Similarly the decades around the turn of the century witnessed the setting up of many university and public school 'missions' and boys' clubs in the poorer city areas.[21]

The reasons for this sudden scramble to enlist the boys of the lower social orders – in fact largely from the lower-middle and upper-working classes – to the cause of British 'muscular' Christianity were undoubtedly complex, but amongst the most significant was arguably an attempt to cement national unity and secure the British Empire through the establishment of the hegemony of the dominant (Liberal-imperialist) ideology over the younger generation. As noted above, this was a time when the status quo was seen as being under considerable threat from outside forces – Germany's imperial ambitions, the weaknesses in the Empire revealed by the Boer War, etc. The earlier part of the period under discussion was also a time when there was considerable anxiety concerning the 'threat from within' as represented by the rise of the labour movement, civil and industrial unrest and the possibility of open and large-scale class conflict. This directly political anxiety seems to have subsided somewhat following the unrest of the 1880s that culminated in the 1889 London dock strike (Stedman-Jones, 1971: esp. ch. 7). However, fears concerning *youthful* – and not directly political – delinquency, violence, hooliganism, etc., persisted into the first decades of the twentieth century. These fears were in turn thrown into particular relief through the more generalized attention that was coming to be directed at youth as a result of the 'national degeneration' debate and through the increasingly clear definition of adolescence/youth as a distinct age grade that was emerging as a consequence of low mortality and fertility and late marriage, universal elementary education and expanding leisure and commercial exploitation.

For a whole range of both objective and subjective reasons, then, the youth question was a much-discussed and often anxiety-provoking issue in late nineteenth and early twentieth-century Britain. One official response to this question was the establishment of the various independent youth organizations that flourished in this period; others were manifested in calls for better and more appropriate education and training for all of the younger generation, and in the establishment of specialized judicial and correctional arrangements for the processing of problem youth.

All of these social institutional developments must, however, be set against further major advances in the establishment of a distinctively modern approach towards the young as an object of study. As noted in the foregoing discussion of the significance of the ideas of Rousseau, the phenomenon of the institutionalization and objectification of adolescence was accompanied, if not actually in the first instance conditioned by, conceptualization. The late nineteenth and early twentieth centuries were a time when developmental and educational psychology took on an ever more professionalized, scientific and empirically based guise, and began significantly to shape policy towards the young, thus contributing to the objectification of the very pattern of division of the pre-adult years that these disciplines claimed to have discovered.

The entry for 'Child' in the *Encylopaedia Britannica* of 1910 commented on these developments thus:

> The physical, psychological and educational development of children from birth till adulthood has provided material in recent years for what has come to be regarded as almost a distinct part of comparative anthropological or sociological science, and the literature of adolescence and of 'child study' in its various aspects has attained considerable importance. In England the British Child Study Association was founded in 1894. . . . In America specially valuable work has been done, several universities have encouraged the study . . . and Professor G. Stanley Hall's initiative has led to elaborate enquiries. (*Encyclopaedia Britannica*, 1910: vol. 6, pp. 136–7)

The same entry went on to provide an extensive bibliography of works of child study – all published in the previous thirty years – and then concluded almost on a note of complaint, itself indicative of the extent of the recent upsurge in 'child study' as an area of expertise in its own right:

> The child, after all, is in a transition stage to an adult, and there is often a tendency in modern 'child students' to interpret the phenomena exhibited by a particular child with a *pari pris*, or to exaggerate child study . . . as though it involved the discovery of some distinct form of animal, of separate value on its own account. (Ibid.)

In the specific context of the definition of adolescence the most significant psychological work in this respect is now generally held to have been the American G. Stanley Hall's massive *Adolescence: Its Psychology and Its Relations to Physiology, Anthropology, Sociology, Sex, Crime, Religion and Education* (1904). A rambling two-volume compendium of speculation and half-digested data, this may nonetheless be seen as the 'first systematic portrayal of that stage of life in the modern world' (Ross, 1972: 333).[22]

Hall's work has long since been rejected by the scientific and professional community and indeed his ideas appear in retrospect as possessing the status of rather weird Victorian pseudo-science. Nonetheless from the point of view of the historian of adolescence these same ideas are of tremendous importance for a whole number of reasons. Basically, what Hall did was to take Rousseau's ideas concerning the stage-like nature of human development, and the special importance of the 'second birth' of puberty and of the adolescent period in general, and re-work these in the light of post-Darwinian biology and evolutionist philosophy. Hall assumed human development to be conditioned by physiological changes and this point of departure, coupled with his own research and observations, led to his postulating the existence of four 'given' pre-adult developmental stages: 'infancy' (the years from birth till 4), 'childhood' (4 till 8), 'youth' (8 till 12 – an odd appropriation of this term for what we would today regard as the years of late childhood or pre-adolescence), and 'adolescence' (puberty at around 12 till the attainment of full adulthood at, according to Hall, the somewhat belated age of 22 to 25).[23]

Hall's developmental *schema* linked the human life-cycle to the history of the human race through the doctrine of *recapitulation*: each individual's passage from birth to maturity re-enacts the same purported stages as those of humanity in its passage to contemporary civilization. It follows from such a doctrine that the period of adolescence, as brought on by the physiological changes of puberty and the 'awakening of the sexual passions', will be of particular importance and also particularly difficult since it is at this time that the individual must, if he or she is to grow to healthy and well-integrated maturity, recapitulate the turbulent period of the passage of (Western) humanity into 'true civilization'. At both the phylogenetic and also the ontogenetic levels, such a transition was primarily effected through the suppression and control of the grosser sexual instincts.[24] Thus, wrote Hall, 'the adolescent stage of life is marked by a struggle between the needs of the organism and the desires of society' (G. S. Hall, 1907: vol. 1, p. xvi). This inner struggle of the adolescent psyche together with its outward be- havioural manifestations Hall chose to label, significantly enough, after the Romantic movement in German literature as exemplified in the writings of Schiller and the young Goethe, as *'sturm und drang'* or, in English,'storm and stress'.

The notion of adolescence as an innately turbulent and difficult period both for those undergoing it and also for society as a whole had been expressed before – it was Hall, however, who put this idea on a fully 'scientific' footing, and who furthermore elevated the imputed characteristic of storm and stress to a definitive and central position within the psychology of the adolescent. Relatively early in his career, when Hall was still primarily interested in the question of youth in relation to moral and religious issues (it is significant that Hall came from a strongly Protestant background and came to developmental psychology via religious philosophy: from both of these he would have acquired the idea – as discussed in Chapter 2 above – of the teenage years as the key time for the undergoing of the experience of religious conversion), he described the storm and stress of adolescence thus:

> . . . lack of emotional steadiness, violent impulses, unreasonable conduct, lack of enthusiasm or sympathy. . . . The previous selfhood is broken up . . . and a new individual in the process of being born. All is solvent, plastic and peculiarly susceptible to external influences.[25]

The idea of adolescence as innately problematic, yet also a time of great individual and social potential (for good or ill), was further elaborated in the chapter in *Adolescence* on 'Feelings and Psychic Evolution', whose import has been summarized thus:

> Hall perceived the emotional life of the adolescent as oscillating between contradictory tendencies. Energy, exaltation and a supernatural activity are followed by indifference, lethargy and loathing. Exuberant gaiety, laughter and euphoria make place for dysphoria, depressive gloom and melancholy. Egoism, vanity and conceit are just as characteristic of this period of life as are abasement, humiliation and bashfulness. One can observe both the remnants of an uninhibited selfishness and an increasing

idealistic altruism. Goodness and virtue are never so pure, but never again does temptation so preoccupy thought. The adolescent wants solitude and seclusion, while he finds himself entangled in crushes and friendships. Never again does the peer group have such a strong influence over him. At one time he may exhibit exquisite sensitivity and tenderness, at another time, callousness and cruelty. Apathy and inertia vacillate with an enthusiastic curiosity, an urge to discover and explore. There is a yearning for idols and authority which does not exclude a revolutionary radicalism directed against any kind of authority.   (Muuss, 1966: 16–17)

Thus the psycho-sexual upheavals ushered in by puberty were seen as giving rise to the many 'paired contradictions' of adolescence as outlined above, and out of these inevitably are born adolescent storm and stress.

What is so remarkable about Hall's description of the psycho-social characteristics of adolescence is of course the extent to which it still coincides with the dominant contemporary view of adolescent psychology, the evidence of such studies as those discussed in Chapter 1 notwithstanding. Thus we still (either along the lines of the classic explanation advanced by Hall of the biological given of the transformations of puberty leading to adolescent storm and stress, or else following the more sociological and relativized post-Eriksonian view of adolescence as a time of identity crisis under the fluid conditions of contemporary society) tend to regard *all* adolescents as troubled, volatile, easily influenced and generally at odds with their elders. On the basis of typifications such as those of Hall (and Rousseau before him) the category of 'adolescent' has increasingly come to be viewed as one which cuts across the other dimensions of social stratification, and adolescence itself has increasingly come to be singled out as a distinct and 'special' entity.

Demos and Demos have reached a similar conclusion concerning the long-term significance of Hall's ideas:

Hall's critics denied the validity of considering personal growth in terms of 'stages'; but we still regard adolescence in just such a context. His critics accused him of having greatly exaggerated 'storm and stress' phenomena, and yet today more than ever we view adolescence in exactly those terms. In fact the special 'cult of adolescence' seems to have lost no strength at all.   (Demos and Demos, 1969: 636)

In the post Second World War period in particular those qualities and values that Hall identified with what might be regarded as the positive side of adolescence – idealism, spontaneity, intuitiveness, honesty, volatility, radicalism etc. – have frequently been held up as of special relevance in a 'new', 'modern' and ever more rapidly changing world. These 'new' values and qualities have been advanced in this context in opposition to the 'old' and supposedly now irrelevant values and qualities that can be associated with maturity. His biographer has stated that Hall himself was 'not happy with maturity', which period as then constituted he equated with mental and ethical rigidity and stasis or even decline, but rather elevated adolescence to the highest position in his regard: 'this golden stage of life which glisters and crepitates . . . the apical stage of human development . . . before the decline of the highest powers of the soul in maturity and age' (Ross, 1972: 332). It should also, however, be noted that as is still the case with the common evaluation of and response to adolescence or youth, Hall's theory embodied at its heart an essential *ambivalence*: on the one hand there is a celebration of adolescence and desire to promote its energy, freedom, potential etc., but on the other there is a fear of these very same qualities and a desire to keep them in check or channel them into 'proper' and ethical forms. Later chapters of this work will explore the contradictions of the contemporary response to adolescence and youth in greater detail.

Some indication of the impact of Hall's *Adolescence* in America at least can be gained from the fact that it sold over 25,000 copies – a remarkable feat considering the work's highly academic tone and sheer physical bulk! A shorter and less 'explicit' one-volume edition, *Youth, Its Education, Regimen and Hygiene* (1906), also achieved considerable popularity as a school textbook and manual for parents, teachers and youth workers.[26] In Britain J. W. Slaughter's *The Adolescent* (1911) provided a popular and accessible distillation of Hallian ideas for the teaching profession (Springhall, 1986: 176). Certainly Hall was the major academic prophet of adolescence for British child-savers and youth workers. The frontispiece of C. E. B. Russell's *Lad's Clubs* bore the following quotation from *Adolescence*:

'Those who believe that nothing is so worthy of life, reverence and service as the body and soul of youth, and who hold that the best test of every human institution is how much it contributes to bring youth to the ever-fullest possible development, may well review themselves and the civilization in which we live to see how far it satisfies this supreme test.'

Some more general sense of the extent to which the Hallian model of adolescence and the associated belief in the special significance of this stage of the life-cycle was dominant in early twentieth-century professional thought can be roughly gauged from the already referred to *Encyclopaedia Britannica* of 1910; this time the entry for 'Adolescence':

. . . the term now commonly adopted for the period between childhood and maturity during which the characteristics – mental, physical and moral – that make or mar the individual disclose themselves, and then mature, in some cases by leaps and bounds, in others by a more general evolution. . . . The sex sense develops, the love of nature and religion, and an over-mastering curiosity both individual and general. This period of life, so fraught with its power for good or ill, is accordingly the most important and by far the most difficult for parents and educationalists to deal with efficiently. (*Encyclopaedia Britannica*, 1910: vol. 1, pp. 210–11)

The rest of this entry then goes on to make recommendations concerning the correct diet, clothing, exercise and educational programme for adolescents and is particularly adamant on the matter of the danger posed to the health and development of the young – but not adults – by town life: 'In an ideal condition children should be brought up in the country as much as possible rather than in the town' (p. 211). In this idea it is perhaps possible to discern another trace of the youth/urban–anxiety connection that has already been noted as a common theme of the social discourse of the period. This is echoed in the entry's concluding remarks which also reinforce the Hallian picture of adolescence as a period with great potential for individual and social peril and stress:

> The adolescent is prone to special weaknesses and moral perversions. The emotions are extremely unstable, and any stress put on them may lead to undesirable results. Warm climates, tight fitting clothes, corsets, rich foods, soft mattresses or indulgences of any kind, and also mental over-stimulation are especially to be guarded against. (Ibid.)

The work of Hall has been dealt with at some length, not out of any desire to attribute to it a unique historical significance, but rather because it marks a further important point in the definition of many aspects of the theory of adolescence as a distinct and important psycho-social state which is still largely taken for granted to this day. Nonetheless it is also necessary briefly to outline the contributions of Freudian and other psychologies of adolescence, if only to point out the way in which these have generally reiterated and served to reinforce the essentials of Hall's original 'storm and stress' model, and have thus added their own weight to the characterization of this period as innately difficult and troubled, if potentially also of the greatest value and importance. It is certainly the case that whereas the work of Hall was fairly soon relegated to an academic no man's land, that of Freud and his followers in this area has been of the greatest intellectual and practical significance throughout the large part of the present century. Especially in the United States, the individual problems of adolescence have to a very considerable extent come to be seen as part of the domain of psychoanalysis and its attendant profession, both in terms of their explication and also their remedy.[27]

The key work in the Freudian canon dealing specifically with the period of adolescence is 'The Transformations of Puberty' in *Three Essays on Sexuality* (1905); for Freud as for Hall the physiological-sexual transformations in individual development that are brought about by puberty can be equated with a 'new birth' after the sexual latency of childhood – the period from around 5 or 6 years of age till puberty. With puberty comes the second and this time enduring phase of conscious sexual feeling, and it is during the adolescent period that the individual is faced with the task of making the final transition to full and 'normal' adulthood through the development of an altruistic heterosexual attachment out of and over against his or her previous narcissism and auto-eroticism. Thus, once again, the notion of adolescence as necessarily stressful is built into Freud's theory, since it is at this time that the individual, if he or she is to progress to well-balanced maturity, must attain emotional independence from his or her parents, while at the same time 'turning outwards' his or her own sexuality, and both of these objectives are only regarded as attainable after a certain amount of stress and friction for all concerned. Note should also be made of what is again the essentially normative nature of the Freudian theory of the psycho-dynamics of adolescence: as with Hall's theory, this stage is regarded as one with its own internal logic which must be allowed to play itself out, and with its own particular and innate problems which must be resolved in order that the final goal of (normal) maturity can then be reached. Unlike Hall, however, Freud regarded the developmental significance of the adolescent stage as of only secondary importance when compared with that of the early stages of infantile sexuality.

Amongst those of Freud's followers to devote more specific attention to adolescence were Anna Freud and Otto Rank. The most significant recent contribution to the psychoanalytic approach to adolescence has been that of Erik Erikson who, in part at least, has relativized and 'sociologicized' the theories of Freud, while at the same time providing us with the influential formulation of adolescence as a period of 'identity crisis' and 'role moratorium' (Erikson, 1975: 239–66; Erikson, 1974). The twentieth century has in general witnessed an explosion in the output of psychologically grounded developmental *schema* and of psychological theories of adolescence, again linked to the growth of psychology and psychiatry as professions and of the 'caring' professions, themselves psychologically based in some large measure. Other, non-Freudian, approaches to this area of study have been made by Eduard Spranger, Kirt Lewin, Alison Davis, Arnold Gessell, Heinz Remplein and many others (see Muuss, 1966). Piaget has also contributed to the theoretical separation out of adolescence as a distinct developmental stage in his work on the development of cognition in general, and in particular on the final shift to adult thought processes or 'formal operations' which he regarded as occurring at somewhere between the ages of 12 and 15.[28] For Piaget it is this new-found mastery of abstract thought that makes the years of adolescence a troubled period, since the adolescent now becomes a systems builder *par excellence*, and thereby romantic and unrealistic, with a desire to change the world.

Just as the late nineteenth and early twentieth centuries saw the emergence of adolescence and the adolescent as objects of professional psychological theorizing, so also the same period witnessed an upsurge in the artistic representation of adolescence. In European literature Romain Rolland's *Jean Christophe* (1904) is generally regarded as the first major modern novel of adolescence, with its detailed portrayal of the torments and turbulence, fierce creativity and lack of clearly defined sense of selfhood of its adolescent protagonist.[29]

The theme of adolescent storm and stress has also been a major one for the twentieth-century American novel, to the extent that the critic Leslie Fiedler has come to speak of the adolescent as 'an archetypal figure for the confusions of our age'.[30] As should be abundantly clear by now, however, the prevalence of such projective connections between images of adolescence and broader social diagnoses is by no means confined to the domain of fiction or to the United States alone. The following chapters will seek to explore how Fielder's maxim might be said to apply – in specific contexts and senses – to the copious *non-fictional* discussion of adolescence and youth in twentieth-century Britain.

4

Responses to youth I:
The early twentieth century

It was the 1918 Education Act that finally established as a social reality the ideal of universal elementary education up until the age of 14, and thus by the same token everywhere institutionized the primary age-grading division between childhood and adulthood. This same Act also committed the government to the development of 'education other than elementary', especially, by implication, for the children of the lower social orders. Demands for universal and free secondary – i.e. non-elementary – education had been growing within the labour movement and other progressive and liberal quarters since the latter part of the nineteenth century, but it was not until the inter-war period that the definition of (universal) 'secondary education' and the planning of a system to bring this objective into being became the major topic for educational debate (Simon, 1974: 162, 176–207, 249–95 and 357–64). The minimum and modal school-leaving age stood at 14 in 1918, was raised to 15 in 1947 and 16 in 1973: for the majority of the population, therefore, the period of full-time schooling has only ever embraced the earlier part of the adolescent years as defined on other criteria. What is significant in the process of the establishment of true universal secondary – as opposed to extended elementary – education, however, is the way in which the former has always been seen as in need of tailoring to a conception of the special characteristics and problems of the period of adolescence.

As early as 1917 a Board of Education Report on 'juvenile education after the war' was making a plea that adolescence, by virtue of its formative nature, be treated as a period for full-time and then part-time education, with the emphasis on learning the skills to equip the individual for adulthood, rather than as one when the majority commenced full-time employment:

Can the age of adolescence be brought out of the purview of

economic exploitation and into that of the social conscience? Can the conception of the juvenile as primarily a little wage earner be replaced by the conception of the juvenile as primarily the workman and citizen in training? Can it be established that the educational purpose is to be the dominating one, without as well as within the school doors, during those formative years between twelve and eighteen?[1]

Perhaps the most explicit and influential connection between the proposed establishment of a universal system of secondary education and the imputed nature of adolescence was made however in the *Hadow Report* of 1926.[2] Under the influence of the educational ideas of R. H. Tawney, himself a committee member, this document advocated that the school-leaving age be raised to 15, and that secondary education be extended to all children through the establishment of 'modern secondary schools', providing practical education for non-grammar-school pupils:

> There is a tide which begins to rise in the veins of youth at the age of eleven or twelve. It is called by the name of adolescence. If that tide can be taken at the flood, and a new voyage begun in the strength and along the flow of its current, we think that it will move on to fortune. We therefore propose that all children should be transferred at the age of eleven or twelve, from the junior or primary school, either to schools of the type now called secondary or to senior and separate departments of existing elementary schools . . . we recommend that as soon as possible, an additional year should be added to the general school life, and that the leaving age should be raised to fifteen. Only in that way can the modern schools and senior departments, which will then be able to plan a four years' course, exercise their full influence on their pupils; only in that way can children be guided safely through the opportunities, the excitements, and the perils of adolescence; only in that way can the youth of the nation be adequately trained for a full and worthy citizenship. (Maclure, 1965: 180)

It was the *Hadow Report* which established our current terminology for the primary and universal subdivision of the years of schooling, thereby in effect advocating the formal institutionalization of a major break in the age grading of the pre-adult years: 'It is desirable that education up to eleven plus should be known by the general name of Primary Education and education after eleven by the general name of Secondary Education' (Maclure, 1965: 183). More than this, secondary education, no matter what its form, was to be 'marked by the common characteristic that its aim is to provide for the needs of children who are entering and passing through the stage of adolescence' (Maclure, 1965: 182). In this manner the age grade of childhood proper came to be associated in educational policy with primary education and that of adolescence with secondary education. Subsequent reports, notably *Spens* (Report of the Consultative Committee on Secondary Education, 1938) and *Norwood* (Report of the Committee of the Secondary Schools Examinations Council on Curriculum and Examinations in Secondary Schools, 1943), whose brief was the question of the establishment of a universal system of secondary education (and which recommended the setting up of the tripartite system on the basis of the doctrine of division by 'innate intelligence', as well as advocating the raising of the school-leaving age to 16), reinforced either directly or indirectly this childhood–primary/adolescence–secondary division (see Maclure, 1965: 193–9 and 200–5 for outlines and excerpts). However, it was not until the implementation of the 1944 Education Act in 1947 that this basic institutional division in the age grading of pre-adulthood became everywhere established and a fact of life (Maclure, 1965: 222–5).[3]

Nonetheless for the majority of the population, and especially of course for the children of the working and lower-middle classes, the period of secondary education did not, and still does not to this day, extend far into the chronological age range of adolescence, if for general purposes we consider this as embracing the years from around 11 till 18 or 21. (Although it should be borne in mind that school-leavers from the lower-middle and skilled working classes customarily left school for a period of craft or trade *apprenticeship*, and thus were in these years still of an institutionalized adolescent or proto-adult status.) Thus in 1938, before the establishment of the tripartite system and the advent of universal secondary education proper, only 38 per cent of all 14-year-olds were receiving full-time education, while the figure for 17-year-olds was 4 per cent, and for 19-year-olds only 2 per cent. In 1962 when the school-leaving age stood at 15 but before the Robbins expansion of higher and further education of the late 1960s, only 15 per cent of 17-year-olds and 7 per cent of 19-year-olds were in full-time education (Ministry of Education, 1963: p. 11, Table 1). In Great Britain the predominantly working and lower middle-class majority have always left full-time education at a relatively early age and have thus enjoyed only a relatively short adolescence in the sense of this period's institutionalization and segregation from the adult world in the secondary school.

Despite being 'proto-adult', by virtue of having already departed from the world of full-time education, the majority of working young people have increasingly come to be still officially defined as *adolescents*, with a consequently special and protected but also inferior status. It is the group of working adolescents, its problems and the potential problems posed to society by virtue of its very existence, that has always formed the prime target for the concern of the various youth organizations, associations and clubs that have flourished in the twentieth century, initially on an independent and voluntary basis, but increasingly, since the Second World War, on a professional and state-sponsored basis.

Let us return, though, to the growth in social awareness of 'youth' as a distinct and potentially problematic entity which was a feature of the earlier decades of the present century. As outlined in Chapter 3 the phenomenon of the flowering of urban working-class youth culture and subculture at around the turn of the century combined with certain prevalent national and social anxieties to produce a situation in which the youth question (basically *what youth was doing* and *what to do with youth*) was a matter of considerable debate. One major focus for this debate was provided by the topic of juvenile delinquency and, as noted, while it is difficult to be sure about trends in the actual incidence of delinquency in this period, the general level of social anxiety about delinquency was running at a high level up until and throughout the First World War.

During the early years of the war, concern was voiced lest the abnormal social conditions of wartime – less parental control, decreased quality and quantity of schooling, greater opportunities for child labour, etc., – be conducive to juvenile delinquency (Leeson, 1917). The official statistics also revealed an increase from a total of 37,520 persons charged before the juvenile courts in 1913 to a peak of 51,323 in 1917 (Burt, 1925: 20). By 1916 the concern at this increase was sufficient for the Home Secretary to appoint a special Juvenile Organizations Committee 'to consider in view of the officially reported increase in juvenile delinquency, what steps could be taken to strengthen and extend the work of voluntary agencies concerned with the welfare of boys and girls' (Carr-Saunders *et al.*, 1942: 13–17).[4]

When the long-term statistical trend over the entire period from the early 1910s to the early 1930s is considered, however, a somewhat different picture emerges. Recorded rates of juvenile delinquency rose briefly in the early years of the First World War and again at the time of the General Strike, but overall the statistics demonstrate a remarkable stability: in 1911 the proportion of persons under sixteen charged in juvenile courts with indictable offences per 100,000 of the population stood at 288, and for 1928 the same statistic was 289.[5] In 1910 the number of juveniles found guilty of an indictable offence stood at 10,786 and in 1930 there were 11,137; over the same period the number of convictions of juveniles for non-indictable offences actually fell by almost half from 14,694 to 7,577.[6]

The various statistical indicators of juvenile delinquency then take an upturn in the late 1920s (an upturn which is incidentally coincident with that of indicators of adult criminality), with the rate of juveniles charged with indictable offences per 100,000 of population rising from 307 in 1929 to 370 in 1933 (Gurr *et al.*, 1977: 158–9).[7] It was however in the mid-1930s, following on from the passage of the Children and Young Persons Act of 1933, that this upward tend really took off, with 439 persons under 16 per 100,000 of population being charged with indictable offences in 1934, 529 in 1935 and 658 in 1936 (Carr-Saunders *et al.*, 1942: 45). Between 1930 and 1938 the absolute numbers of juveniles[8] convicted rose from 11,137 to 27,875 in the case of indictable offences and 7,577 to 15,310 in the case of non-indictable offences (Halsey, 1972: pp. 527–8, table 15.1).

Nonetheless by the 1920s juvenile delinquency was already becoming established as a topic for investigation for British academics, even if it was not seen as a particularly pressing social problem of the period, and the major study of the decade was undoubtedly Cyril Burt's *The Young Delinquent* (1925).[9] Burt set the tone for much subsequent British work in this area in his adoption of an essentially medico-psychological case study approach to his problem and in his attempt to apportion the respective impacts of psychological and environmental factors in the causation of delinquency. He also echoed the thoughts of the earlier child-savers in his rationale for the separation out of juvenile delinquency as a distinct object of study:

> To treat delinquency in the young as a separate topic, as a problem apart from criminality in adults, may seem, at first sight, a fault in procedure; there are however, two strong reasons that unite to render this advisable. The juvenile offender is easier to study; and at the same time he is easier to reclaim. (Burt, 1925: 19)

The theme of juvenile delinquency truly returned to the limelight in the 1930s along with the rapid rise of delinquency statistics in this decade and the phenomenon of mass juvenile and youth un-employment as ushered in by the Great Depression.[10] Un-employment amongst juveniles (i.e. in the 14–17 age range) hovered around 150,000 in the early 1930s at the lowest point of the Depression and declined to around the still considerable total of 100,000 in the later part of the decade (Gollan, 1937: 156). For a number of commentators the level of juvenile unemployment at this time, especially in hard-hit urban areas, was sufficient for a direct connection to be made between this factor and juvenile delin-quency. J. H. Bagot's study of juvenile delinquency in Liverpool over the period 1934–36 argued that unemployment was an important influence in the production of delinquency in boys in the 14–17 age range (Bagot, 1941). Similarly in 1937 the Report of the Commissioner of the Metropolitan Police 'cited the primary importance of unemployment among youth as a cause of crime and added that this was a view widely held by officers' (Gurr *et al.*, 1977: 167).

It should be stressed, however, that the connection that was being drawn in the 1930s between juvenile unemployment and rapidly rising juvenile delinquency statistics was only one relatively minor aspect of the much wider area of then-current concern that can be subsumed under the heading 'youth unemployment'. At this period – unlike in the 1970s and 80s – the major youth unemployment problem was not seen as being primarily to do with unemployment amongst school-leavers or juveniles. The use of 'boy labour' was still a prevalent feature of the labour market, and as a consequence of this the sector of youth hit hardest by unemployment was in the 18–25 age range. As one contemporary commentator on the plight of 'workless youth' remarked, 'if the problem of unemployed children is serious, that of unemployed young people of eighteen or older is doubly so' (Gollan, 1937: 159). In 1931 unemployment in the 18–24 age range stood at approximately 542,000, in 1935 the figure was 416,000, and in 1936 it was 317,000.[11] (The overall level of unemployment during the Depression reached a peak of 2,557,000 in 1932 and had fallen to 1,621,000 by 1936) (Pilgrim Trust, 1938). A major theme of the social and political discourse of the Depression years was, as one might reasonably expect, that of the real and anticipated consequences of mass unemployment, and in a number of ways these were regarded as particularly serious for youth. The Pilgrim Trust's classic report on the personal impact of unemployment reserved the following special considerations for the topic of the social-psychological implications of youth unemployment:

> When prolonged unemployment comes at this age . . . it is bound to have different effects from those of long unemployment on a more stable and mature nature and this is the reason for the large numbers of young men who 'don't want to work' (Pilgrim Trust, 1938: 224)

This idea of the supposed demoralization of young workers as a result of relatively long-term joblessness recurred throughout the various studies commissioned at this time to enquire specifically into the nature and consequences of youth unemployment. Of these, the most significant text was Cameron, Lush and Meara's *Disinherited Youth*, a report of the results of extensive fieldwork into the condition of unemployed 18–25-year-olds in Glasgow, Liverpool and Cardiff in the summer of 1937 (Cameron *et al.*, 1943). In the introduction to their report Cameron *et al.* pointed out the special significance assumed by the youth unemployment problem in the 1930s:

> While there has aways been a conflict between young and old, recent years have thrown into prominence one particular aspect of it which the community has characterized as especially a young

person's problem. . . . Today if young people show bewilderment and confusion at the network of social machinery surrounding their lives, it is not a cause for wonder . . . [they have been taught to expect permanent full-time employment and yet] for many this was not so, and therein lies the crucial problem of young people today. (Cameron *et al.*, 1943: 1)

One major finding of this report was that the incidence of unemployment was considerably higher amongst those young men who had left school at the minimum age of 14 than amongst those who had left later, and that moreover this effect did not significantly diminish with age.[12] This idea led the authors to expand upon the idea of youth-as-national-asset which was already well established as a major strand of the youth question, and which now resurfaced with renewed vigour in the discourse surrounding youth unemployment. Inadequate educational provision for the mass of young people was not merely tied up with the problem of youth unemployment, it also posed real questions for the future of Britain as a free and democratic society:

The relationship between standard of education and unemployment, as revealed in this analysis, leaves no grounds for complacency. On the contrary, it forces the conclusion that to leave matters as they are, to allow another generation of our youth to scramble into the labour market with the inevitable recurring periods of unemployment, and then jealously to guard and to strengthen their liberties by alert participation in a democratic society, is to ask the impossible. (Cameron *et al.* 1943: 21)

These anxieties and the consequent urgent call for the nation to improve dramatically its educational and social provision for youth were returned to in the report's conclusion, here with the additional element of a sidelong and apprehensive glance at the burgeoning centrally directed youth programmes of the fascist and communist states:

Perhaps the time has come if it has not already passed, when we must face squarely some fundamental questions on youth in the

community today. . . . Today it appears more and more necessary that a capacity for social and political responsibility should be
made part of the skilled equipment and stock in trade of the
citizen of tomorrow.

   . . . the youth problem today is essentially a human problem
concerning as it does the apprentice citizen or citizen-in-the-
making.

   In other highly industrialized countries we have seen, in the
past decade, how the youth problem has been tackled in a manner
odious to lovers of freedom and democratic institutions . . . we
must find our own solution. What is it to be?   (Cameron *et al.*,
1943: 87)

The then-much-discussed question of the emotional and mental
impact of unemployment upon the young also received a good deal
of attention from Cameron *et al.* with particular reference to the
volatility that is imputedly characteristic of adolescent psychology:

   It seems fairly clear that the effects of unemployment upon the
   personalities of youth have a marked influence on their future
   manhood. . . . Lacking the stability of age and experience they
   are emotionally more liable to become drifters. For many
   self-confidence is shattered, and this, in itself, becomes a barrier
   to further employment. . . . Their decreased sociability, irrita-
   bility and sometimes open violence, are common manifestations
   of heightened emotional instability due to unemployment . . . or
   . . . some are apt to become fatalist and adopt as a protective
   measure the 'don't care a damn' attitude.   (Cameron *et al.*,
   1943: 69)

The idea that mass youth unemployment might produce a
dangerously demoralized and apathetic younger generation (see
also the remarks of the Pilgrim Trust report on this topic above)
would seem in fact to have been the dominant one in the period's
projection of the likely social and political consequences of this
undoubtedly real and serious problem. It may have sometimes been
assumed or asserted in the popular debates of the period that the
phenomenon of youth unemployment – and unemployment in
general – carried with it the potential for large-scale political
upheaval. This possibility, however, was one that was almost

entirely rejected in official and academic analyses of the problem, where, unlike in certain later eras, a fear of youthful apathy, not activism, ruled the day. The following final quote from Cameron *et al.* suggests something of the flavour of the prevalent attitude:

> The overwhelming majority of the men [in the survey] had no political convictions whatsoever. . . . It has perhaps been assumed too readily by some that, because men are unemployed, their natural state of want and discontent must express itself in some revolutionary attitude. It cannot be reiterated too often that unemployment is not an active state; its keynote is boredom – a continuous sense of boredom. This boredom was invariably accompanied by a disbelief which gave rise to cynicism. (p. 78)

The youth question in the inter-war period, in as far as this applied to the mass of young people, therefore came increasingly, as the 1920s gave way to the 1930s, to be dominated by the problem of youth unemployment – itself only one aspect of the period's major social issue, that of the Great Depression and unemployment as a whole. It is perhaps for this reason that images of working-class youth from this period seem relatively 'unspectacular' and under-emphasized when compared with those of the pre-First World War era or those of the 1950s, 60s and 70s.

However, a different picture emerges with respect to the image of *middle-class* youth in the inter-war period, and indeed with respect to the further elaboration of the concept of youth at around this time. To backtrack to the early post-First-World-War period, it would seem to be the case that the aftermath of the war was accompanied by a *sense* at least of intergenerational discontinuity of a scale and intensity previously unknown. The numerical commitment of the younger generation of 1914–18 to the hostilities, the rates of mortality amongst young front-line troops, and by the end of the war the sheer sense of enormous unnecessary waste of life that was then current, meant 'the young' were now widely seen as opposed to 'the old' in a quite unprecedented manner. In the early 1920s there emerged in one form or another in all of the combatant nations a cult or myth of the 'lost youth' of the war, needlessly sent to their deaths by the 'old men'. One aspect of this was manifested in a sense of specialness and group identity amongst veterans and a need to 'keep the faith' with fallen comrades through pilgrimages to the former battlefields of Flanders, the erection of war memorials, charitable work amongst the permanently wounded, etc.[13] More directly, amongst many young intellectuals and political activists there developed a sharp sense of intergenerational animosity.[14] George Orwell, looking back on the immediate post-war period in *The Road to Wigan Pier* (1937) summed up this feeling when he wrote that:

> By 1918 everyone under forty was in a bad temper with his elders, and the mood of anti-militarism which followed naturally upon the fighting was extended into a general revolt against orthodoxy and authority. At that time there was among the young a curious cult of hatred of 'old men'. The dominance of 'old men' was held to be responsible for every evil known to humanity and every accepted institution. . . . At that time we all thought of ourselves as enlightened creatures of a new age, casting off the orthodoxy that had been forced upon us by those detested 'old men'.   (quoted in Hynes, 1972: 19–20)

At the same time, and stemming from the same mood, there emerged in 'progressive' quarters a heightened sense that only *youth* and the *values that it stood for* was capable of creating the truly new, modern and above all better society that was now so desperately needed. The idea of the possibility of and need for a 'New Generation' had been current in European thought since at least the nineteenth century; the effect of the war was in Robert Wohl's phrase 'to democratize and internationalize' this idea (Wohl, 1979: 222). As Wohl has pointed out, the tendency to think about society and history in terms of generations feeds off a sense of discontinuity and disconnection from the past, and the First World War provided a powerful boost for this growing tendency in modern European thought (Wohl, 1979: 2).[15] This generational mode of socio-historical analysis was itself formalized in the post-war theories of François Mentré in France, Karl Mannheim in Germany and José Ortega y Gasset in Spain. The work of the last two was translated into English in the 1950s and undoubtedly made its own contribution to that later period's preoccupation with the closely interrelated concepts of generation and youth.

Ortega developed a system for the dynamic of history in terms of the different perceptions of the present, and differential power, of the three major generations that he saw as 'contemporary' but not 'co-eval' in any given historical moment:

> Until he is twenty-five years old man normally does little but learn, receive information about the things that make up his social environment.
>
>   . . . in these years he comes up against the aspects of a world which he finds already made. The young man [soon] too takes his place in world making. But as he mediates on the world in force (the world of the men who in his time are mature) . . . his problems, his doubts are very different [from those which] young men felt when they mediated on the world of those who were then mature (men who are now very old) and so on backwards.
>
>   . . . every historical present, every today, involves three distinct times, three distinct todays [i.e. those of the three major 'contemporary' generations]. Or to put it another way the present is rich in three vital dimensions which dwell together in it whether they will or no, linked with one another, and, perforce because they are different, in essential hostility to one another. For some 'today' is the state of being twenty, for others forty and for still another group sixty; and this, the fact that three such very different ways of life have the same 'today' creates the dynamic frame, the conflict, and the collision which form the background of historic material and of all modern living together.   (Ortega y Gasset, 1959: 40–2)

Writing a little earlier than and quite independently from Ortega, Karl Mannheim was also interested in the possible relationship between generational divisions and historical change, but his analysis was pitched at a more explicitly sociological level. Mannheim argued that at any given moment the category of (younger) generation may or may not take an actual and objective political significance and self-consciousness, depending upon the nature and realities of the specific socio-historical context. This in turn led him to distinguish between three generational categorizations:

(i) 'generational status' – a mere aggregation of individuals on the basis of common unreflexive generational member-ship;

(ii) 'generational actuality' – where a concrete bond and sense of shared identity and consciousness is created between all the members of a given generation as a response to its 'concrete historical problems'; and

(iii) 'generational unit' – where differing and possibly opposed responses to the same problems lead to a subdivision of the generation as actuality. (Mannheim, 1952: 303–4)

Mannheim argued that in a rapidly changing social order it was the younger generation, because of the decelerating rate of adult socialization, that was most 'sensitive to the present'. He also argued that because of the process of the biographical 'stratification of experience' – with early experience taking precedence and stabilizing into the outline of a world view – each historically contemporary generation would tend to view the same present in a different light. According to Mannheim these factors *may* result in a significant social, cultural or political interaction, in either or both directions, between younger and older generations:

One is old primarily in so far as he comes to live within a specific individually acquired framework of useable past experience, so that every new experience has its form and its place largely marked out for it in advance. In youth, on the other hand, where life is new, formative forces are just coming into being and basic attitudes in the process of development can take advantage of the moulding power of new situations.

. . . The up-to-dateness of youth therefore consists of their being closer to the 'present' problems (as a result of their potentially fresh contact . . .) and in fact that they are dramatically aware of a process of destabilization and take sides in it.

. . . The extent to which the problems of younger generations are reflected back upon the older one becomes greater in the measure that the dynamism of society increases.

. . . With the strengthening of the social dynamic however the older generation becomes increasingly receptive to influences from the younger.   (Mannheim, 1952: 296–302)

It is therefore from the 1920s and 30s that it is possible to trace the rise of generational theorizing and the conflation and sometime equation of the concepts of *generation* and *youth* which has been so characteristic of much of the post-Second-World-War period's response to the youth question. Similarly it was from this time onwards that the *concept of youth* in its broadest sense increasingly came to be loosened in its connection with chronological age and ever more closely associated with ideas about social, political and cultural renewal and change (Wohl, 1979: 224).[16]

In terms of the emergence of adolescence/youth as an increasingly significant *category* and *concept*, and of the elaboration of a range of associated images and meanings, influential developments were also occurring during the inter-war period in the United States. Indeed when reference is made to youth in the historical context of the 'Roaring Twenties' the first image that comes to mind is of the culture of jazz, flappers and prohibition, and of the 'flaming youth' as portrayed *par excellence* in the writings of F. Scott Fitzgerald, which is widely believed to have inhabited this milieu. Further attention was drawn to the supposed existence in inter-war America of a pronounced intergenerational discontinuity and conflict through the artistic and literary production and well-publicized lifestyle of the 'Lost Generation', such young expatriates as Gertrude Stein, Ernest Hemingway, *et al.*

Such characterizations were and are undoubtedly in large part myth rather than a historical reality, but nonetheless the point remains that American society in the 1920s was undergoing a range of social upheavals: immigration, the transition from a predominantly rural to urban society, the sense at least of unprecedented prosperity, the spread of cinema, radio and the motor car – all of which undermined the sense of continuity between generations, and which together provided the basis for the emergence, especially amongst more privileged youth, of distinct and apparently radical lifestyles. (In addition the 1920s were certainly also a decade in which there occurred a relative emancipation of large sectors of 'ordinary' youth from at least some of the outward aspects of the rigid moral and behavioural code of the pre-war era. In the United States and also in Great Britain a working-class youth culture centred on the commercial dance-hall flourished – and provided cause for a certain amount of adult alarm – as did the female fashions of the day, with the characteristically short length of skirt.)[17] Even if the whole phenomenon of flaming youth had a much narrower basis in reality than is generally believed, public *concern* about the younger generation and its activities reached a peak in the United States at this time that was unsurpassed until the 1960s.

Significantly it is also from the context of the USA in the 1920s
that it is possible to date the identification of adolescence/youth as a
distinct object for properly sociological and anthropological scrutiny and analysis. One aspect of this phenomenon was the development of a specifically sociological approach to the topic of juvenile
delinquency with the publication of Frederic Thrasher's *The Gang*
in 1927. This extensive study of Chicago gangs firmly associated
delinquency with urban social disintegration and stressed the role of
the street gang for its members as an increasingly 'necessary'
transitional institution in a society that was seen as characterized by
a growing rift between family and society and childhood and
adulthood. As in Great Britain, the Depression years also ushered
in a whole range of American policy documents and studies dealing
with aspects of the youth employment problems (see K. Davis,
1935).

Another key work in this respect was Margaret Mead's *Coming
of Age in Samoa* (1928) which can be seen not only as an attempt to
test the validity of the doctrine of universal adolescent storm and
stress, but also an investigation through the comparative method
into why at that particular time the younger generation was (or so it
seemed to Mead and her contemporaries) so troubled and such a
problem for society. This new-found concern with youth and
apparent generational discontinuity was both exemplified and also
reflected upon by Mead when she wrote that:

> The spectacle of a younger generation diverging ever more
> widely from the standards and ideals of the past, cut adrift
> without the anchorage of respected home standards or group
> religious values, terrified the cautious reactionary, tempted the
> radical propagandist to missionary crusades among defenceless
> youth, and worried the least thoughtful among us. (Mead,
> 1973: 9)[18]

The idea of the emergence within American society of a distinct
and self-contained adolescent/youth culture was also taken up in
the studies that now began to appear of the world of the
comprehensive High School. Here, the argument ran, the fact that
all American young people spent their adolescent years in the
company of their peers, within the institutional confines of the High
School, was having the consequence that a separate adolescent

culture was emerging with its own system of norms and values quite apart from those of adult society. As early as 1929 Robert and Helen Lynd were noting in their study of 'Middletown' that:

> The High School, with its athletics, clubs, sororities and frater-nities, dances and parties and other 'extracurricular activities', is a fairly complete social cosmos in itself, and about this city within a city the social life of the intermediate generation centers.   (Lynd and Lynd, 1956)

Perhaps the classic early statement of this argument,[19] and certainly the most influential for subsequent sociological analyses of adolescence/youth in both the USA and Great Britain was put forward, however, by Talcott Parsons in 1942:

> It is at the point of emergence into adolescence that there first begins to develop a set of patterns and behaviour phenomena which involve a highly complex combination of age grading and sex role elements. These may be referred to together as the phenomena of the 'youth cultures'.   (Parsons, 1954: 87)

In what it should be pointed out was an entirely theoretical statement, Parsons too stressed the importance of the formal system of High School education for the crystallization of a separate youth culture which he regarded, in contrast to the 'dominant pattern of the adult male role', as being characterized by the following features:

(i) 'irresponsibility' and an emphasis on 'having a good time';
(ii) the prominence of sport as an avenue of achievement (as opposed to adult occupational achievement);
(iii) *vaguely* negative feelings towards the adult world ('a certain recalcitrance to the pressure of adult expectations of discipline');
(iv) physical attractiveness as an (especially female) source of peer-group status.

Parsons argued that this youth culture was a product of the tensions in the relationship of younger people and adults that were inherent in contemporary society, but at the same time he saw growing up as being facilitated by temporary participation in youth culture patterns. Such participation, he argued, was functional in that it eased the (male) individual's transition to the universalism and achievement orientation of adult society at large: 'From the athletics hero or the lion of college dances the young man becomes the prosaic businessman or lawyer' (Parsons, 1954: 98).

In retrospect it can be fairly readily seen that Parsons's formulations and those of his post-war followers concerning 'the youth culture' and its component norms and values were and are at best only applicable to one particular youth subcultural strand amongst largely *middle-class* students in the *American* High School (see J. S. Coleman, 1962). Even within this specific milieu subsequent empirical studies have substantially undermined the idea of the existence of a homogenous 'culture of the High School student', cutting across all other divisions, and clearly any attempt to apply these ideas to the quite different context of post-war British adolescent/youth/college culture would be highly misleading.[20] Nonetheless Parsons's essay gave considerable academic legitimation to the idea that there was emerging in post-war Western societies a separate youth culture, uniting the entire cross-section of the younger generation in a way of life quite different from, and possibly even opposed to, that of the parent generation. This essentially erroneous way of thinking about the youth question, especially in the British context, came to dominate much of the increasingly intense and ever more sociologically couched discussion of this topic that was to characterize the period from the 1950s to the 1970s on both sides of the Atlantic. The notion of 'generation over class' has indeed been a major motif of the post-war British cult of youth as a whole.[21]

By the Second World War the stage had been set. Within the range of variation by social class the years of adolescence – and in some cases youth – had been universalized as a transitional but nonetheless distinct age grade between childhood and adulthood. Professional and scientific theories had been developed to account for the special nature of this time of life and to define its psycho-social characteristics, and these had furthermore come to be appropriated by the general 'common sense' of our culture. There had also emerged a wide variety of adult-run agencies seeking to cater for the 'needs' and 'problems' of this time of life at both individual and social levels. Various sub-groups within the younger generation had started to develop, in a semi-autonomous manner, a range of subcultural responses to the material (including generationally specific) circumstances of their lives. At the same time the topic of adolescence/youth had become a significant component in the social, economic and political discourse of the period. Society as a whole was coming to be increasingly preoccupied with what seemed to be an ever-widening gulf between the generations, and consequently with all aspects of the youth question.

Out of the interplay of these factors, their amplification and the addition of new elements, was to emerge in British society from the 1950s onwards the full flowering of the cult of youth and the emergence into the public eye of what could be termed the 'youth spectacle'.

5
Responses to youth II: Post-war Britain

The prominence and variety of form of the *youth spectacle* in the mass media of post-war Britain can be seen as reflecting – and itself contributing towards – the coming to the fore over this period of 'youth' as a category of particular socio-cultural significance. In the first instance a range of objective economic, demographic, social institutional and social structural changes have served to make this particular age-grading division a more clearly differentiated and consequent one than previously. If, however, during the same period the *idea* of youth has also taken on a special *subjective* significance – or, more accurately a whole range of significances – this is by virtue of its 'metaphorical utility' in the ongoing project of the general and particular making sense of what was (and is) a seemingly rapidly and fundamentally changing social order. It is this additional complementary and subjective dimension of the phenomenon of the rise to prominence of youth that explains not only a good deal of the youth spectacle's complexity and all-pervasiveness, but also the gulf between 'image' and 'reality' that is to be found within the youth spectacle at nearly all its levels.

Thus, while the emergence of youth as a distinct age grade has in many ways been an objective phenomenon with objective significance for contemporary British society, the full nature and degree of the significance of the category of youth in the post-war period can only be grasped through an examination of the forms and origins of the common subjective meanings of youth and media-transmitted images of youth that have grown out of and alongside the objective realities. It is the sum total of these meanings of youth, both 'positive' and 'negative' (and also often ambiguous or 'mixed'), that constitutes the *cult of youth* in post-war Britain. These meanings are transmitted and shaped in our society largely through the mass media images of the *youth spectacle*.

This chapter and the next will be devoted at their most basic level to an outline of the objective and generally 'externally imposed' changes in the material condition and social situation of the age grade of adolescence/youth that have contributed towards the ongoing process of the definition of this time of life as a distinct entity. Official policy as such towards the young has in its own right been shaped by certain common assumptions and images in relation to the perceived nature of youth itself, and beyond these in relation to the perceived condition and direction of post-war Britain overall. A number of key educational and recreational policy statements of the 1950s and 60s will therefore be examined as embodying the part-real, part-metaphorical connection that was increasingly coming to be drawn at this time between the youth question and the diagnosis of the very state of the nation. For the purposes of the present work such studies constitute not merely a valuable *resource* to be drawn upon in the charting of the changing situation of post-war youth but also a topic for analysis in their own right. Finally youth has also increasingly become in the post-war period a topic for extensive political debate, social scientific investigation and artistic representation. These areas will be considered in general terms as a further exemplification of the varieties of professional response that have been called forth by – and have themselves influenced – the rise to prominence of the category of youth in contemporary society. Once these objective changes and professional responses have been considered the way should then be clear, in the concluding chapters of this study, for an examination of the extensive and *essentially subjective* phenomenon of the cult of youth in post-war Britain.

Firstly, then, let us examine the historical and social structural parameters within which the age grade of youth has further separated out in the post-war period and within which the cult of youth has developed.

The school-leaving age was due to have been raised from 14 to 15 on 1 September 1939, thus realizing a reform suggested in the 1918 Education Act, but owing to the outbreak of hostilities this measure was indefinitely deferred and did not in fact finally come to be implemented until September 1947. More than this, however, the mass evacuation of city schoolchildren at the outset of the war, and the extensive destruction and official requisitioning of school buildings in the war's early years in particular, resulted for a while in the severe disruption of the entire system of elementary education. After the initial period of mass evacuation (at one time about one-half of London's school population had been moved to safe country areas, while the figure for the Lancashire conurbations was anything up to two-thirds) and the consequent widespread closing down of schools in urban areas, many of the evacuees began to return home (Calder, 1971: 43).[1] However, by January 1940 only one-quarter of the school population in evacuation areas had resumed full-time education, with another quarter receiving part-time schooling, another quarter home tuition, while the remaining quarter – about 430,000 children in all – were still receiving no formal education (Calder, 1971: 57).

At around this time about two-thirds of London's schools had in any case been requisitioned for war purposes, and this pattern was common throughout most of the other major urban centres, with the comparable ratio for Manchester for example standing at six out of ten. After a partial recovery of the educational system during the latter stages of the 'phoney war', the Blitz, over the period from September 1940 to May 1941, served to compound the effects of the initial period of educational disruption. During this period about one-fifth of the nation's schools were damaged by bombing, and when this was added to the effects of requisitioning the consequence was that many children either did without education altogether – and absenteeism was high even when there was a school to go to – or else at best were crammed into what were already grossly over-crowded classes (Calder, 1971: 260). All in all it was not until around 1943 that the British elementary education system settled down again into anything approaching its pre-war normality.

The impact of this educational disruption upon the young was to be discerned for some years after the end of the war. Thus in 1949 one educationalist was remarking that 'the boys and girls who are now leaving the primary schools [who would have been under school age at the outbreak of hostilities] have lost up to five years of formal education' (Calder, 1971: 260). At around the same time a rate of illiteracy that was far above pre-war levels was being detected in the post-war intake of National Servicemen and, at a more general and also more tenuous level, it was now coming to be thought by some at least that the experience of childhood in the war years might have had lasting and serious psychological conse-quences for large numbers of the younger generation. Thus it was coming to be argued that the violence of the war, with the bombing bringing the civilian population for the first time very much into the front line, and the widespread breakdown in the 'normal' processes of socialization that was supposed to have occurred at this time, with absent fathers, overworked mothers, no school, etc., were somehow responsible for the apparently unprecedentedly 'violent', 'disturbed' and 'anti-social' character of post-war British youth.

Because of the time lag involved in the process of 'war babies' growing into post-war 'problem adolescents' this line of explanation of the 'uniqueness' (and supposedly unique delinquency) of contemporary youth did not begin to surface fully until the late 1950s and early 1960s. One example of this argument is to be found in T. R. Fyvel's study of 'rebellious youth in the welfare state' (Fyvel, 1963). Fyvel perceived there to have been, along with the emergence of the Teddy boys in the mid-1950s, a 'flare up of [youthful] violence' and saw as a partial explanation of this trend 'the expression of a particularly disturbed generation, a delayed effect of the war' (Fyvel, 1963: 51).[2]

Such arguments were given a more formal and rigorously academic statement in Leslie Wilkins's *Delinquent Generations* which set out, in accordance with the 'childhood conditioning' social psychological paradigm then made fashionable through the work of such researchers as John Bowlby, to 'examine and test the theory that children born in certain years (for example wartime) are more likely to commit offences than others, and that this tendency remains from childhood to early adult life' (Wilkins, 1960: 1). From the manipulation of the official statistics on the rates of conviction of juveniles for indictable offences in the post-war period, Wilkins claimed to have found:

(i) that children born in the years 1935–42 were more delinquent over the whole post-war period than those born in any other seven-year period;

(ii) that the highest delinquency rates were to be found amongst those aged 4–5 years at some time in the war (and that the disturbance of socialization at this age was therefore particularly harmful);

(iii) that these findings applied equally to both England and Scotland despite differences between rates and types of delinquency between the two countries;

(iv) that youths aged 17–21 years in 1955 were *even more delinquent* than that foretold by the author's own year-of-birth analysis.

The final point is particularly significant here since it demonstrates not merely the 'war-as-cause-of-post-war-juvenile-delinquency' theory but also a sense of even further heightened anxiety concerning the apparently unprecedented lawlessness of post-war British youth. Wilkins was fairly explicit in his singling out of the Teddy boy phenomenon as an additional and supplementary factor in this respect, and in his insistence that, whilst a highly significant factor, the *war alone* was not a sufficient explanation for what was now occurring:

One of the most disturbing features of the pattern of post-war criminal statistics is the recent crime wave among young adult males between seventeen and twenty-one years of age. The crime wave among males has been associated with certain forms of dress and other social phenomena.

The recent crime wave phenomenon among young males cannot be dismissed as 'only' to be expected in view of their childhood experiences.   (Wilkins, 1960: 9–10)

By the time of its publication in 1960 the arguments of *Delinquent Generations* were, however, already proving ill-founded and outdated, since the generation born in the first few post-war years was now manifesting an even higher rate of delinquency than that of its immediate predecessor.[3] (This can now be seen as part of the general upward trend – outlined later in this chapter – for all statistical indicators of juvenile and adult crime throughout the post-war period.) On the whole, then, such 'explanations' probably demonstrate that adults thought that the young *ought* to have been disturbed by the war – it had after all been *the* major experience of most of the parent generation. In the situation of Britain from the mid-1950s onwards, where contemporary youth was widely seen as a new and different – not to mention particularly problematic – entity the notion of the war as a 'cause' of this sprang readily to mind. (See also the discussion of the prevalence of the *idea* of generational discontinuity – and of 'generationalism' itself as a mode of social theorizing – in immediately post-*First*-World-War Europe in Chapter 4 above).

To return, though, to the period of the war itself, it is certainly the case that these years were witness to a sharp increase in the number of convictions for juvenile delinquency. The number of law-breakers amongst the under-17s in England and Wales rose by over one-third between 1939 and 1941, and over the same period the figures for malicious damage and petty stealing amongst this age group rose by 70 per cent and 200 per cent respectively (Calder, 1971: 260).

As has previously been pointed out, however, such figures need to be treated with a good deal of caution; they can be taken either as simply indicative of a massive increase in the 'real' incidence of juvenile crime, or else they can be seen as pointing to a new degree of adult awareness of youth, and its (potential) status as a social problem, brought on in its own right by the disruption of the war. The fact that magistrates ordered six times as many birchings of juveniles in 1940–41 than pre-war is perhaps one piece of evidence which suggests that the dramatic rise in juvenile delinquency figures during the war was partially the product of a new official awareness and nervousness of youth, and a tendency on the part of adults to project their anxieties and frustrations on to this age group (Titmuss, 1950: 339–40).

If there was a new official awareness of youth and its associated (real and imaginary) individual and social 'problems' engendered by the war, this certainly seems to have manifested itself also in more positive provisions and reforms aimed at this age grade. During the war the discourse surrounding youth began to be linked, in official thinking, with the broader topics of post-war national reconstruction and the future of Britain and its democracy (themes and connections which were then elaborated upon throughout the post-war era). A wartime survey of the condition and needs of British youth noted that: 'today there is more talk about the claims of youth and probably more general recognition of the necessity of dealing with the question than ever before in this country' and suggested that the current problem of youth was essentially an *educational* problem, to be tackled via such measures as the raising of the school-leaving age, the provision of day continuation classes for school-leavers and the provision of improved recreational facilities for young people.[5]

It was during the war years, then, that concern over the general lack of adequate provision for the leisure needs of that group caught in the potentially troublesome transitional years between school and full adulthood – whose plight had been dramatized by the effects of the war – finally resulted in the setting up of a state-controlled youth service. In the pre-war period, although local education authorities had been empowered since the 1918 Education Act to give financial and other types of aid to voluntary youth organizations, as well as to provide their own facilities for youth, such provision as did occur was uneven and piecemeal in the extreme. It was not until November 1939 that the Board of Education Circular 1486, 'Service of Youth', recorded the Board's decision to take direct responsibility for the welfare of youth as part of an integrated system of national education (Thomas and Perry, 1975: 6–12).

For the purposes of the youth service, 'youth' was defined as the age range between 14 – then the school-leaving age – and 21 years, thus encompassing the group of 'pre-adult' workers, the provision for whose 'profitable' use of leisure time was then considered to be a particularly pronounced gap in the state's overall programme for the education and socialization of the younger generation. Initially, indeed, the youth service was conceived of as catering only for those *who had finished formal education* and were under 21, but in practice this restricted definition has been fairly liberally interpreted to include young people as a whole.

Following Circular 1486 a National Youth Committee (later the Youth Advisory Council) was set up to advise the Minister, and a special branch of the Board was formed to administer grants. Local education authorities were also urged to set up youth committees and to co-operate with the local branches of the various voluntary youth organizations. Because of this decentralization, the extent and type of official provision for youth outside of formal education has always been subject to a considerable degree of regional variation. Nonetheless from 1939 final responsibility for the youth service has rested with central government, from 1944 under the newly formed Ministry of Education and from 1966 under the Department of Education and Science.[6]

The various pre-war and wartime reports and official documents leading up to the 1944 Education Act and the introduction of the tripartite system of universal secondary education were then all much concerned in one way or another with the question of the expansion of the state's provision for youth, or adolescence as it was then more commonly termed, both inside and outside the school. It has been noted in Chapter 4 above how in the pre-war years the idea of universal secondary education had come to be equated with the education of the adolescent. Now, during the war, the programme of educational reform in the secondary or adolescent sector that was to culminate in the 1944 Act – with its implementation of 'secondary education for all', its raising of the school-leaving age, its proposal for the compulsory continuation of all school-leavers in part-time education and its reassertion of the need to expand the youth service – was perceived as vital to the national interest, and to the long-term project of post-war national reconstruction. Thus, prominent in the introduction to the 1943 White Paper on Educational Reconstruction, the document that immediately preceded the 1944 Act, it was stated that:

In the youth of the nation we have our greatest national asset. Even on a basis of mere expediency we cannot afford not to develop this asset to the greatest advantage. It is the object of the present proposals to strengthen and inspire the younger generation. For it is as true today as when it was first said, that 'the bulwarks of a city are its men'.   (Maclure, 1965: 206)

This notion of the *whole of* youth as a national asset and its implicit identification of the condition of youth with the condition of the nation was, as already noted, perhaps first widely advanced in the late Victorian and Edwardian era, as was the plea that this 'asset' be fully developed in the future interests of the nation. These ideas – and their corollary that society ignored them only at its extreme peril – now came to be much repeated and elaborated by post-war educationalists, youth workers and social commentators of all ideological persuasions. There has been throughout the post-war period, a persistent concern with the 'wastage' of the talents of much of youth and with the possible implications of this for British society.

The most pronounced aspect of the post-war period's formal institutional response towards youth, and therefore one of the most important aspects in the overall process of the institutionalization of the (semi)autonomous status of this age grade, has been the ongoing process of the expansion of secondary and higher education. The destruction of school buildings and the partial collapse of the state educational system occasioned by the war, the imperative need to provide extra educational facilities for the bulge of schoolchildren shortly to be passing through the system as a result of the post-war baby boom, and the zeal of the post-war Labour government to implement in full the provisions of the Butler Act as an integral part of the general package of 'Beveridge' social reforms, were all factors contributing to the high priority that now came to be accorded to the project of the rapid and far-reaching expansion of national education.[7] Over the period 1947–58 spending on public education doubled in real terms and increased by 75 per cent as a proportion of the national income; whereas in 1955 net public educational expenditure stood at 2.8 per cent of the national income, by 1965 this figure had risen to 4.1 per cent (Halsey, 1972: p. 168, table 6.2).

Mention has already been made of the raising of the school-leaving age to 15 in 1947 and 16 in 1973; more significant than this, however, from the point of view of the formal institutionalization and social spread of the age grade of youth has been the rise in average school-leaving age over this period. As with the proportional increases in educational expenditure outlined above, this increase in 'staying on' began to take off from the economic boom of the 1950s onwards. (Over the fourteen years of Conservative government from 1951 to 1964 the number of schoolteachers also rose from 215,000 to 287,000, places at teacher training colleges more than doubled, the number of students in full-time higher education trebled and the number of university places rose by 60 per cent.)[8] Thus the percentage of 15–18-year-olds in secondary schools in England and Wales rose from 12.5 in 1951 to 19.6 in 1961, 30 in 1968 (Halsey, 1972: p. 163, table 6.1) and 45 (after the raising of the school-leaving age to 16 in 1973) in 1977 (CSO, 1979).

Despite the advances made in the provision of secondary education in the 1950s and 60s this was still a period in which there was a growing official and public awareness that the existing system of state schooling was in many respects woefully inadequate and wasteful of ability, and that these defects were nowhere so pronounced as in the education of the 'ordinary' (working-class) non-academic adolescent. This realization once again drew heavily upon the theme of youth-as-national-asset in its expression. The late 1950s and early 1960s saw the publication of a number of classic studies in the sociology of education demonstrating the systematic disadvantage under which working-class children laboured in the tripartite system of secondary education, and in 1954 an official report on 'Early Leaving' presented for the first time statistical evidence on the influence of social class upon school performance, with particular reference to the disproportionate number of pupils from middle-class backgrounds to be found in the grammar schools (Floud *et al.*, 1956; Douglas, 1964; Ministry of Education, 1954).

The themes of the inadequacy of existing provision for older pupils and of working-class educational under-achievement were taken up specifically by the Crowther Report of December 1959 whose terms of reference were 'the education of boys and girls between the ages of fifteen and eighteen' (Ministry of Education, 1959). The findings of Crowther and the report's indictment of the inadequacies of the existing system provoked considerable comment in the popular press with, for example, the *Daily Sketch* stating that it would 'shake every parent' and the *Daily Herald* commenting that it showed that 'our poverty-stricken education must be revolutionized'. The *Daily Mirror*'s front page headline of Friday 11 December 1959 proclaimed 'a revolution in our schools: the most vital report ever written on education is out today'. Inside the same issue the *Mirror* hailed the report as 'social, educational and political dynamite' and provided a four-page guide 'for every parent' to Crowther's recommendations. The same paper's centre spread was devoted to an examination of how 'Britain is letting her teenagers down' and stressed the idea that without the rapid implementation of Crowther's suggested reforms 'Britain cannot keep her place in the world'. Seldom has the popular press evinced such a serious concern for the education of the younger generation.

A major recommendation of Crowther had been the raising of the school-leaving age (RSLA) to 16. As with official pre-war recommendations concerning the universalization of secondary education, Crowther's rationale for RSLA was based in part upon certain taken-for-granted assumptions concerning the psychology of adolescence and its consequent problems:

By around thirteen pupils have reached a stage of growth when any word that harks back to childhood is misleading and resented. They think and speak of themselves as 'teenagers' and the word, though not yet standard English, is descriptive enough of the troubled and exciting time of adolescence which lies half within and half beyond the school life of most English boys and girls.   (Ministry of Education, 1959: 109)

The subheadings under which this part of Crowther's case for making secondary education 'the education of the adolescent' and therefore for extending the minimum leaving age to 16, was stated are revealing in their own right: a section on 'The Years of Adolescence', outlining the conventional wisdom concerning the physiological and emotional changes and problems of this period was followed by a discussion of the developments in cognitive abilities and bodily skills occurring at this time and therefore of 'The Adolescent's [Educational] Needs'. Under 'Standards of Life' the then, as now, much-discussed issue of the need for moral education of the young in a world of seemingly rapid change and diverse and often competing value systems was taken up, again in conjunction with the standard assumptions concerning adolescent psychology:

Adolescence is a period of uncertainty, unwelcome uncertainty, about life as a whole and man's place in the universe, about what is real, what is true, what is the purpose of it all, and what matters. The adolescent is just as conscious of the different metaphysical assumptions that are made in different circles as he is of the different ethical assumptions. . . . The adolescent needs help to see where he stands, but it must be given with discretion and restraint. He does not want to be 'told' but he wants a guide, and a guide who will be honest in not over-stating a case.   (Ministry of Education, 1959: 114)

Finally, under the subheading of 'The Assertion of Independence' this section of the report speculated upon the question of whether secondary schooling could cater for the growth of independence that is necessary to adolescent boys and girls (the answer was 'yes') and further underlined its previous remarks on the then-current underdevelopment of youthful talent and ability in English education.

More than expounding a range of common assumptions concerning the social psychology of adolescence in contemporary society, however, the Crowther Report also combined these with a special

concern for specifically *teenage* problems (the nature and significance of the then-emergent category of 'teenager' will be discussed
shortly) as well as once again identifying reform and expansion in
the field of the formal socialization of the young with ideas
concerning the 'national interest':

> There are two main arguments for raising the school leaving age.
> One starts from the social and personal needs of fifteen year olds,
> and regards education as one of the basic rights of the citizen; the
> other is concerned with education as a vital part of the nation's
> capital investment. . . . A boy or girl of fifteen is not sufficiently
> mature to be exposed to the pressures of the world of industry or
> commerce. . . .
>
> The onset of puberty is earlier than it used to be. . . . But this is
> not true of the emotional and social consequences of pu-
> berty. . . .
>
> This is surely the period in which the welfare of the individual
> ought to come before any marginal contribution he or she could
> make to the national income. . . .
>
> Secondary education is, then, in our view, essentially the
> education of the adolescent. And adolescence coincides much
> better physically than it does psychologically with the present
> length of the compulsory secondary course. Until they are
> sixteen, boys and girls need an environment designed for their
> needs. Each extension of the school leaving age obviously brings
> the schools increasingly difficult emotional problems. . . . We
> may hide, but we do not solve teenage problems simply by letting
> boys and girls leave school. . . . It is true that the protective side
> of education is likely to be quite ineffective if the educational side
> is unsatisfying, but we are convinced that there are sufficient
> important, fresh educational interests which can be aroused in
> boys and girls which are today left only half-exploited, or barely
> touched upon, when they leave school.   (Ministry of Education,
> 1959: 108–16)[9]

The theme of the urgent need to improve England's educational
provision for youth out of considerations of 'national interest'
(which were nonetheless of secondary significance as far as the
report was concerned when compared to the individual/
developmental arguments outlined above) was further underscored

in Geoffrey Crowther's remarks to *The Times* on 11 December
1959, on the subject of his committee's conclusions:

> Public interest in educational policies is steadily rising, and we
> think it should not be difficult to convince the public that there is
> as much need for a twenty year programme of educational
> development as there is for a similar programme of railway
> modernization or of atomic generation of electric power.
>
> We may find it difficult to conceive that there could be any
> other application of money giving a larger or more certain return
> in the quickening of enterprise, in the stimulation of invention, or
> in the general sharpening of those wits by which alone a trading
> nation in a crowded island can hope to make its living.   (p. 6)

The Times itself largely concurred with Crowther's indictment of
the inadequacies of the existing system. In its editorial of the same
day it went on to throw its weight behind both the report's
recommendation for RSLA and also its call for improved technical
education (it is interesting to note that Geoffrey Crowther claimed
to have invented the term 'numeracy', at that time a neologism) for
school-leavers in terms which had been familiar in the youth
question debate since the turn of the century:

> But raising the age (expensive as it is especially in teachers)
> should round off the schooling of the great majority of children
> and add to *national efficiency*. It is a reform that pays its way. . . .
>
> [There is] much human waste in the lower reaches of technical
> education. . . .
>
> . . . [a] scandalous waste of talent . . . now persists.   (p. 13)

The Crowther Report has been considered in some detail here
because it can be seen as a key document in marking one aspect of
the final point of separation out in Britain, around the late 1950s and
early 60s, of the age grade of adolescence/youth as a distinct entity,
both in *conceptual* and also – interrelatedly – in *formal institutional*
terms. Subsequent official educational documents of the 1960s,
notably the Newsom Report, *Half Our Future* (Ministry of Education, 1963a)[10] repeated the call for RSLA made in Crowther, and
demonstrated a further and closely related concern for the undoubtedly real inadequacy of current secondary educational provision, in

this case for the 'ordinary', academically 'average' or less than average, or under-privileged adolescent:

> Despite some splendid achievements in the schools, there is much unrealised talent especially among boys and girls whose potential is masked by inadequate powers of speech and the limitations of home background. Unsuitable programmes and teaching methods may aggravate their difficulties and frustration express itself in apathy or rebelliousness. The country cannot afford this wastage, humanly or economically speaking. If it is to be avoided several things will be necessary. The pupils will need to have a longer period of full time education than most of them now receive.   (Ministry of Education, 1963a: 3)

Newsom's call for more and better education for the young person of average and less than average ability was seen as particularly pressing at the time because of what was widely perceived as the increasing level of skill and flexibility that was coming to be demanded of the workforce, especially in the growing scientific and technological sectors. 'Trained and technical manpower' was in short supply (this was a period of more or less full employment) and was likely to become more so, unless major corrective action was taken, as the modernization of the British economy proceeded. Indeed, it was implied, without the provision of such manpower, coupled with better all-round education, such modernization would be seriously impeded: 'the need is not only for more skilled workers to fill existing jobs, but also for a generally better educated and intelligently adaptable labour force to meet new demands' (Ministry of Education, 1963a: 5).

This then-widespread perception of the nation's economic circumstances and requirements inevitably led to the conclusion that there existed an urgent need to tap the as yet *largely unrealized potential* of the 'less able half' of the younger generation (hence the significance of Newsom):

> These developments [in the labour market, industry and technology] are still at a relatively early stage, but the trend is clear and should be setting the vocational pattern to which our educational system is geared. Other advanced industrialized countries are also having to look critically at their educational systems, and

attempts are being made to measure the national reserves of ability.

Can our pupils be regarded as one such reserve of ability? Will a substantial investment in their education produce people capable of fulfilling the industrial roles indicated above?

. . . There is very little doubt that among our children there are reserves of ability which can be tapped. . . . One of the means is a longer school life.

There are still too many boys and girls who, otherwise, will leave at the earliest permissible moment, whatever their potential abilities, because outside pressures are too much for them. Again and again teachers confirm that the pupils with whom we are especially concerned stand to gain a great deal in terms of personal development as well as in the consolidating of attainments from a longer period of full time education – but it is just these boys and girls who most readily succumb to the attractions of the pay packet and the bright lights it com- mands.   (Ministry of Education, 1963a: 6–7)

(Note also in the final sentence above the image of the 'pull' exerted on prospective school-leavers by 'teenage affluence' and 'consumer society': these latter images, amongst the period's most powerful, will shortly be extensively discussed in their own right.) Nonethe- less, and leaving such worthy sentiments aside, Newsom's arguments for RSLA, as with Crowther's before it, continued to return to the question of the nation's future and position in the world:

Besides, in the national economic interest we cannot afford to go on waiting. . . . Others are already ahead of us. . . . In the United States nearly two thirds of the population are at High Schools until the age of eighteen . . . France . . . has already raised the school leaving age from fourteen to sixteen.   (Ibid., p. 7)

Newsom also demonstrated the concern, particularly prevalent in this period as a whole, that contemporary conditions were in many crucial respects *qualitatively different* from those of earlier (pre-war) times, and that since these would (supposedly) have an

especially pronounced impact upon the young, educational provision should be adjusted accordingly.

> There are some aspects of our times which must affect anyone
> growing up today, and of which education ought to take an ac-
> count. This is a world in which science and technology are
> making spectacular extensions to human experience: it is also
> the world in which the threat of nuclear war has been present
> ever since the boys and girls now in school were born. . . . The
> conditions under which our pupils will work and live out their
> lives may be very different, even from what their parents now
> know.
>   . . . This is a century which has seen, and is still seeing,
> marked changes in the status and economic role of women.
>   . . . In Western industrialized countries, the hours which
> must necessarily be spent in earning a living are likely to be
> markedly reduced during the working lifetime of children now
> in school.
>   . . . These are issues especially relevant to the present
> day. (pp. 27–8)

As in the case of Crowther, Newsom's recommendations were
on publication accorded a great deal of prominence in the
national press. The *Daily Mirror* of 17 October 1963 still found
room on its front page, underneath its lead story of Macmillan's
resignation from the premiership, to characterize the report as
'Vital: to our Children', while a double-page centre-spread featured an extensive summary of Newsom, and quoted its chairman
thus:

> There is very little doubt that among our children there are re-
> serves of talent which can be tapped if the country wills the
> means.
>   My mental image as I worked on this report was the boy in
> the leather jacket and jeans – and the girl in the tight skirt and
> the beehive hair-do. They will probably be married in five
> years time. The boy will probably become a labourer and the
> girl a factory worker on the production line.
>   What can we do to help them become Full Persons – to help

them break through the barriers society has rigged against them?

The *Mirror*'s own verdict was that 'There's nothing much wrong with today's fifteen-year-olds . . . they have responded to enlightened teaching . . . they read better . . . they behave well.'

The Times of the same day also took up the youth-as-asset and economic investment theme in its leading article, 'Half Our Children':

A merit of the report is that it brings forward evidence that longer schooling does in fact increase human efficiency. For example, the nation's literacy, as measured by reading tests, has risen markedly since the age was raised to fifteen after the war.

The Government's task is to apportion spending on education, which is bound to increase greatly, most profitably between the various sectors.

[The Robbins Report on higher education was due for publication the following week and the Plowden Report on primary education in approximately three years, it was noted.]

The lower reaches must be kept in balance with the higher, and the apprentice not forgotten for the graduate.

This kind of concern for and image of youth is very far removed from the more visible area of 'deviant youth' that has been a major feature of much of the youth spectacle overall. In the late 1950s and early 1960s at least, the youth question and *youth spectacle* – witness *The Times*'s and especially the *Daily Mirror*'s interest and comments – embraced the mundane as well as the exotic, the ordinary as well as the deviant.

The idea then current of the need to draw upon and develop the 'human resource' that was, specifically, the 'less able' half of the younger generation, that was at the heart of Newsom, became a significant one in the period's educational and political rhetoric and discourse. It was moreover an idea which both major political parties attempted to appropriate as their own. The then Conservative Minister of Education, Edward Boyle, publicly reacted to the Report by describing it as 'immensely important' and drawing an explicit connection between improved education (including RSLA to 16) for the less able and the very future of the nation:

> The sort of society we are going to have in Britain will depend on doing our best for average and below average children.[11]

While just three months later as part of his election campaign Harold Wilson was castigating the Conservative record on education thus:

> At present, as recent reports have shown, half the talent, energy and drive of this nation is going to waste, as a result of our vicious system of so-called elite education. . . . What the Conservatives have completely failed to provide are the funds and the drive required to give first rate education to the majority of our children who crowd the classes of very often dingy primary and secondary modern schools and are shoved out on the labour market at the age of fifteen.[12]

The theme of 'youth-as-national-asset' and the idea that the potential of youth was currently sorely and dangerously under-developed, perhaps especially in the case of 'ordinary' adolescents, was also echoed in the late 1950s and early 60s in a range of further professional and official statements on other, related, aspects of the youth question. Alongside the policy statements and debates on schooling as such discussed above, the period also witnessed an outpouring of discussion and analysis on such topics as the recruitment and training of young workers, the apprenticeship system, art education, further education, the supply and training of teachers in further education, the provision of sporting facilities and – of course – the youth service.[13] As in the case of the Newsom Report the question of the inadequacy of Britain's existing supply and training of skilled and adaptable labour loomed large in much of this literature. This was particularly strongly exemplified in the debate surrounding what was generally agreed to be the outmoded nature of the British apprenticeship system. It was already becoming clear by the mid-1950s that not only was Britain suffering from a shortage of *skilled* workers, but also indeed that her provision for the industrial training of *all* young workers, whether prospectively skilled or not, was in many respects inadequate and (supposedly) inferior to that provided elsewhere.[14] Thus, writing in the late 1950s, Kate Leipmann argued that:

> Apprenticeship is, generally speaking, the only accredited form of training for industry in this country, and it covers only a minority of young workers.
>
>   . . . [but] the highly mechanized and intricately organized economic system of the day has little use for the 'ox-like man' [a reference to the ideas of R. W. Taylor]; in modern conditions the whole working population is required to be literate, machine minded and adaptable. Training for industry for all young workers is of supreme importance for their own sake as well as for the sake of the country's productivity.
>
>   Therefore besides the question of how all those within the apprenticeship system are to be adequately trained, there arises the second question of what part apprenticeship is to play in the training of that majority of young workers who are at present outside the apprenticeship system.   (Liepmann, 1960: 194)

Liepmann went on to argue that training for industry was now so important to the nation's future that the *state* should assume primary responsibility in this area: at present old-fashioned restrictive attitudes to industrial training and retraining on *both sides of industry* were directly at variance with the larger national interest:

> In leaving the majority of workers, who are outside the apprenticeship system, without the training which is required in the national interest the attitude of the two sides of industry is the same, for different reasons: the employers' reason is the costs of training: the craft unions' motive is that of maintaining exclusiveness of training as a means of protecting the privileges of their members.   (Liepmann, 1960: 196)

The idea that Britain's provision for industrial training was hopelessly inadequate and out-dated in the face of 'modern' conditions and that this was to the nation's considerable detriment in the international 'league table' was also a prominent one in more directly accessible aspects of the period's social and economic commentary. In general terms the theme of industrial and technological training can of course be regarded as a perennial one for the youth question; what varies is the degree of prominence accorded to this issue from one period to the next and its specific form and wider frame of reference.

Thus an article in the *Observer* of 4 June 1961 by Andrew Shonfield, the economic editor of that paper, set out to reveal and dissect 'The Apprentice Scandal' (p. 3) and laid out a series of 'crucial facts which affect the country's future'. First and foremost there was what was seen as the current acute shortage of skilled workers: 'for years now it has been our most serious bottleneck: it has helped to keep the rate of economic growth in this country significantly lower than in any other industrial country in Western Europe'. The 'organized complacency about medieval craftsmanship' and 'outdated traditionalism' of the British system of industrial training also once more came under attack: 'there is surely something wrong with a system of training which seems to leave Britain less equipped to take advantage of the new industrial opportunities than her competitors.' Contemporary industrial conditions were, again, seen as requiring a new flexibility in the workforce:

> With the modern pace of technological change, particular skills rapidly become outmoded. What the nation needs is people who do not feel so dependent on some specialised ability that they begin by resisting and slowing down the process of change, and then are unable to adapt themselves confidently to new techniques.

Shonfield went on to list a number of further shortcomings in the apprenticeship system as it then operated: it did not provide for the general education of the worker, the traditional five-year period of indenture was unnecessarily long, the necessity for prospective skilled workers to become apprenticed by the age of 16 at the latest was iniquitious and counter-productive. The overall conclusion was that 'there is a serious national weakness here'. It was necessary to '*plan* on a national scale for the types of skills that we are going to need in the years ahead'. . . . 'The extra 400,000 school leavers who are moving into industry during the years of "the bulge" [a reference to the working through of the post-war 'baby boom' in the nation's demographic structure] 1961–3, present an opportunity that will not be repeated soon'.

Finally the areas of concern expressed in the post-war period's debate on schooling and industrial training were further supplemented and in many respects synthesized in the growing body of literature that addressed itself to the question of the 'transition from school to work' as a topic in its own right.[15] Surveying this literature in 1966 Michael Carter wrote that:

It is . . . apparent now . . . that the country's failure to provide adequate opportunities for school leavers is detrimental, in ways both direct and indirect, to its economic and social well being.   (Carter, 1966: 11)

In this upsurge of official and professional concern for the education and training of youth *at all levels* it is possible to discern a more generalized anxiety concerning the future of the nation at large. It is also possible to see a further and decisive step in the process of the identification of adolescence/youth as a distinct age grade with a status of its own. As early as 1947 the Clarke Report was noting that full employment (in marked contrast to the situation pre-war) and relatively high pay (note again the foreshadowing of the topic of 'teenage affluence') were combining to render the 'young worker' someone to be reckoned with:

. . . outside working hours at any rate . . . [the young worker] acquires a new independence with an income of his own; when juvenile workers are scarce, as they are now, and are likely to continue to be, he quickly realises that he may not be so unimportant as he seemed at first; and after two or three years his income may be larger compared with his needs and with his contribution to his maintenance than at any other period of his life.   (Ministry of Education, 1947: 47)[16]

Or again:

Much more than hitherto he has time and money of his own to spend as he will, at his own free choice.   (p. 67)

The two themes of youth-as-national-asset and the emergence of adolescence/youth as a distinct age grade were indeed sometimes explicitly combined, as in this statement by Michael Carter of one of the major arguments for the extension of further education (a project that was central to many of the major policy statements discussed above)

> Colleges of further education could also play a fundamental part in resolving the problem of how to fit adolescents into the wider society. The country has not yet faced up to this issue of what place to accord boys and girls during the time when they are too old to be 'treated like school kids' yet not old enough to assume the full status of adults. By making part time attendance at further education college normal for all those who do not continue their education in other ways, the country would provide an anchor for its young people. That such an anchor is desirable seems clear. (Carter, 1966: 219)

As previously noted, the minimum school-leaving age was finally raised to 16 in 1973, thus implementing Crowther's recommendation that the early adolescent years be spent within the separate confines of secondary education. In this manner early adolescence at least came universally to be formally institutionalized as a distinct age grade between childhood and the world of primary schooling, and adulthood and the world of work.

At a lower numerical level than the extension of secondary education described above, but perhaps of even greater significance with regard to the formal institutionalization – and prolongation – of the age grade of *youth* has been the process of the expansion of all varieties of higher or tertiary education that was a pronounced, highly visible and much-commented-upon feature of the post-war educational scene. In 1954 in Great Britain 5.8 per cent of the post-secondary age group entered full-time higher education of one kind or another (as opposed to 2.7 per cent in 1938) and by 1962 this figure had risen to 8.5 per cent (Ministry of Education, 1963b: p. 16, table 4). In the wake of the Robbins Report into higher education in the United Kingdom in 1963, the mid to late 1960s and early 1970s witnessed a period of considerable further reorganization and expansion in all areas of this field with, most notably, the establishment of the 'New Universities': Sussex, East Anglia, York, Essex, Kent, Warwick and Lancaster in England, and Strathclyde, Stirling, Heriot-Watt and Dundee in Scotland. At the same time, existing universities and polytechnics were expanded, there was a rapid increase in the number of advanced places in technical colleges, and the colleges of advanced technology (CATs) were promoted to full university status (Halsey, 1972: 194–7).

This programme of expansion was in part a response to what the Robbins Report described as the 'educational emergency' of the immediate need to provide enough places in higher education to cater for the children of the post-war 'bulge', who were then reaching the ages of 17 and 18. Beyond this it was argued that in the field of higher education also Britain was beginning to lag behind other nations, thus jeopardizing her prospects for continued growth and prosperity, and indeed her entire 'position in the world'. To quote from Robbins:

> . . . when we compare published plans for future development [of higher education] many other countries are far ahead of us. If, as we believe, a highly educated population is essential to meet competitive pressures in the modern world, a much greater effort is necessary if we are to hold our own.   (Ministry of Education, 1963b: 268)

Robbins's diagnosis of the inadequacy of Britain's system of higher education and of the dangers of the latter met with widespread concurrence in the media. The *Daily Mirror* of 13 November 1963 carried this editorial response to the Report: 'Where are all the Young Men Going? Young talent has been or is being wasted and frustrated. Brainpower, vital to Britain's future has been and is being wasted.' *The Times* of the same day devoted an unusual double-page spread to an outline of the 'Sweeping Proposals for Higher Education in Robbins Report' (pp. 8–9) (perhaps predictably a good deal more space than had been allocated to Crowther or Newsom on publication) and noted that in terms of the overall level of opportunity for university entry Great Britain was well 'Below U.S. and Soviet':

> A much greater effort [in this area] will be necessary in future if we are to hold our own and they [the Robbins Committee] conclude, 'Both in general cultural standards and in competitive intellectual power, vigorous action is needed to avert the danger of a serious relative decline in this country's standing'.

The same article then went on to note once more that 'reserves of untapped ability [are] greatest in the poor sections of the community'; while an editorial article (p. 13) welcomed Robbins's recommendations in general, whilst expressing reservations about the need to preserve academic standards. This latter question was in turn the major one around which the discussion of Robbins revolved in *The Times*'s correspondence columns in the following few days.

The Robbins Report projected the need for the provision of 560,000 places in all kinds of full-time higher education by 1980–81 – the figure for 1962–63 had stood at 216,000 (Ministry of Education, 1963b: p. 15, table 3). By 1965–66 the total number of students in full-time higher education stood at 309,400 and by 1975–76 the Robbins' target was well on the way to being met with the total then at 514,800 full-time students (Central Statistical Office, 1979: p. 139, table 5.37). In the thirteen-year period from 1962–63 to 1975–76 the total student population in full-time higher education more than doubled. By 1974–75, 10.6 per cent of 18–20-year-olds were students on full-time or 'sandwich' courses in higher education, while 5.2 per cent of 21–24-year-olds were similarly engaged (CSO, 1979, p. 138, table 5.26).

Thus for a small but growing and often highly socially visible (predominantly middle-class) minority of the younger generation the years from 18 to 21 plus have come to be spent in the state of 'studenthood'. In its purest form this entails living away from the parental home – probably for the first time if one excludes the large proportion of ex-public-school pupils – in the company of what is effectively an *age set* which occupies moreover a still essentially pre-adult status. Students have only a fairly low level of disposable income – compared say to that of many young workers – but at the same time they enjoy a considerable amount of free time and, within limits, freedom of thought and action. In the late 1960s and early 1970s this generationally specific context was to produce one of the most significant facets of the entire post-war spectacle, that of student radicalism.

The final aspect of the formal institutional response to youth in post-war Britain was the setting up of a state-sponsored youth service to cater for the leisure needs of the young in general, and in particular those of young workers. By the late 1950s it was coming to be widely thought that the youth service was in a critical condition, with much talk of insufficient facilities, inadequate buildings, an acute shortage of trained personnel, and a membership that was both proportionately small and generally uninspired by the somewhat staid programme which was at that time on offer. It was estimated that in the late 1950s only one (old) penny of every pound allocated to education from both central government and local authority sources was being spent on the youth service, and – a particular cause for concern at this time – only one in three of the relevant age group had any formal youth organization affiliation (Ministry of Education, 1960: 1).

It was against this backdrop that the Albermarle Report, *The Youth Service in England and Wales*, appeared in February 1960 as the first major public statement about the youth service, and was greeted as had been the Crowther Report a few weeks before with considerable public interest. The *Daily Mirror*'s front page headline of 4 February proclaimed the 'Scandal of Our Youth Service' and devoted a good deal of space to outlining Albermarle's findings concerning the inadequacy of existing state provision for youth. A centre-page spread on 'The Youth Scandal' argued that:

> Table tennis in old Church Halls is *square*. . . . Youth club leaders who use high-faluting phrases like 'character building' are *square*. . . . Youth organizations who would rather see a canteen than a coffee bar in their clubs are *square*.

The Mirror's 'verdict' was that the 'state of the youth service at present was 'scandalous', but it was 'splendid' that 'here is one government report that is not being pigeon-holed'. Likewise *The Times* agreed that the low level of priority and provision currently accorded to the youth service was deplorable, in an editorial of the same day entitled 'A Neglected Service'.

More than *exposing and commenting on* the inadequacy of the existing youth service, however, the Albermarle Report responded to and reflected the common perception that the Britain of the late 1950s and early 1960s was undergoing a period of rapid and fundamental upheaval, of which the recent emergence of youth as a distinct and significant social category was an integral part. In the first page of its introduction, the report stated that 'several aspects of national life, to which the youth service is particularly relevant, are today causing widespread and acute social concern'. The Albermarle Report then went on to cite as instances of such causes for concern the likely effect on the existing youth service and on society at large of the (real enough) late 1950s 'bulge' in the adolescent population, and the (far more questionable) 'fact' that many adolescents were responding to rapid social change 'in ways which adults find puzzling and shocking' (Ministry of Education, 1960: 1).

Albermarle itself made fairly explicit the connection between the youth question and 'broader issues of social change' that was widely being made when it expressed the view that 'the "problems of youth" are deeply rooted in the soil of a disturbed modern world' (p. 2). What of course it failed to grasp, along with the other major statements on the youth question of the period, was that such a connection was at least as much a metaphorical or projective one as it was objective.

Following the recommendations of Albermarle a ten-year plan was instituted for the reform and expansion of the youth service over the period 1960–70. By the time this period of development was nearing completion and the follow-up report *Youth and Community Work in the Seventies* was published in 1969, it was possible for the authorities to claim that many of Albermarle's original proposals for expansion had in fact been met. Thus, whereas there were only 700 full-time youth leaders in 1960, an emergency training scheme had raised this to 1,300 by 1966 and 1,500 by 1969 (YSDC, 1969: 11). Over the same period a £28-million building programme had been initiated, the Department of Education's grants in the area of the youth service had increased from £299,000 to £1.9 million, and local authority grants had increased from £2.58 million to £10 million. In the same ten years the total number of youth groups assisted rose by 112 per cent and expenditure per head of related population rose from £0.07–£2.65 to £0.42–£6.27 (YSDC, 1969: 12). In 1957–58 the estimated population in the youth service age range had stood at approximately 3.5 million while in 1967–68 it was approximately 5 million; over the same period, taking LEA youth work activity alone, the number of centres roughly doubled, as did the number of part-time youth leaders and the number of financially assisted youth groups. The number of full-time youth leaders nearly quadrupled and expenditure per head of population trebled from £0.74 to £2.03 (Halsey, 1972: p. 170, table 16.29). These increases in youth service provision, while still small in absolute terms and a small proportion of total educational expenditure, do at least give some idea of the growing feeling over this period that the 'special' needs of youth should be more 'properly' and adequately catered for by the state, and that the activities of youth should thereby be brought further under adult supervision and control.

The mere fact that the youth service was only involving a minority of its target group was now coming to be seen almost as a social problem in its own right. The Albermarle Report estimated that the youth service of the late 1950s was reaching approximately 'one in three' of the total adolescent population, and considered this level of provision inadequate, a sentiment that was widely echoed in the general reaction to the report's findings. In 1969, by the time of *Youth and Community Work in the Seventies*, this proportion was still much the same, with the figure quoted of 29 per cent of young people 'attracted by the youth service' (YSDC, 1969: 16).

A fairly typical example of the official response to the 'problem' of 'unattachment' is to be found in the description by Mary Morse, first published in 1965, of a National Association of Youth Clubs sponsored experiment in which three youth workers were sent incognito into three English towns, in an attempt to get to know and 'help' unattached youth. The latter group, while not 'extremely delinquent' was seen as 'basically dissatisfied, bored and resigned, with few prospects and no direction' (Morse, 1965: 45).[17] Indeed, according to Morse 'it could be seen that their [very] inability to join a youth organization was no more than one expression of a much wider pattern of unstable behaviour' (Morse, 1965: 75). Such statements provide a rationale for the further attempted formal institutionalization and control of youth, and lying behind this yet another expression of the generalized anxiety 'about youth' that was so prevalent at this time.

Let us return, though, to the Albermarle Report itself as both a key *resource* and also a key *topic* for the charting of the rise of the post-war period's cult of youth. This report listed a range of economic, social, institutional, demographic and physiological factors which were, by the late 1950s, combining to produce a considerable stepping up of the process of the differentiation of the age grade of adolescence/youth *at both objective and subjective levels*. (These factors were largely seen as objectively 'given'; what is of interest in retrospect is the range of *subjective meanings* that can be seen to be associated with them.)

Firstly, then, Albermarle noted the effect of the post-war population bulge, which meant that 'for every five 15–20-year-olds today [1960] there will be six in 1964'. Youth service and general educational provision was therefore seen as in urgent need of rapid expansion on demographic grounds alone. Secondly it was pointed out that the ending of National Service (in 1963) meant that 200,000 young men in the age range 18–20 who would previously have been 'contained' in the armed forces, were now going to be found in normal civilian life, thereby placing an extra strain on leisure facilities, etc.

It was further noted that adolescents were now taller and heavier and that children were maturing earlier, with as yet largely unknown but potentially major (or so it was thought) psycho-social consequences. The topic of the earlier physical maturation of the young was in fact a frequently discussed aspect of the youth question in the 1950s and 60s, often in conjunction with, and sometimes as a partial explanation of, the more general idea that post-war 'teenage culture' represented a qualitatively new phenomenon. Scientifically, the fact of earlier maturation was borne out in the much publicized work of J. M. Tanner on the physiology of adolescence, which demonstrated amongst other things how the average age of the onset of menstruation in Western countries had declined from around 17 in the mid-nineteenth century to around 13 in the late 1950s (Tanner, 1962). Popularly the adult response to earlier physical maturation amongst post-war British youth was exemplified in a series of feature articles run by the *Daily Mirror* over the period 15–19 September 1958, under the general title of 'The Beanstalk Generation'. The first of these was a centre-page feature by Keith Waterhouse beneath the headline 'Our Children Are Changing' and a large picture of a teenage girl:

She is only 13 but . . . already her hair has a home perm. She uses lipstick. She wears light face powder . . . she has been wearing a bra for a year now . . . in her pocket she is carrying her own key . . . her fingernails are varnished . . . this is one of *five* dresses in her wardrobe. She has pinups of Elvis Presley in her room. . . . She is wearing nylons. She has been wearing them for *two* years. . . . She is wearing high heels. She is going out on a date. . . .

[She is the] figure-head of a challenge: a challenge of our

changing children – youngsters of today are growing up *faster and sooner* than any other generation.

(Waterhouse then went on to refer to the work of Tanner on the declining average age of menarche, etc.)

The concluding article of the 'Beanstalk Generation' series (19 September) – advice to parents by 'Agony Aunt' Mary Brown – provides an even more graphic illustration of the then widespread perception of the 'difference' of contemporary youth: a difference which was seen as partly physiologically grounded but which also involved a range of significant imputed cultural factors:

> Now you face a bewildering challenge. The speed up of physical development in the young and the hot house forcing from American films, TV, and some youth magazines.
> . . . To talk about 'when I was your age' will leave your early developer unmoved.

After noting that there was a *'changing pattern of women's lives'* with a trend towards earlier marriage and a shorter overall period of child-rearing, the Albermarle Report next went on to express concern at the rising figures for *juvenile delinquency* over the previous decade (the overall rates for convictions in the 14–21 age range then stood at 2 per cent for boys and 0.2 per cent for girls). There seemed to the Report to be a 'new climate of crime and delinquency' in society, and this moreover was seen as posing the particular puzzle of 'delinquency in affluence'. Various possible explanations were in turn advanced to account for this – the Bomb? boredom? the cushioning of the Welfare State? – and the bland general conclusion reached that 'society does not know how to ask the best of the young' (Ministry of Education, 1960: 16).

The next factor discussed after that of juvenile delinquency was the general shortage and inadequacy of *housing* at this time. Following this, the question of the current expansion in secondary and further *education* (see above) was raised, after which there was some discussion of the possible impact upon youth of the creation in the post-war period of a comprehensive system of *social security*. It was noted that young people now had money to spend (Albermarle estimated an average of £3 per week) and that this was leading to something of a specialized teenage consumer boom. Finally, under the heading of *employment*, it was noted that the children of the post-war population bulge were now beginning to leave school and thus to place more pressure upon the Youth Employment Service, and under that of *life at work* the argument was advanced that the problems of the transition to work (see above) were particularly acute in times – such as the whole of the post-war period – of rapid industrial change.

The problem – and prevalence – of *youth unemployment*, especially amongst school-leavers has of course in the 1980s become one of the major areas of official and public concern over youth.[18] The period around the publication of the Albermarle Report, was, however, one of relatively full employment, and this extended to the employment of the young. Allowing for regional and sectional fluctuations, the whole of the period from 1945 to 1968 was one in which the labour demand for young people outstripped supply and there was therefore little youth unemployment, or concern over or discussion of this topic. Rather, as noted above, the *shortage* of juvenile labour, and the inadequacy of Britain's provision for the training of young workers to become the skilled and flexible workforce that would be so necessary in the future was widely considered to be a major problem in its own right. In her enquiry into the adequacy of the apprenticeship system under 'modern' (late 1950s) conditions, Kate Leipmann even went so far as to argue that British employers were then having to 'scrape the barrel' as far as juvenile labour was concerned:

> Since the last war, conditions of full employment in general and of scarce juvenile labour in particular have meant that Youth Employment Officers have had no difficulty (barring a few problem cases) in helping school-leavers to find employment of some sort. Indeed, the big demand for young workers has absorbed even boys and girls of small competence who would in other conditions be unplaceable. This is one of the reasons for complaints about the alleged low educational level of the average modern school-leaver.   (Liepmann, 1960: 64)

The implications of full youth employment in terms of the social mobility of the young, and thus the possibility of intergenerational strain, were at this time also a topic for (mild) anxiety. In the third

instalment of a series devoted to 'Problems of Adolescence' in the
Observer (8 June 1958), Marie Battle wrote that:

> Full employment and improved educational facilities have
> permitted a boy or girl to choose more freely than before from a
> wide range of possible vocations, professions or trades. If the kind
> of life chosen represents a departure from the family tradition, it
> will necessitate a revision of moral and social values which is bound
> to increase the tension between the adolescent and the family.

The expression of such views provides clear exemplification of the
ability of statements about and concern over 'contemporary youth'
to stand in metaphorical or projective relation to almost any wider
social anxiety or analysis: even the fact that there was seemingly no
shortage of occupational opportunities for the young could
apparently provide occasion for alarm!

Beyond its discussion of the basic 'objective parameters' of the
situation of youth in the post-war period the Albermarle Report must
however be located in its own specific socio-cultural context, as a
benchmark for the high degree of attention that was coming in the
late 1950s to be levelled at the category of adolescence/youth, and the
way in which the *concept* of youth was coming to be employed as a key
term in the project of making sense of a rapidly changing society. This
latter point becomes particularly apparent when the report switches
its focus of interest from the relatively 'hard' objective factors of the
'changing [social] scene' to that of the 'world of young people' and the
'less tangible changes in society' which were widely regarded as
having an impact upon society's 'mental climate' in general, and in
particular upon that of the young (Ministry of Education, 1960: 29ff).
The idea of youth's sensitivity to social change as developed by
Mannheim and Ortega y Gasset was restated quite boldly:

> Adolescents are the litmus paper of society. Subject to continuous
> and considerable mental, emotional and physical changes, as yet
> unregulated by the formal demands in the daily life of the
> breadwinner or housewife, adolescents are unusually exposed to
> social change.   (Ibid., p. 29)

Nevertheless the Albermarle Report was generally remarkably
level-headed with regard to much of the subjective, distorted and

exaggerated component then commonly to be found in statements about contemporary youth. It cited and *rejected* a whole range of clichés that were current concerning the youth of its day: that the young were 'a generation of teenage delinquents', that they had 'rejected family life', that they were 'featherbedded by the Welfare State', they were 'materialistic', 'couldn't care less', had 'no moral values' (Ibid., p. 32). The mere fact that an official report could enumerate such a list of adverse images of youth (a list which moreover still has a remarkably contemporary ring) is in its own right indicative of the degree of often unwarranted attention and comment to which this age grade was subjected throughout most of the post-war period.

As in the case of the other major educational and recreational policy statements of the 1950s and 60s discussed in this chapter, the Albermarle Report was basically optimistic and positive in its conception of youth. Provided that the youth service could in future provide *association* of the right kind, *training* of the right kind and above all *challenge* for the young, there was in its view a vast reservoir of talent and idealism to be tapped from amongst this age group. Once again, then, beneath the much publicized image of deviant youth it is possible to discern here a continuing awareness of youth as a sorely underdeveloped national asset. This most fundamental and most objectively anchored theme of the youth question can be traced back to at least the beginning of the present century and it persists – alas still chiefly at the level of rhetoric – right down until the present day. Perhaps at no time since the era of Crowther, Albermarle and Newsom, however, has there been such an explicit recognition of the *potential* of youth alongside of that of the problems of youth.

6
Responses to youth III: Images of youth culture

For the Albermarle Report, a major consideration with respect to the changing situation of contemporary youth had been that young people as a group had 'money to spend' to an extent which had not previously been encountered. This question of the new-found spending power of the British teenager (and indeed of teenagers throughout the Western world) is an important one, since in the most direct sense it provides the material base for many of the most distinctively contemporary aspects of the further differentiation of adolescence/youth.

The rise of youth – or 'teenagers' – as a distinct consumer group was a phenomenon of the post-war economic boom. It has been noted in the previous chapter how the whole of the period from 1945 to 1968 was one of relatively full employment in the youth sector of the labour market; more than this, however, it seemed at the time at least that the young as a group were 'the outstanding financial beneficiaries of the post-war situation'. Certainly by the late 1950s average teenage earnings had increased by more than 50 per cent in real terms from pre-war levels (M. Abrams, 1959).

The newly 'affluent' teenager of the 1950s was, hardly surprisingly, never to be faced with the problem of having nothing upon which to spend his or her money. By the end of the decade commercial interests were already becoming highly successful in their exploitation of this new market for goods and services, and were pondering moreover upon how further and more effectively to plumb this still relatively novel and unknown field of business enterprise. This, then, was the background for the publication of Mark Abrams's *The Teenage Consumer* (1959) and *Teenage Consumer Spending in 1959* (1961). These surveys into the extent, incidence and distribution of the new teenage spending power were produced as *consumer research* and their very existence testifies to the emergence of the youth market in this period, and the growing awareness amongst entrepreneurs that there were rich pickings to be had, especially on the basis of a fuller knowledge of exactly *who* was spending (or could spend) *how much* on *which products*.[1]

Abrams's starting point was the rather curious definition of teenagers as 'those young people who have reached the age of fifteen but are not yet twenty-five years of age and are unmarried' (M. Abrams, 1961: 3). On these criteria there were then in Great Britain approximately 5 million teenagers: 2.75 million males and 2.25 million females. Of this total approximately 4 million teenagers were at work and 'earning comparatively high wages and salaries' – £8 per week on average for young men in industry and £6 for young women – while the remainder, either still at school or else in National Service, were generally considerably worse off, economically speaking. It was, however, perhaps rather misleadingly, to the overall spending power and average rates of expenditure of the entire teenage group as above defined that Abrams devoted most of his attention. It was estimated that on average male teenagers, both employed and not employed, spent 71s 6d per week, while the figure for the same categorization of females was 54s. Allowing for deductions this represented a total annual expenditure of £830 million.

As Abrams pointed out, this figure represented only 5 per cent of total national consumer spending for the year in question, but also, as he was at pains to emphasize, this expenditure was of special significance in as far as it was concentrated in certain areas. Teenagers, as defined by Abrams, were much less encumbered than adults with the financial burden of providing for the necessities of life – housing, food, household durables, heating, light, etc. – and indeed were generally effectively subsidized in these areas the whole of the time that they remained resident in the parental home. (In this connection it has been pointed out that teenagers in the 1950s and 1960s were in large measure only 'affluent' by virtue of their parents also being 'affluent', itself a product of the general economic boom and full employment of the period (Frith, 1978a: 36).) In short, teenagers *en masse* had for the first time a substantial amount of money to spend on 'luxuries', and could dominate the market in many sectors of the burgeoning leisure industry:

Nearly one-fifth of all teenagers' uncommitted money goes on clothing and footwear; another 17 per cent is spent on drink and tobacco, and another 15 per cent on sweets, soft drinks, meals and snacks etc. in cafés and restaurants; a good share of the balance goes on entertainment goods – 'pop' records, gramophones, romantic magazines and fiction paperbacks, visits to the cinema and dance hall.   (M. Abrams, 1961: 5)

At the same time Abrams estimated that teenage spending as a percentage of all consumer spending stood at 37.1 per cent in the area of bicycles and motorcycles, 42.5 per cent for records and record players, 29.3 per cent for cosmetics and toilet preparations, 28.2 per cent for cinema admissions and 30.5 per cent for 'other entertainments' (M. Abrams, 1961: p. 4, table 1).

What can be discerned here is the establishment of the 'economic base', in terms of consumption at least, upon which an apparently new and distinctive 'Youth Culture' emerged in the post-war period:

By and large then, one can generalize by saying that the quite large amount of money at the disposal of Britain's average teenager is spent mainly on dress and on goods which form the nexus of teenage gregariousness outside the home. In other words this is *distinctive teenage spending for distinctive teenage ends in a distinctive teenage world.*   (M. Abrams, 1961: 5)

Abrams's work has been criticized by later sociologists of youth on a number of grounds, some rather more justified than others. Clearly his definition of the category of 'teenagers' as those aged 15–24 and unmarried is somewhat arbitrary, perhaps especially at its upper end, and probably presumes an identity of status and interests between all unmarried 15–24-year-olds which is quite unjustified. Also through his emphasis on the average expenditure in various areas of *all* teenagers, both those in full-time education and also those in full-time employment, he tends to gloss over the very real differences of material and economic circumstances, and therefore of culture, between these two groups. The former group, with its relatively low income from pocket money and part-time jobs, is thereby made to appear as economically better off and therefore more 'emancipated' in certain respects than in fact it was (and is), thus helping to reinforce the 'myth of the affluent teenager', while conversely (although this point seems to have gone unvoiced) the latter group is actually made to appear worse off economically.[2]

Abrams cannot be accused, however, of glossing over the differences in teenage spending that are to be found along the dimensions of social class and sex – and thus of contributing directly towards the myth (then prevalent) of 'teenage classlessness', or to the gender blindness that has until fairly recently been a feature of much of the sociology of youth.[3] Although at the time of its initial reception this aspect of the work seems to have been rather ignored under the impact of the notion of generalized teenage affluence – and clearly the fact that the latter was singled out as Abrams's major 'finding' is significant in its own right – it was in fact made reasonably clear through Abrams's statistics that male teenagers had more money to spend on average than did females (see above), that working-class girls were worse off than middle-class girls (an average weekly expenditure of 47s by the former versus 68s by the latter), and that whereas middle-class boys and girls were more or less equals in terms of their level of expenditure, the average working-class boy was considerably better off in this respect than his female counterpart. Working-class boys as a whole – probably because of their greater proportional engagement in full-time employment than their middle-class peers and their often higher initial incomes – were, in terms of weekly expenditure, the best-off group of all. For 1959 Abrams found that the average working-class boy spent 72s per week whereas the average middle-class boy spent 70s (M. Abrams, 1961: p. 6, table 2). There are no easily comparable statistics for the present, or indeed for any time since the original survey, but the situation in terms of breakdown by class and sex probably remains much the same. As has been pointed out, the specifically *teenage* market was and is dominated, at least in money terms, by young male unmarried workers, and for this reason the aesthetic of the teenage consumer market – as opposed to the extended youth market which emerged from the mid-1960s onwards – has remained a largely working-class aesthetic (Frith, 1978a: 19).

The rise of the affluent 'teenage consumer' in the late 1950s was all the more visible and remarked-upon a phenomenon by virtue of being set in contrast to the austerity of the immediate post-war period and the material sparseness which had characterized the youth, in the 1930s, of most of what was then the parent generation.

(It should, however, perhaps again be stressed that what is primarily under discussion here is the predominance of certain socio-cultural images and even 'myths' with only a partial basis in objective economic and social reality.) The general emergence of the consumption-based facet of teenage culture in the late 1950s, and the complementary process of the expansion of an essentially new sector of commercial enterprise to service – and create – its demands, through the provision of pop records, cosmetics, fashions, motorcycles and motor scooters, soft drinks, TV programmes, magazines, etc., marks an important moment in the history of the definition of the age grade of adolescence/youth, in the growth of the youth spectacle and in the establishment of the cult of youth.[4] Abrams's studies marked and charted this real-enough phenomenon of the emergence of the post-war teenage market whilst themselves contributing significantly – if unintentionally – to the further emphasis and dissemination of such then-central (semi-mythical) images of youth as 'teenage affluence' and 'teenage classlessness'.

In so far, precisely, as it was and is based upon passive consumption, teenage culture and indeed the 'teenage role' itself can be seen as (merely) the creation of *commercial* exploitation. This was a view that was much espoused in the late 1950s and throughout most of the 1960s. Looking back from the later vantage point to the initial period of the 'creation of the teenager' David Downes argued thus, for example:

> The concept of the teenage role is the product of external cultural forces, but the celerity with which it became rooted testifies an immensely powerful generational need it fulfilled. The logic of Abrams' work on the 'teenage consumer' is that, in order to sell to this very prolific market, the image of the 'teenager' had to be created, the precise achievement of pop culture.   (Downes, 1966: 130)[5]

More recent sociological work in the field of youth subculture, notably the contribution of the 'new subcultural theory', has argued that we should not merely view the young *en masse* as *passive* consumers but rather as at least potentially *active* in this respect, 'making something out of what is made of them' through their *bricolage* of the artefacts of consumer society. Following on from this point it has been emphasized how there is an extent to which most youth subcultural formations and phenomena can be regarded as in the first instance the spontaneous creation of a subsection of youth itself, to which the market then sooner or later *responds*. At the same time we have been urged to discard as of doubtful validity and utility such generic classifications as 'teenagers' and 'youth culture' and focus attention rather upon the specifics of social-class-based subcultures at particular historical moments.[6]

Together these points provide an invaluable corrective to the narrow economic determinism of the argument that sees *all* youth subcultures, groupings, styles and youth-related phenomena as *merely* the creation of the manipulative forces of consumer capitalism. They apply of course with the most force in the area where they were initially developed: the analysis of the succession of relatively tightly bounded, high visibility, fringe delinquent, working-class youth subcultures – the Teds, the mods, the skinheads and (perhaps) the punks – that has been so characteristic a feature of the British social scene, and of the youth spectacle, since the early 1950s. As outlined in Chapter 1, however, the 'new subcultural theory' is far from problem free, even in its analysis of such spectacular subcultures. These problems become considerably more acute when the focus of attention is shifted to the majority of more or less 'conventional youth'.

At the very least the *market*, as Downes has argued, has played a considerable role in the provision of new youth-orientated products, in the spread of youth styles and therefore ultimately in keeping the category of youth in one form or another in its position of high visibility throughout the post-war period. Spectacular youth subcultures may once at least have had their initial 'moment of originality': even here, however, commercial exploitation has invariably soon set in, diffusing the outward trappings of the subculture into wider youth – and perhaps eventually even 'adult' – society.[7]

Empirical surveys reveal the majority of contemporary British youth as being essentially conventional: there is no reason therefore to suspect this group of being any *less* susceptible to the lure of the latest fashions and products than is the adult population as a whole. At the present moment it would also seem to be likely that those young people who *do* adopt some or all of the outward trappings of spectacular subcultural affiliation generally do so more out of conformity to a largely pre-established and 'commercial' style than out of any deep-seated sense of intergenerational or inter-class antagonism. (As previously noted, the whole area of the relation-ships between youth subcultural affiliation, individual and group identity and the genesis of style, whether commercial or otherwise, is sorely in need of genuinely empirical research.) Even young people who are overtly rebellious and 'resistant' to formal coercion and authority in the shape, e.g., of the school or the youth club, are attracted – and perhaps particularly so – to the informal but ultimately exploitative world of commercial youth culture. At the level of immediate experience the latter does at least provide a certain freedom of expression, and a 'free space' away from, and possibly in opposition to direct (middle-class) adult intervention. As Paul Corrigan has written concerning the role of 'commercial institutions' (e.g. the commercial dance-hall) in the life of working-class near-delinquent youth in Sunderland:

> The *aims* of commercial institutions are, primarily, to make money. As far as the boys are concerned, for a certain amount of money you can buy a certain amount of freedom, since the aim of the institution [unlike that of the school or the youth club] is not primarily to interfere with the behaviour or ideas of those that enter them.   (Corrigan, 1979: 113–14)[8]

Since the mid-1950s, then, the forces of the *market* have together with those of the *media* played a central role in the actual creation of many aspects of youth culture and in the exploitation – and thereby ultimately in the absorption into 'safe' mainstream culture – of a number of possibly original and potentially 'subversive' youth (sub)cultural phenomena.[9] The point at which this intervention of market and media to 'diffuse and defuse' occurs would seem to vary from one instance to the next, but occur it does, even when the youth-related phenomenon under discussion can in one way or another be regarded as having been at the outset spontaneous and 'youth created'. It may well be that as professional sociological understanding of the mechanisms involved in the establishment and diffusion of youth trends, styles and subcultures has grown, so too has that of the cultural entrepreneurs. Thus a period of nearly two years seems to have elapsed between the original appearance of the mods in the early 1960s and their elevation to the status of full-blown folk devils in the media, accompanied by the large-scale commercial exploitation of mod by the market (S. Cohen, 1980: 178–91). In the case of the punks on the other hand, media and market manipulation seem to have followed on immediately from the 'moment of originality' – if there ever was such a thing – of punk-as-subculture, and may actually have been simultaneous, or even determining, processes right from the outset.[10]

The final key embodiment of the post-war period's official response to the youth question is to be found in the Latey Report on the Age of Majority, whose terms of reference were 'to consider whether any changes are desirable in the law relating to contracts made by persons under 21 and to their power to hold and dispose of property, and in the law relating to marriage by such persons and the power to make them wards of court' (Committee on the Age of Majority, 1967). From the point of view of the present study, Latey is of significance as a manifestation and exemplification of the post-war cult of youth in a number of senses. It bears eloquent witness, both in itself and via the testimony of its witnesses, to the sheer volume of adult attention that was at this time focused on the youth question, whilst simultaneously giving expression to the range of attitudes towards youth then current, from the most favourable to the most hostile. The report's own assessment of 'contemporary youth' – and that of the majority of its evidence – was however in the main markedly favourable: to this extent Latey can be viewed as a particularly clear statement of the positive cult of youth that was perhaps a peculiar feature of the late 1950s and early 1960s.

As the Albermarle Report had done before it, Latey noted the widespread minority stereotyping of youth then current, but rejected such negative images and evaluations as exaggerated and unrepresentative (and, significantly, as the product of media manipulation and adult anxiety):

It is easy for those not closely in touch with young people to get an entirely wrong idea of what they are like. The very word 'teenager' conjures up horror images of pop fans screaming at airports, gangs roaming the streets and long haired rebels being rude to their headmasters; and some of the older generation react with an automatic shudder.

We think this is the result of two things. First, the press. 'Dog bites man' is not news, 'Man bites dog' is. 500 thugs vandalize a seaside town and the public gets front page headlines on it; scores of thousands lead normal decent lives and little is written about it. . . .

We would certainly like to see more written about the enterprising responsible and vigorous young people about whom we have had so much evidence; and we think that on the whole the live media of television and radio can do a better job in this than newspapers . . . the discussion programmes show the young themselves in action, and the excellent account they give of themselves certainly presents a better picture than the headline news in the popular dailies.

And the second thing that contributes to this false picture of the young is the reaction of those generations which grew up when times were harder, when the young had less economic power and so less opportunity to express themselves.   (Committee on the Age of Majority, 1967: p. 25, paras 58–61)

The central issue for Latey's enquiries was whether contemporary youth could be considered as being 'more mature' than its predecessors, since this would in the main determine whether or not there was a case for lowering the age of majority from the then-current 21 years. Again this report acknowledged a strong current of opinion that subscribed to an essentially pessimistic view of contemporary youth and which could see no reason to suppose that the young possessed any greater maturity than their forebears. As one witness argued, neatly summarizing most of the negative themes then prevalent in the youth spectacle:

I look to the contemporary scene for signs of increased responsibility among the young and I see: the hooliganism of 'mods' and 'rockers', the hysterical behaviour of pop fans, the growing number of unmarried mothers and the high proportion of pregnant brides under twenty-one, the increase in drug taking, purple hearts and pep pills, the increase in venereal disease among the young . . . and I do not feel that this suggests any grounds for assuming that 'they mature so much earlier nowadays'.   (Ibid., p. 26, para. 62)

The Latey Committee, however, rejected this viewpoint and argued forcefully that since the vast majority of contemporary youth was shown by the evidence to be 'sensible' and 'responsible', there was in fact a strong case to be made on these grounds alone for the age of majority to be lowered to 18. Its other major argument here was that *not* to lower the age for free marriage and full contractual capacity might actually do more harm than good: 'To keep responsibility from those who are ready and able to take it on is much more likely to make them irresponsible than to help them' (ibid., p. 27, para. 71).[11] Juvenile delinquency was a real enough social problem – and the rise in its incidence a cause for alarm – but age of majority legislation should be brought into line with the qualities and aspirations of the mass of conventional youth: 'we must not legislate merely for a fistful of felons,[12] but for the vast majority of young people. . . .' (ibid., p. 31, para. 89).

The case for seeing contemporary youth as 'mature' – and probably *more mature* than its predecessors – and therefore for the lowering of the age of majority – was supported by the 'wholly encouraging' and 'surprising' evidence of a wide range of professional bodies, which, as Latey characterized the British Medical Association for example, were 'not exactly known for the wild and revolutionary nature of [their] views generally'. The BMA itself elaborated upon the then-much-discussed topic of the earlier *physical* maturity of the young (see above) by arguing that there was a link between physical maturation on the one hand and psychological maturation on the other: 'there is good evidence . . . that children who are physically advanced for their age score higher in mental tests than their contemporaries. . . . It is our view that there are no psychological reasons for placing the age of majority at 21, or any psychological objection to lowering the age . . . certainly, from the physical aspect and very probably from the psychological aspect the adolescent of today matures earlier than in previous generations' (Ibid., p. 28, para. 74).[13] The Justices Clerks' Society and the Church of England Board for Social Responsibility also thought that it would be more 'consistent' and appropriate to contemporary conditions if the age of majority be lowered to 18 in all respects. The opinion of the National Union of Teachers was not unanimous on these questions, but the Marriage Guidance Council was decidedly in favour of the age of free marriage coming down.

The Judges of the Chancery Division and of the Probate, Divorce and Admiralty Division were nearly unanimous in thinking that the age of majority needed to be lowered in order to bring it into line with contemporary conditions: 'the age which is appropriate to the conditions obtaining at one period may not be fitted to the conditions obtaining at another . . . we think that 18 should be substituted for 21 as the age at which a marriage can be contracted without consent and the wardship jurisdiction end' (ibid., p. 29, para. 77). The Town Clerks to District Councils 'praised the good sense and responsibility of young people with one voice' and were likewise in favour of a substantial lowering of current age limits. Finally, representatives of the business world in the shape of witnesses from finance, property and trade bodies – perhaps not surprisingly in view of the new-found economic power of British youth at this time – were also unanimous in wanting the age of majority lowered.

Latey concluded that 'All these witnesses and many more give us a picture of the young very different from that which emerges from a hysterical concentration on the delinquent minority'. Contemporary youth was if anything perhaps a little *too* conventional on the whole:

> Indeed, [it continued] those of us who remember our own wild youth with something softer than utter disgust found ourselves almost depressed by the image of the honest, sober, hard working, credit-worthy young, ready and eager to settle down for life, which was so often presented to us. . . .   (ibid., p. 30, para. 84)

In a later section the report went on to consider the relationship between its own area of investigation and the question of the formal education of youth (ibid., pp. 40–1, paras 126–32). Here it welcomed the then-still-projected raising of the school-leaving age, arguing that 'the young, advanced as they are, need far more training in human relations' and indeed in the 'mechanics of modern life' in general, and that RSLA could and should provide the time for exactly this. The concluding paragraph of this section will perhaps also serve as a summary of Latey's central argument that for a number of reasons – themselves closely related to the perceived pattern of overall social change in the post-war era – contemporary youth was 'different' and that the age of majority should be adjusted in recognition of this 'fact':

> Young people today, as the old never tire of remarking, are not what they were. They are largely literate and educated; they are

far better off financially and far more independent of their parents; they are taught to think and enquire for themselves and mostly do so; and their experience of life is wider. The question is not whether this is a good thing or a bad thing but what we are to do about it. . . . In giving [the young] adult status at eighteen we are doing no more than recognizing the simple facts.   (Ibid., p. 41, para. 132)

The subsequently implemented recommendation of the Latey Committee was therefore that the legal age of majority be lowered to 18. (The question of lowering the *voting age* to 18 was at this time also under investigation by the Speaker's Conference on Electoral Law, and the 1971 General Election duly became the first for which the 18–21 age group was enfranchised.)

The *Latey Report* remains nonetheless a somewhat internally contradictory document: at several points it was forced to acknowledge the existence of strong arguments and currents of opinion quite at odds with its own eventual conclusions and recommendations, and two committee members dissented sufficiently to produce their own Minority Report, urging that the age of majority should remain at 21. Even here, however, there can be found the perception that post-war youth was in many respects 'something new', and a recognition of the sheer extent of adult attention that was currently directed at youth:

Thus the young of this generation are probably more in the limelight than ever before. Indeed some would think that the youth of this country have focused upon them the eyes of the world. They have striven – a little too self-consciously perhaps – to break away from precedent; they have succeeded too. They have become aware of themselves and their elders have become aware of them.   (Ibid., pp. 130–57)[14]

Latey's 'contradictoriness' – and the underlying claims and counter-claims of its evidence – can perhaps best be seen here as a manifestation of the range of attitudes towards youth that coexisted at this period, of the vehemence with which many of these were held, and of the extent to which the youth question figured in the overall social discourse. The report's predominantly favourable

evidence and its recommendations – dissenting opinion notwithstanding – can likewise be interpreted as a manifestation of the high
esteem in which 'contemporary youth' was then held in significant
and influential sectors of adult opinion. The broader desire implicit
in the report to accord full adult status to 18–21-year-olds – which in
some respects runs counter to the trend towards the expansion and
formal institutionalization of adolescence/youth as a distinct age
grade noted elsewhere – can also be viewed as a function of the
generally high status enjoyed by youth in this period: a status that
was perhaps itself the product of relative youthful affluence and full
youth employment.

The media response to the Latey report was mixed, but once
again generally positive evaluations outweighed the negative. *The
Times* of 20 July 1967 devoted considerable space on its front page
to Latey's recommendations under the headline of 'Proposal to
Lower Age of Majority' and quoted the committee as saying that
'we have had impressive evidence that the young are quite capable
of conducting their own affairs with sense and honesty'. Better
education, physical maturity, affluence and greater sophistication
were identified as factors of special significance in this respect and it
was emphasized that, according to the report, the highly publicized
delinquent minority was just that. Another more evaluative article
(p. 3) commented upon the 'racy humour' of Latey: '[it] champions
British youth in a language they can understand and [has been]
widely acclaimed as one of the most readable of Government White
Papers'. A *Times* leading article of the same day, 'The Age of
Majority' (p. 9), rehearsed Latey's principal argument yet again
and concluded that 'in broad outline the Committee's case is
therefore a good one'. On 21 July a further *Times* piece noted the
reactions to the report that were then emerging: 'Proposed new deal
for teenagers welcomed' – the National Marriage Guidance Council, the Married Women's Association, and the HP Trades Association, to name but a few, were all strongly in favour of its
recommendations, and the British Youth Council was quoted as
saying that the Committee's proposals 'prove beyond doubt our
contention that young people both want and deserve more responsibility' (p. 2).

The *Daily Mirror* of 20 July 1967 proclaimed on its front page that
Latey was 'Swinging! A Charter for Teenagers' and again commented upon the Report's 'racy' language and 'bright and blunt

manner'. The *Mirror*'s editorial was – quite predictably – all in favour of the Latey recommendations: 'the sane sensible and responsible youngsters will remain sane, sensible and responsible [if the age of majority is lowered]; they are the vast majority . . . the truth is that young people do grow up *earlier* . . . the law ought to be brought up to date'. A full-page article inside the same issue of the *Mirror* devoted itself to a comprehensive outline of Latey's proposals with extensive quotes from committee members and witnesses, under the headline of 'Breakthrough for the Rights of Teenagers'. Even the *Mirror*'s political cartoonist got in on the act with an incongruous blend of then-current youth spectacle themes: Harold Wilson and George Brown are pictured outside a 'psychedelically' decorated Houses of Parliament and are addressing the Speaker thus: 'What with the swinging teenage charter and Prince Charles at the next opening of Parliament we thought. . . .' (This was also the 'Summer of Love' of 1967.)

The above discussion has perhaps strayed a little far, however, from the topic of the new 'teenage affluence' and the supposedly classless Youth Culture of the late 1950s. It is time now to return to a consideration of some of the initial responses to these perceived phenomena as are to be found within the social scientific discourse on youth itself.

The post-war period has been witness to a considerable expansion of research and publication in what might broadly be characterized as the academic field of 'youth studies'. Those engaged in this field in both Britain and America were often themselves aware of the special significance and attention that was at this time coming to be focused upon this age grade, and to which they themselves were contributing. For example in the USA, where this upsurge in interest in adolescence/youth pre-dated the equivalent occurrence in Britain by a number of years, Gessel, Ilg and Ames (1965) remarked thus in the introduction to their classic study of the developmental psychology of adolescence, first published in 1956: 'The social approaches to the study of the adolescent personality . . . have assumed new significance in an age of cultural crisis and global cold war' (p. xii). In a similar vein, writing some nine years later in the preface to a volume based upon an interdisciplinary symposium on the 'problems of youth in a changing world' M. and C. Sherif (1965) commented that 'the topic of this book is one of the most timely of our age. . . . In the throes of their own personal transition from childhood to adulthood, youth also faces a world of transition' (p. vii).

In the specifically British context a good idea of the general degree of professional attention that was being focused upon the youth question in all its manifestations in the early 1960s is to be gained from Raison's anthology of articles on 'youth' in *New Society* over the period 1962–65. Writing in 1966 in his introduction to this volume Raison commented thus:

> The youth question – and whether there is a youth question – has dominated much discussion about society in the past year or two. Juvenile delinquency, juvenile sexual behaviour, juvenile ethics, juvenile culture, juvenile spending, the gulf between the generations – these are themes that have recurred over and over again in writing, broadcasting, conferences and private conversation. (Raison, 1966: viii)

The titles of the pieces contained in this collection together provide in their own right an inventory of most aspects – some of which have already been encountered – of the youth question and the youth spectacle at this particular time. Beyond this, however, it is also possible to discern here a certain almost timeless quality, in as far as with certain omissions and modifications of terminology, many of the same titles could pass as those of articles written only yesterday.[15] Thus amongst others we find pieces on 'Adolescence 12 to 18: The Body'; 'Adolescent Personality'; 'Adolescent Values'; 'Teenage Idols'; 'What to do about Pep Pills'; 'Moral Education in Chaos'; 'The Teenage Criminal'; 'New Facts on Teenage Marriage' and 'Young Marriage' as well as two rather more time-bound articles on the then-current, highly visible, problem adolescents – the mods and rockers.[16]

In terms of key texts that have subsequently had ramifications for the more general area of theorizing about adolescence specifically, some sort of high-water mark for the definition of adolescent psychology had been reached in 1950 with the publication of Erikson's *Childhood and Society*. As previously noted, it is to Erikson that we owe the theoretical formulation of the idea of adolescence as a period of 'quest for identity' and 'role moratorium' that has come to be the dominant taken-for-granted assumption – along with the closely related imputed characteristic of storm and stress – in our culture concerning the 'innate' psychology of this stage of life. In *Childhood and Society* Erikson demarcated eight stages of the human life-cycle, each characterized by its own particular crisis or conflict in the sphere of ego development (Erikson, 1975: 239–66, esp. 252–5). The crisis of adolescence was seen as being that of 'identity v. role confusion': this, according to Erikson, was particularly pronounced and protracted in advanced Western societies, as in such societies vocational and sex roles were becoming increasingly ill-defined and/or numerous. The loss of clear-cut and pre-given roles for the contemporary adolescent to *grow up into* meant that a fairly lengthy period of time was needed for a viable adult identity to be formed; thus adolescence became a period of 'psycho-social moratorium'. In this period the adolescent supposedly tested extremes in his or her beliefs and actions, before normally settling down to some middle course. It was out of these features that, according to Erikson, the adolescent characteristics of confusion, instability, marginality, idealism, etc., arose, and thus also the prevalence at this time of life of stormy conflict with the older generation.

As discussed in Chapter 1, such theoretical formulations concerning the innate 'psychological difficulty' of the stage of adolescence would seem, even in their modified Eriksonian variety, to be considerably out of accord with the rather humdrum realities of this time of life as experienced by most young people. Empirical evidence demonstrates overall a remarkable *continuity* of values rather than a conflict between generations, and growing up as relatively smooth and gradual, rather than a process involving violent jumps and swings. Pronounced adolescent storm and stress at an individual/psychological level, and intergenerational conflict at a group/sociological level, would seem to represent the exception rather than the norm.

Nonetheless the storm and stress model of adolescent psychology, with its identification of the 'special' – and particularly fraught – 'characteristics' of this time of life has continued to be taken for granted in large sectors of professional and popular opinion, along with the closely related idea that adolescence should be singled out as an entity *sui generis* on 'innate' psychological grounds alone. The question of the expressly psychological 'problems of adolescence' – usually couched in the relativized form of the inherent difficulties of this stage of the life-cycle in a complex and rapidly changing society

– has indeed formed a minor, if constant aspect of the post-war period's youth spectacle.

One example of the post-war 'media-ization' of the topic of the 'problems of adolescence' is to be found in the series of articles on this topic by psychologist Marie Battle that appeared in the *Observer* over the period May to July 1958, which has already been encountered with reference to the specific problem of the 'identity quest' and greater social mobility of the young leading to intergenerational tension: 'a perennial problem but one that has been greatly intensified in the post-war years', according to Battle (8 June 1958). The first article in the same series (25 May) noted the minority stereotyping of the young that was then, as now, a common feature of the response to youth, and went on to suggest that the 'fact' that adolescents were somehow more 'spontaneous' and 'less inhibited' than adults was at the root of adult resentment of the young:

> [the] difficulties surrounding the discussion of adolescence have been exacerbated by the way in which the subject is sometimes publicly treated, with the words 'juvenile' and 'delinquent' automatically linked together. There is a great deal of natural adult resentment of adolescents, due largely to those young people's giving direct and untrammelled expression to desires that are inhibited in most grown ups.

Subsequent articles proceeded via a series of case studies of individual adolescents to exemplify a number of the difficulties that could be experienced by adolescents' parents in contemporary Britain, whilst continuing to stress the positive side of adolescence. Thus, while it was stated at various points that adolescents could be and often were inconsistent, moody and self-centred, it was also argued that they were honest and valued tolerance. One article in particular (29 June) stressed the value of the much-vaunted quality of 'adolescent idealism' in the following terms:

> It would be idle to speculate about the exact nature of the world's debt to this adolescent idealism. . . . But it is certainly greater than most of us imagine. Repeatedly it has enriched

our culture by reminding us of exactly those things that we had almost forgotten.

The idea of adolescence as inevitably psychologically problematic, but at the same time of tremendous potential for both individual and society, also found a more popular expression in the writings of such figures as the *Daily Mirror*'s 'agony aunt' of the late 1950s and early 1960s, Mary Brown. (Advice to parents and the young themselves on the 'problems of adolescence' has of course continued to constitute a major stock in trade of agony aunts, child psychiatrists, developmental psychologists and other concerned professionals, down until the present day.) The pronouncements of Mary Brown on the specific topic of the implications of the earlier physical maturity of post-war British youth, ('The Beanstalk Generation') have been encountered above, but the former theme was generally blended in her discussion with a consideration of imputed adolescent *psychology*, and of the particular psycho-social factors inherent in contemporary society that were seen as combining to render this time of life both more 'problematic' and also more 'important' than previously.

In a characteristic *Daily Mirror* article of 29 May 1956 on 'Teenage Troubles', Brown wrote of Terry, aged 17, who was 'unreasonably jealous' of Angela, 16, who 'would never say sorry', noting that in other respects 'these two were a pleasant, normal pair whose only fault was a youthful tendency to take themselves too seriously'. The problem was that while Terry and Angela were 'grown up physically' they were not yet 'mature emotionally'. Brown's advice to the young themselves was that:

> Adolescence is a strange new world of intense feeling . . . you live on an emotional see saw . . . you are sure you are being awkward and clumsy. . . . We all go through the same experience. These experiences are natural at this stage of your emotional growth. Teenagers are emotional toddlers.

In a later article (11 March 1957) Brown replied to parents' letters on the topic of how to cope with their teenage offspring. One such letter and its reply together neatly illustrate the widely held belief – again possibly throughout the whole of the period since 1945, but perhaps especially in the late 1950s and early 1960s – that a gulf was opening up between generations due to the sheer pace and extent of material progress and social change:

> *Letter:* 'My husband and I went without a lot for our daughter [but] clothes and boys are all she thinks of. . . .'
> *Answer:* 'I think our criticism is more than tinged with envy. It irks us to see our youngsters taking for granted so much that we never had in our own youth. . . .'

The same reply went on to restate the positive image of contemporary youth which was increasingly coming to be advanced as a counter to the negative image of the delinquent minority: 'In Britain today more than half a million of them [teenagers] work voluntarily for the community'.

The connection between 'youth' and ideas about the future and social change is further exemplified in Brown's reply in the same feature to a letter asking 'How can I understand my teenagers?' (The question itself is revealing in its implication that 'teenagers' were somehow a race apart: another idea that was particularly in evidence in the late 1950s and 60s):

> The answer is that complete understanding of both sides is hardly possible. Youth's eyes are on tomorrow. Most older people look backwards. . . .
>
> Youth is naturally idealistic. Youth naturally longs to serve. I believe that if we let our young people see we expect the best from them we get it.

Here it is possible to discern once more the imputation of the quality of 'adolescent idealism' along with a popular expression of the idea, more formally stated in the theories of José Ortega y Gasset and Karl Mannheim, that while the older generation thinks in terms derived from the past, youth 'looks to the future'. This conception is essential to the *metaphorical* interconnectedness of the themes of youth and social change in the social, cultural and political discourse of the post-war period.

The image of the rebellious, disturbed, mixed up (yet) idealistic and honest adolescent that was already established by the early decades of the twentieth century has then continued to exert a firm grip on popular thought and iconography, perhaps with a special power in the 1950s and 60s. Two fictional texts, much at evidence in the early post-war youth spectacle and which widely captured the imagination of young and old alike, also spring immediately to mind in this connection: J. D. Salinger's novel *The Catcher in the Rye* (1951) and Nicholas Ray's film *Rebel Without a Cause* (1955). In Holden Caulfield, hero of *The Catcher in the Rye*, there can be seen the further modernization and in many respects the culmination of the tradition of the fictional adolescent hero whose sufferings and problems are partially pre-given but also partially socially conditioned, and whose gaucheness, innocence, candour, and refusal to compromise cast a highly critical light upon the superficiality and empty sophistication of adult society. If the fictional adolescent can be seen as the 'archetypal figure for the confusions of our age' then Holden Caulfield is perhaps the archetypal contemporary adolescent; it is in him that many of the our popular ideas about adolescent psychology find their expression and also in part their source.

Rebel Without a Cause can be read in the same way: the tragedy of adolescent innocence confronted with adult experience, and the potential for social critique thus generated. However, while Holden Caulfield remains in some respects a timeless figure, the figure of Jim, the 'Rebel' of the film's title as portrayed by James Dean, was much more closely a creature of his times, an icon for the 'different' and special status of youth in the post-war world and for the growing sense of intergenerational disjuncture that characterized the 1950s. Thus while Jim/Dean in *Rebel* was undoubtedly a confused adolescent in the classic mould, he was also firmly established in the film as a denizen of the already flourishing American High School youth culture. This emergent awareness of youth as a 'new' phenomenon and autonomous age grade was reflected in the viewpoint of the film in which, in the words of its director, 'youth is always in the foreground and adults are, for the most part, shown only as kids see them' (Herndon, 1974). (In this, of course, it shares a common feature with the first person narrative of *The Catcher in the Rye*.)

Dean provided, then, a kind of *model* (in his screen roles and in his life and death: as with most true stars, fiction and reality fuse at some point into myth) which defined one version of contemporary youth not only for the parent generation but also for the post-war generation itself.[17] (The other archetype of adolescence/youth to be found in the Hollywood cinema of the early 1950s was Marlon Brando in Laslo Benedek's *The Wild One* (1954). Here there can be found an image of overtly delinquent and sexually aggressive youth to counterpose against Dean's more passive and sensitive, although still disturbed and near delinquent, persona.) Following his tragic yet somehow 'heroic' and 'appropriate' death, James Dean emerged as the first media-created *idol* and *icon* of post-war youth.[18] This is a phenomenon which was in later years, especially in the context of rock music rather than cinema, increasingly to come to play a central role in the youth spectacle, and thus in the (self)identification of youth as a meaningful socio-cultural categorization in its own right.

In the area of sociology proper the parallel conception to that which has regarded adolescence/youth as a distinct and problematic entity by virtue of its innate characteristics, has been the notion of the emergence of a distinct 'Youth Culture', uniting the younger generation *en masse*, and thus cutting across the stratification of society by social class. This idea was already taking shape in the context of the sociological analysis of the American High School culture of the 1930s and 40s, but it was in the 1950s and early 1960s that it reached its peak as a way of thinking about the youth question on both sides of the Atlantic.

It has been pointed out that there has, almost from the outset, been a tradition within the sociology of youth that has been concerned with the differences to be found in youth subcultural formation along the dimension of social class. Nonetheless this class-based approach more or less disappeared from the mainstream of sociological thought during the period from roughly the mid-1950s until the early 1970s, to be replaced by the idea of 'generation over class' and consequently of the coming into existence of a unified Youth Culture (Murdoch and McCron, 1976: 10–18). Murdock and McCron have argued that the predominance at this time of this way of thinking about youth can be attributed to its consonance with the ideology of democratic pluralism: beyond this, and in a much less subtle sense, it would seem at least partly explicable in terms of an initial and 'naive' response to the appearance of phenomena and social types that had not previously been widely encountered. The apparent emergence of a distinct and highly visible teenage culture, and of 'the teenager' as a social type, which began in the USA sometime in the 1940s, and which finally arrived in Britain in the late 1950s, naturally encouraged the first analysts of these processes to take 'generation' as their prime variable (as in the general thrust of Abrams's work on teenage consumer spending). A similar 'naive analysis' can be discerned in the initial academic theorizing that accompanied the appearance, some ten years later, of the concept – and reality – of 'Counter Culture' and 'Extended Youth'. In this manner much sociological analysis in the post-war period has itself contributed to the establishment of the cult of youth, through its emphasis, which now seems misguided at least, upon the essential identity and unity in one way or another of successive younger generations, and the distinctiveness and separateness of these *vis à vis* their elders.

The classic post-war sociological statement of the idea of the emergence of a distinct Youth Culture, and one which seems to have been highly influential in its day in a quite generalized manner was James S. Coleman's *The Adolescent Society* (1962). This study was in most respects a continuation of the earlier work of Parsons and others on the American high school as the locus for the formation of a distinct Youth Culture. To this basically unoriginal conception, however, Coleman brought a whole barrage of sophisticated empirical techniques.

On the basis of an extensive questionnaire and sociometric study of ten Illinois high schools, Coleman claimed to have discovered that the dominant informal student culture and value climate of *all* the schools in question was quite distinct from, and perhaps in opposition to, the formal adult value system of the school as an institution. In essence Coleman argued for the existence of a separate Youth Culture whose own values were reinforced, if not created, through the process and experience of schooling itself:

> [the adolescent] is cut off from the rest of society, forced inward toward his own age group, made to carry out his whole social life with others his own age. With his fellows he comes to constitute a small society, one that has most of its important interactions within itself. . . . As an unintended consequence society is confronted no longer with a set of individuals to be trained toward adulthood, but with a distinct social system which offers a united front to the overtures made by adult society. (J. S. Coleman, 1962: 3–4)

Coleman saw the 'fundamental competition' within the informal student social system as being for *peer group status* and this he regarded as being derived from a mixture of 'athletic achievement, good looks and dressing well, doing well in school, maintaining a good reputation while still being willing to have fun, having a car but not being a fanatic about cars, knowing popular songs without being addicted to popular music' (ibid., p. 144). As has been pointed out subsequently by a number of commentators, such dominant peer-group values are in fact far from being in opposition to those of adult Middle America, nonetheless Coleman's study was widely taken as further proof of the emergence in post-war Western societies of an autonomous, unified and even anti-adult Youth Culture.[19]

This 'Youth Culture Thesis', reinforced by the interrelated notion of 'teenage affluence', remained the dominant professional and popular conception concerning *British* youth throughout the 1950s and 60s (e.g. Laurie, 1965). During this period, however, in the American context a continued awareness of the importance of social-class-based subdivisions within youth as a whole *did* persist in the specialized field of the study of juvenile delinquency.[20] In Britain something similar seems to have occurred in the sociology of education and of the transition from school to work. As noted in the previous chapter, one common image of youth to be found in post-war British discussion of the youth question was that of 'youth-as-national asset'. In the sociology of education this idea has manifested itself in a continuing concern for and analysis of the roots of the systematic under-achievement of working-class children and adolescents in the educational system as a whole, and in particular the proportional under-representation of the latter group in grammar schools and higher education.

In the 1960s this concern with the processes involved in the under-achievement of working-class adolescents in secondary education – and therefore implicitly with wastage of youthful ability and talent – was combined in the British sociology of education with a Coleman-type methodological approach to the study of the school as an informal social system. Studies by Sugarman, Hargreaves and Lacey all demonstrated, in one way or another, how clique formation amongst secondary school pupils was structured along a dimension of social class, and how the subculture of working-class under-achievers came to be increasingly anti-school, drawing rather upon the oppositional elements in adult working-class culture and on the then-burgeoning commercial Youth Culture (Sugarman, 1967; Hargreaves, 1967; Lacey, 1970). Taken together, these studies represent an important moment in the reintroduction of the dimension of class into the study of British youth, and thus in the demolition of the myth of the primacy of generational differences.[21] Outside the school, after pioneering studies in the sociology of urban working-class youth by Downes and Wilmott, this reinjection of class into the sociology of youth has of course been taken up most notably in the analyses of 'spectacular working-class youth subcultures' of the 'new subcultural theory' of the 1970s.

At a popular as well as social scientific level the peak of the idea of generation over class was reached in Great Britain and the United States in the late 1960s and early 1970s when radical/counter cultural youth was seen by many commentators as actually becoming a 'class' in its own right.[22] Along with the emergence of 'the teenager' this represents one of the two high points of the cult of youth. It is towards the post-war cult of youth in its various forms and manifestations that the attention of the following chapters is directed.

7

The cult of youth I: Teds 'n' Teenagers

Perhaps more than by anything else, youth has been recurrently brought into the field of general public attention and concern as an emergent and problematic category in post-war British society by the succession of spectacular fringe delinquent working-class youth subcultures, and the array of more diffuse but no less visible 'ideological' middle-class youth movements that have over the past thirty-five years or so been a prominent and constant feature of the general social scene. It is with reference to this range of more or less clearly defined youth subcultures and groupings, all undoubtedly real enough and more or less 'spontaneously created' socio-cultural phenomena, but nonetheless all rapidly transmuted into spectacle, the focus of adult concern and official reaction and the stuff of commercial exploitation, that it is possible to discern the workings of the interplay of objective reality and the construction of subjective image and meaning from which the concept of youth has derived much of its current significance.

More than this, however, the foregoing discussion has already established in outline how youth was at certain times seen as a highly significant and meaningful concept and 'class' to be isolated for the purpose of social analysis and commentary. Thus there have been moments in post-war British history when, in one way or another, the ideas of youth and generation have been employed as prime variables for the mapping of the major features of contemporary society, and for the prediction of the trend of future social changes. Such *generic* images of youth are embedded in the post-war youth spectacle and are in turn explicable in terms of their relationship to broader perceptions of the nature of social change and the 'state of the nation' over the period in question.

The first major theme of the youth spectacle in the post-war years was provided in the early 1950s by the emergence of the Teddy boys, a style and subculture with its origins in the working-class districts of south and east London, but which was to spread numerically and also geographically, mainly to other urban centres, as the decade progressed. There had been earlier semi-formulated and sometime remarked-upon styles and groupings amongst near delinquent urban working-class youth in the 1930s and 40s: 'razor gangs', 'wide boys', 'spivs', 'cosh boys', etc. The Teds, however, with their highly distinctive mode of dress – appropriated from a post-war Saville Row 'Edwardian look' for young gentlemen, but soon adapted and embellished – and their reputation for sudden violence, were the first true high-visibility working-class youth subculture of the period, and certainly its first major 'folk devils' and 'problem adolescents'.[1] The image of the Teddy boy as a new and particularly problematic social type first crystallized in the mass media and in the popular imagination following a particularly violent and seemingly pointless murder on Clapham Common in 1953.[2] Nonetheless it should be noted that in the early days of the Teddy boy phenomenon the image of this group was far from entirely negative, being coloured in part by the generally favourable image of post-war British youth (or 'teenagers') that was emerging in the mid-1950s, by the (perennial, and in a sense probably quite 'correct') idea that it was only a minority that was genuinely 'bad', even within the subculture, and by the then-widespread concern for the realization of the 'true potential' of the young. These themes were expressed in a *Daily Mirror* piece of 5 July 1955 by Tony Miles, on one of the current periodic attempts to institutionalize 'un-attached youth':

There's hope among the teacups in the TEEN CANTEEN – where the boys in Slim Jim ties find they belong.

. . . As a class the Teddies are often branded as trouble makers through the headline antics of a few. Individually I found the boys I met in the canteen personable, friendly and responsive to trust – given the chance.

Before the 'Teen canteen' had come along the local Teds had been 'outcasts' – bored, wandering the streets and consequently fre-quently in trouble: now they were redecorating the premises, forming self-governing committees and themselves taking care of any trouble that might occur.

The Teddy boy phenomenon was also 'news' for the popular press – as with all subsequent youth subcultures and styles – at the simple level of the reporting of the latest developments in fashion, although in this case it soon came to be acknowledged that the 'Edwardian look' had acquired a real power to stigmatize its wearers:

Now the Boys are Roamin' in the Roman Look.
The dapper boys who led the Edwardian revival are now swanning around town in a crisp creation with short jacket and natural shoulders. [Note the anticipation of the early mod style here.]
Said Ken, 24, 'I stopped wearing Edwardian clothes – long jackets, cuffs, the lot – when the cheaper imitations occurred. Anyone wearing Edwardian got a bad reputation.' (*Daily Mirror*, 14 July 1955)[3]

A slightly later *Daily Mirror* (27 July 1955) carried the front page headline 'No Teddy Boy Suits for Soldiers' and went on to report how new conscripts had had their Edwardian 'civvies' confiscated by their commanding officers.

Other less-then-entirely negative Teddy boy images are to be found in stories concerning 'reformed Teddy Boys': 'When a Teddy Boy turns to Sermons . . . Bob Cochran wants to battle for the souls of Britain's boisterous bop-loving teenagers with swingtime hymns and straight-talk sermons' (*Daily Mirror*, 22 August 1956) and in the – again perennial – cry of minority stereotyped youth itself against the role in which it has been cast:

I am fed up with adults who always run us teenagers down, moaning and groaning about us hanging round coffee bars or street corners. I am a Teddy Boy but I don't do either. I'm far too busy – with 100 other lads – at the youth club. (*Daily Mirror*, 'Live Letters' 24 April 1959)

Of course the fact that such essentially dissenting views could be expressed – and indeed that the necessity was felt to express them – still points to the fact that as the 1950s wore on the Teddy Boy was coming to be ever more minority-stereotyped in an overwhelmingly negative mould. The association between youthful delinquency and violence and the increasingly visible, remarked-upon and wide-spread Teddy boy style and subculture was reinforced by the media's reporting of so-called 'Teddy Boy riots' in dance-halls and other public places from 1954 onwards, and in particular by the disturbances accompanying the arrival, in 1956, of rock 'n' roll in this country (of which more shortly). The zenith of the 'Teddy Boy movement' and its associated moral panic seems to have been reached over the period 1956–58, with the last year witnessing serious race riots in London's Notting Hill and also in Nottingham, in which Teds were centrally implicated, even while the press, both popular and serious, was at pains to point out that these clashes could not simply be attributed to the Teds alone.

The *Daily Mirror* of 1 September 1958 (front page headline '400 Clash in "Colour" Riot') noted that in Notting Hill 'Each time the riots began after gangs of white youths had jeered at coloured people . . . [and they then] developed into violent pitched battles'. The next day's issue reported further arrests in new ' "colour" riots' and again spoke of white 'teenage youths' (sic) as the instigators. A front-page Vicky cartoon went further in the minority stereotyping of the Teds by depicting a 'racialist thug' in full Edwardian drag being addressed by the ghost of Adolf Hitler: 'Go on boy, I may have lost the war but my ideas seem to be winning'. The riots continued throughout most of the first week of that September, and the *Mirror* continued to elaborate a small range of variations upon the themes of Teddy boys, hooliganism, racialism and fascism now established: its front-page headline of 3 September was 'Black v. White: What we must do' and the editorial of the same day urged maximum sentences for 'white hooligans' – 'spineless louts and bully boys, with their razors and broken bottles'; the issue of 5 September carried another Vicky cartoon equating the Teds with the Nazis and quoted a speaker at the TUC conference as suggesting that 'evidence is accumulating that those who promoted pre-war racial hatred are once again fanning the flames of violence.'

The Times similarly made a good deal, in its customary under-stated yet circumlocutious manner, of the role of youth and especially the Teds in the Notting Hill and Nottingham riots, with a number of references over the period 1–3 September to the central involvement – undoubtedly real enough in its way – of 'gangs of youths'. (This despite the fact, also garnered from *The Times* of the same period – 2 September 1958 – that the 'Nottingham Rowdies' who were imprisoned for their part in the riots ranged in age from 16 to 45.) The Chief Constable of Nottinghamshire was quoted as saying that the Nottingham disturbances should not, strictly speaking, be considered as a 'racial riot' at all: 'the people primarily involved were irresponsible Teddy Boys and persons who had had a lot to drink' (2 September). In one of those 'coincidences' of timing that seems to occur fairly frequently in the youth spectacle, *The Times* of the following day (3 September) carried both a report of an address delivered to the British Association by Leslie Wilkins on his work on the particularly 'crime prone' nature of the post-war generation (once more Wilkins stressed that the 'destabilizing effect' exerted on the young by an early childhood spent during the war years was a *necessary* but not *sufficient* explanation) and also a detailed investigation by its 'Special Correspondent' into the Notting Hill disturbances which had then just reached their peak. The latter article conceded that the riots could not be 'explained away' simply, and should be viewed as a product of deep-seated prejudices – held *across generations* – in certain sectors of society; it still managed however to portray the Teds in the lurid light of full folk devil status: 'London Racial Outburst Due to Many Factors: Hooligan Invaders and Wild Charges':

> . . . The trouble has been written up as race rioting; and it has been written off as mere hooliganism of gangs of excited Teddy Boys. It is nothing so simple as either of these two things.
>
> It is no good dismissing the evening pursuits and bottle throwing and lynch mobs as the work of Teddy boys. After all some of the young men of Notting Dale are Teddy Boys. They get reinforcements from all over the town because these stunted pallid thugs like the chance of violence without dangerous odds. But having listened to what some of the fathers and little brothers of Notting Dale were saying in the daytime one felt that quite a few must be proud of their teenage sons.
>
> [These are nothing but] young roughs, hunting in packs . . . unless the boy-thugs are put down with a heavy hand and a real effort is made that justice is both done and seen to be done . . . tension, and then trouble, must spread.   (p. 7)

Another article on the same page further implicated the Teds in the race riots, and further contributed to the stigmatization of this group, in its account of the Magistrates' Court proceedings against some of those arrested in Notting Hill: 'Throughout the morning groups of people, many of them in Teddy Boy dress, gathered on pavements or street corners near the courthouse. . . .' The magistrate in charge of proceedings had ordered that weapons seized from the accused be placed in a box in court; this produced a fearful assortment of 'flick knives, stilettos, razors, bicycle chains, choppers, a club and a carving knife', according to *The Times*. Such media stories and images concerning the prevalence of such weapons, and campaigns against this alarming 'new' phenomenon were in themselves a fairly prominent feature of the youth spectacle at around this time. The flick knife itself often served as a symbol, in the mass media and popular imagination alike, for all that was (supposedly) most wrong, and threatening and different about early post-war youth.

A *Times* leader of the same day: 'The Hooligan Age', combined comment on both Leslie Wilkins's recent pronouncements on post-war levels of juvenile delinquency and the riots as such. The 'Teddy Boy phenomenon' could not be explained by the war alone but represented a 'crime wave of a different type' from that encountered previously. The Nottingham and Notting Hill disturbances originated, according to *The Times*, in the activities of 'gangs of youthful thugs' and were yet another 'manifestation of the youthful ruffianism long endemic in both areas'; the *racial* form taken by the current disturbances could be viewed as the 'reaction of ignorant folk against strangers of any sort' and the overall and sobering conclusion to be drawn was that 'the Stormtroop mentality exists in England too'.

By the end of the 1950s the Teddy boy style, and possibly also the subculture itself, was in decline and had in fact become rather passé, at least among the youth of London and the South-East. The moral panic was beginning to abate as well, perhaps partly because the contemporary image of youth as conveyed via the youth spectacle was becoming a far more complex and ambivalent one. Nonetheless 'Teddy Boy gangs' continued for some while to figure in the headlines, in association with the more generalized theme of the (unprecedented level of) post-war juvenile delinquency and violence, as in the *Daily Mirror*'s front and centre page story of 19 March 1959 concerning a then widely publicized murder trial. Here the front-page headline was 'A Knife Killer is to Hang', the killer in question being one Ronald Marwood aged 25, an ex-grammar-school boy but one with 'old Teddy Boy connections'. The centre-page feature described the context in which the crime – the murder of a policeman – had been committed: 'the jungle of Seven Sisters Road, Holloway, where rival Teddy Boy gangs have been terrorizing the district for months'. Marwood had knifed the policeman outside a dance-hall 'where 200 teenagers were rock 'n' rolling'.

In stories such as this the negative image of the Teddy boy spills over into what were, strictly speaking, other areas of the youth question. It is perhaps worth noting in passing here how by the later years of the decade the appellation 'Teddy boy' had become a generalized term of abuse for any individual or group that was perceived as 'rowdy', 'violent', 'dangerous' or whatever. Almost any group of young people could be referred to in a derogatory and often semi-ironic fashion as 'a crowd of Teds', and the young John Osborne was referred to by a critic as 'an intellectual Teddy Boy'. *The Times* similarly carried a story in which the drivers of high-powered motor boats were described by an irate yachtsman as 'water-borne Teddy Boys'. The use of such negative imagery, drawing on youthful minority stereotypes (as in Norman Tebbit as 'the Chingford Skinhead') continues as a common rhetorical device to the present day.

The representation of the Teddy boy in the mass media, and in particular in the popular press, then, provides the first example of how in the post-war period images of certain highly visible, delinquent (although probably only on the fringes) working-class youth subcultures have been used as highly negative minority stereotypes, expressing many of the anxieties current in adult society. Rock and Cohen have argued that the representation of 'the Ted' in the press can be understood in terms of the 'allegorical personification of evil': 'He seems to stalk', they write, 'like some atavistic monster through much of the otherwise prosaic newspaper reporting of the fifties' (Rock and Cohen, 1970: 289).

More than some vague idea concerning the 'personification of evil', it is probably the case that the minority stereotyping of the Ted was tied up fairly closely with a common and growing perception from the early 1950s onwards that Britain 'was not what it used to be': at home the austerity of the immediate post-war period was now being succeeded by the beginnings of the new era of 'affluence' with all of its (perceived) social and cultural transformations, while abroad the Empire was dissolving and the nation was losing – or had in reality already lost – its status as a first-rank economic and political power. Everywhere scientific and technological innovation was proceeding apace, with largely unforeseeable consequences (except that, as has already been noted, it was widely felt that Britain was losing – but could not afford to lose – her 'lead' in this area also) and what was seen as society's established value system itself seemed under threat in the new climate of apparent change on all fronts. In short, what was regarded as the certainty and stability of the old order was perceived to be disintegrating fast, and the Teddy boy as a 'new' and threatening social type, himself the child of post-war flux, provided the ideal screen on to which many of the most deep-rooted anxieties about and hostile evaluations of the new order could be projected.[4]

Such minority stereotyping of the Teds was itself a part of the more general phenomenon of the (conscious/unconscious, explicit/implicit) employment of the concept of youth – in a whole range of fashions and senses – in the analysis and critique of the state of post-war Britain. Sometimes statements about *all of* 'today's youth' were linked with highly generalized denouncements of perceived contemporary trends and mores, as in the following speech of the President of the Methodist Conference, delivered in Leeds in 1956 and reported in *The Times* of 3 July 1956 under the headline 'Methodist President's Warning of a "Moral Landslide"':

> What a moral climate in which to grow up! Let us face the fact that a generation is growing up that fears neither God nor man, which neither believes in itself nor anyone else, a generation all dressed up with nowhere to go.

Much of contemporary youth was fine but there was a significant sector that was a 'menace' to both the community and the church, the President continued:

> The neglect until recently of religious teaching in day schools, the absence of religion from the home, the theory that man is little more than a sophisticated animal, the background of broken family life – from all that what could you expect to emerge, other

than what has emerged? The type of youth whom I am thinking about is more sinned against than sinning. . . .

Such diatribes are of course sufficiently vague and all-encompassing to be a perennial feature of the youth question and spectacle: before anything else they demonstrate the general utility of statements about youth to almost any wider social critique; they were however perhaps particularly in evidence during the post-war period proper.

Sometimes however – and this is perhaps a unique feature of the post-war youth question – statements about contemporary youth in general reflected a far more favourable analysis both of youth itself and also of the perceived trend of society. Another speech from 1956, this time delivered by J. F. Wolfenden, then Vice-Chancellor of Reading University (reported in *The Times* of 18 May 1956, under the headline 'Youth Not Going to the Dogs: Behaviour Affected in Changing World') exemplifies such more favourable analyses along with the related perception that in line with changed social conditions, post-war youth itself was an essentially 'new' kind of entity.

Wolfenden first of all noted the 'unusually difficult background in growing up' encountered by contemporary youth because of the 'speed and stress and tension and ceaseless change' of modern life. The young were 'not without their faults' but their behaviour should be understood in the context of the 'unstable background' and 'constant expectation of continuing change' in which they lived. Contemporary youth was characterized by:

A sort of excitement, a kind of emotional hectic flush, as if their metaphorical pulse-rate has to be high to keep pace with the speed of what is happening around them, so that everything about them is in a harsher, higher, noisier key.

It was therefore necessary to beware of assuming that 'change, restlessness and even apparent rudderlessness' were 'inevitably and necessarily bad'. There were undeniably 'some signs of selfishness' amongst the young, but there was also considerably increased enterprise and initiative. The young were earning bigger wage packets and it was no use deploring the fact that it was having an effect upon their attitudes and activities. Youth clubs were currently 'dull, drearily furnished, badly lighted, [and] administered by obsolete techniques', Wolfenden concluded, and every effort should now be made to bring these up to date and into compatibility with the needs – and spending power – of the new generation.

From the outset the image of the Teddy boy was closely associated in the youth spectacle with the idea, and reality, of juvenile delinquency in general and of 'senseless' acts of violence against the person in particular. Increasing levels and rates of juvenile delinquency during the after the war served to focus a good deal of adult attention and concern upon youth, and its real and supposed needs and problems. At the same time, as already noted, the purported psychological impact of the experience of a childhood spent in wartime came to be widely advanced as an at least partial explanation for the supposed 'disturbance', 'violence', 'delinquency', etc., of the post-war younger generation, which was in any case generally viewed as a new phenomenon, both in terms of its extent and also its 'quality'. It was certainly the case that, for whatever reasons, the number of juveniles convicted of serious offences rose fairly dramatically during the 1950s. Over the period 1955–61 the number of males convicted of an indictable offence in the 14–17 age group more than doubled, from around 13,500 to in excess of 28,000 (the 1938 level had been around 11,500) while figures for the 17–21 age group almost exactly repeated the same pattern (Fyvel, 1963: p. 15, table 1). Similarly there was over the period 1956–61 an approximately threefold increase in convictions for crimes of violence against the person, in both under-21 age groups.[5]

In Britain this increase in the level of juvenile delinquency – centrally associated in image with the emergence of the Teddy boy as a social type, but always also acknowledged as a broader social phenomenon – came to be a much-discussed social problem of the late 1950s and early 1960s. The period's rising juvenile crime statistics were themselves the subject of a fair measure of media attention, as exemplified in a *Daily Mirror* article of 2 October 1958, 'More Teenagers are Turning to Crime' . . . 'a sharp increase in crimes committed by young people was revealed in Home Office figures yesterday', or again in the *Mirror* of 20 September 1963:

'POP STAR MAY HELP IN TEEN CRIME QUIZ'

A new enquiry into the causes of teenage crime is to be set up by the Home Secretary . . . who is alarmed at the latest crime figures.

He is considering inviting a 'pop' singer or some other personality well known to teenagers to join the enquiry. [Indictable offences in the 14–17 age group had risen by 200 per cent for boys and 300 per cent for girls from their pre-war levels, the article then went on to note.]

This post-war increase in juvenile delinquency was singled out as particularly significant and disturbing as the fastest-rising sector (by age) in a crime rate that was in any case rising fairly rapidly overall from the mid-1950s onwards.[6] As R. A. Butler, then Home Secretary, responded to a question in the House in 1958:

The number of persons found guilty of indictable offences has increased in all age groups and for both sexes. The proportionate increase is most serious in the age group seventeen and under twenty-one and nearly as high in the age group fourteen and under seventeen years.   (Reported in *The Times*, 1 August)

This trend was all the more puzzling in that it occurred within the context of an 'affluent society' that had recently made considerable advances in educational welfare provision for the young. R. A. Butler, in 1958 again, reported on the 'upward curve' that juvenile delinquency had taken over the past three years:

[This is] particularly disturbing when it occurs after the most massive educational and social reforms for a century . . . the effect of alleged prosperity upon the individual is not sufficiently understood.   (*The Times*, 10 June 1958, '"Sad fact" of Rise in Juvenile Crime: Mr Butler on Need of More Spiritual Force')

As suggested above, the image of flick knives, bicycle chains and other such weapons in the hands of contemporary youth served as a kind of symbol and point of focus for much of the early post-war period's pronounced anxiety over juvenile delinquency and youthful violence. The flick knife itself actually became the centre of a kind of moral panic in the late 1950s (or perhaps a major element of a more generalized Teddy Boy/juvenile delinquency moral panic). The supposed spread and use of such weapons amongst youth was then widely taken as yet another indicator of something being seriously wrong with at least a significant sector of the younger generation and therefore, by implication, with contemporary society at large. As a high court judge remarked during his summing up at the trial of a 'teenage knife murderer':

> Years ago, not so many years ago, it used to be thought un-English and despicable for a man to produce a knife during a fight. Now, alas, it seems that the production of a knife is thought by young men to be merely an earnest of manhood.   (Reported in the *Daily Mirror*, 13 September 1958)

The *Mirror* of the previous day had carried a full page account of the same trial: 'Boy of 16 in Death Knife Court Drama' . . . 'teenage flare up during a rock 'n' roll dance in Hoxton' (the accused had pleaded in mitigation that, 'nearly everybody I know carries a knife just to be big headed') and continued, with most of the popular press, in the following months to feature 'flick knife stories' prominently. This seems to have reached some form of climax in the spring of 1959 when the same paper launched a national campaign to alert parents and adults in general to the dangers of the 'flick knife craze' and to persuade delinquent youth to surrender its weapons:

> 'BAN THIS THING'
> Week after week in this country people are being threatened and wounded and – sometimes – killed [with flick knives] . . . [they are] the latest craze among the cosh boys. The modern brainwave of the dead end kids. The new 'romantic' way to show you're a man.   (*Daily Mirror* editorial, 6 March 1959)

A full-page feature inside the same issue by the *Mirror*'s crime reporter, Tom Tullett enquired:

> Teenagers, have you got a flick knife?
> . . . the grave menace of these murderous weapons is grow- ing. . . . Teenage murders have shocked the nation . . . almost daily there are reports of young people being stabbed. . . . Are you sure your SON hasn't got a knife?

And so the *Mirror*'s flick knife campaign continued throughout March and April of 1959 with almost every new issue giving prominence either to accounts of 'teenage flick knife attacks' (see e.g. the Marwood case as outlined above) or else to features detailing the inventory of offensive weapons received under its 'amnesty':

> 'A Private Peep for Parents into the *Mirror*'s Horror Postbag': All the horror weapons pictured on this page, the front page and the back page have been sent to the *Mirror* by parents and teenagers from all over Britain.   (Accompanying a double-page picture of a fearsome assortment of knives, knuckledusters, coshes, guns, etc., *Daily Mirror*, 18 March 1959.)

Nor were the images of post-war juvenile delinquency outlined above confined to the outpourings of the press, popular or otherwise. All of the images and (implicit) analyses of early post-war juvenile delinquency as a new and disturbing phenomenon that have been encountered above are also to be found in the period's more or less serious and academic youth question discourse. As T. R. Fyvel wrote at the close of the 1950s, on the topic of the ever-rising juvenile delinquency statistics:

> These figures of actual law breaking are only part of the post-war story. Equally noticeable during the fifties was the appearance among a section of working class youth of a more intensified gang life, characterized by a hostility towards authority in every form, which could flare into violence upon a trivial cause. Coupled with it went a sort of stylized warfare between the gangs themselves, especially those wearing exaggerated Teddy boy suits, and a fashion for carrying improvised offensive weapons. In fact, if one regarded only the outward picture, a disturbing dichotomy seemed to be at work. As British working class youth was becoming more urbane, as more modern schools and housing estates went up, so more boys seemed to drift into the new gang warfare, and to walk about carrying flick knives or such things as bicycle chains 'for defence'.   (Fyvel, 1963: 17–18)

Such a statement elides what were in many respects the separate images and questions of 'Teddy boys', juvenile delinquency, and 'all (working-class) youth'.

For Fyvel also the roots of this post-war wave of delinquency were to be found primarily in such *distinctively contemporary* perceived social ills as the boredom inherent in the affluent society, the 'breakdown of the family' and traditional authority patterns, materialism, too much sex, etc.: 'the current unrest of youth is a new phenomenon, illuminating aspects of our society at which it is worth looking very carefully' (Fyvel, 1963: 13).[7] As these supposedly fundamental shifts in culture and social structure were seen as operative in *all* advanced industrial societies – including Sweden, which had of course been neutral in the war – the new wave of youthful delinquency was regarded by Fyvel and many other commentators as essentially an *international phenomenon*, endemic to the post-war economic and social climate. Fyvel indeed went so far as to speak of the 'teddy boy international', citing the much-publicized delinquency of American street gangs, and such exotic contemporary youth folk devils as the German *Halbstarken*, the Swedish *Skinnknuttar* (leather jackets), the French *Blousons noirs*, the Japanese *Taiyozoku* (children of the sun), the Australian *Bodgies* and the Russian *Stilyagi* (style-boys) as manifestations of the same imputed complex of social dislocation. (Fyvel, 1963: 18–24, 138–205). The extent to which the supposed delinquency of these various 'groups' was real is clearly a question which cannot be answered here; nonetheless the above international listing of juvenile delinquents is, if nothing else, indicative of the way in which the 'j–d' (to borrow the once popular American term) became a highly visible social type in many advanced societies in the 1950s and 1960s.

Beyond this, the period's concern over juvenile delinquency can clearly be interpreted, in terms of the workings of the process of the minority stereotyping of (all) youth as delinquent, as a vehicle for the expression of further-ranging adult anxieties in a rapidly changing society. The theme of 'post-war affluence' producing *internationally* a generation of juvenile delinquents and degenerates persisted well into the 1960s. At the end of 1964 (the period of the mods and rockers moral panic in Great Britain) a *Reader's Digest* article of quite incredible sensationalism on the topic of 'The World's Wild Youth' was proclaiming that 'throughout the world growing numbers of young people are being gripped by an alarming fever of hooliganism, recklessness and moral anarchy', and backing up its thesis that affluence carried the seeds of juvenile delinquency with lurid tales concerning the delinquent youth of England, France and Brazil (!) and – especially – the excesses of the *raggare* of ultra-prosperous Sweden. (Lucy, 1964). 'How', the anguished cry went up, 'can the efforts of nations to raise their living standards avoid producing a diseased harvest of anti-social children?' (ibid., p. 48).

Against such outbursts of the near-hysterical minority stereotyping of youth it is nonetheless necessary to set the constant, if understated and unspectacular, opposing theme and image of the 'unsung majority' of youth who are basically decent and who in fact exhibit great potential for social and moral good if only given the right opportunity. As previously noted, such a view abounds in much of the post-war period's official and policy response to the youth question, especially in conjunction with the theme of youth-as-national-asset. It has also surfaced from time to time – but perhaps especially in the late 1950s and early 1960s – into the youth spectacle proper (see also the 'anti-stereotypical' images of Teddy boys discussed above, and J. F. Wolfenden's remarks to the effect that contemporary youth was 'not going to the dogs') often in the face of a youth-centred moral panic. Thus, as a direct counter to the *Reader's Digest* article already referred to, it is possible to cite another, again the product of a period when deviant youth was seldom out of the news: 'Let's Stop Maligning British Youth' by one Michael Randolph (January 1957). The title speaks for itself here, and could indeed have been produced, as could the article itself with a few modifications of specifics and detail, at any time right down until the present.

Another example of the 'media-ization' of an *anti-stereotypical* image of youth is to be found in the *Daily Mirror* of 28 October 1958, a time when the same paper was much engaged in the purveying of stories concerning juvenile delinquency, 'Teddy boy riots', etc.:

'"I PUT THE BLAME ON GROWN UPS" – SAYS AN ARCHDEACON'

Adults – not young people – are to blame for the faults of modern youth, said an Archdeacon yesterday. And he added that in any case the young people of today were a good deal BETTER than those of his own generation. [People spoke of the young in terms of dishonesty, laziness, drink, sex and violence, but, the Archdeacon continued:] Generally these judgements are made by middle-aged and elderly people who, I fancy, want to find someone to blame for the sort of world they themselves have created.

Or again in *The Times* of September 1956, also the month of the rock 'n' roll riots moral panic:

'THE COURSE OF NATURE: GOOD WORK BY YOUNG BIRD
WATCHERS'
In an age of rock 'n' roll it is good that so many young men and boys – and girls too – should be content to spend almost the whole of their leisure time in such worthwhile occupations as bird-watching.
. . . Field clubs throughout the country agree that their best work in this respect is done by young people.

Such stories concerning the specific activities of (presumably predominantly middle-class) 'worthy youth' are of course also very much a stock in trade of the routine reporting of the local press.

In Britain a peak of the equation of youth *en masse* with juvenile delinquency seems to have been reached, along with the notion that the latter phenomenon was becoming more violent and more group-based than ever before, around the late 1950s. The temporary tailing off of the predominantly minority stereotypical depiction of the young that then followed was associated with the emergence of another constellation of images of youth, in this case of a far less unambiguously negative nature. These images were focussed around another new youthful social type: 'the Teenager'.

Even the most rabid and unperceptive of contemporary commentators on the Teddy boy phenomenon could not fail to have an at least partial awareness of the subculture's working class, near lumpen proletarian, status and membership. The same obvious location in terms of social-class background however, just did not apply to the Teenager, who was emerging as a major focus for the youth spectacle just as the post-war austerity was giving way to the economic boom of the 'never had it so good' years of the late 1950s and early 1960s.[9]

It has been suggested that the socio-political discourse, and cultural spectacle as a whole, of this period was dominated by what can now be seen in retrospect as a complex of interlocking social myths whose key terms were 'affluence', 'consensus' and 'embour-geoisement'.[10] Thus, as the economy as a whole expanded, the working class in particular was seen as enjoying the fruits of this in a new and quite unprecedented degree of material prosperity. At the same time, and in part seemingly because of this generalized affluence, the old class warfare of pre-war British politics was widely regarded as having been replaced by a new centrist consensus, with a moderate form of Conservatism remaining in power at the expense of an increasingly divided and 'irrelevant' Labour party.[11] Finally the range of social stratification and inequality was seen as becoming less extreme, with the old class boundaries dissolving under the impact of the new affluence and social mobility, and the working class in particular being swallowed up by the ever-expanding middle range of society.

In the domains of the youth question and the youth spectacle, one expression of these myths is to be found in the idea of the coming into being of a unified and consumption-based 'Youth Culture', cutting across the traditional and now 'outdated' stratificatory dimension of social class that had so fundamentally – and, it was increasingly argued, fatally – divided the older generation. The same myths also found their apotheosis in the closely related, and itself at least semi-mythical concept of the Teenager. What made a Teenager was his *age* and *generation* coupled with a distinctive pattern of consumption, not his social origins.

In this case it could also be *her* age, generation and pattern of consumption since, unlike the case of the period's youth *subcultures*, images of girls were far from marginal to the discussion of 'Teenagers'. As noted previously, one aspect of the feminine side of the image of the Teenager is to be found in much of the then-current topic of the 'earlier maturity' of the young. Teenage girls were also associated particularly closely with images of the supposed class-lessness and consumerism of the 'affluent society' – it was after all even more remarkable that such trends should be affecting working-class *young women* – as in this *Daily Mirror* feature from 10 February 1960 on the (highly mythologized) lifestyle of Leicester's young female hosiery workers:

'BOOM GIRLS! THEY RUN SPORTS CARS AND PAY FOR BOY FRIENDS
ON DATES'
The teenage girl in a model frock brought her £1,000 red sports

car to a stop outside the dance hall . . . she wasn't a rich
industrialist's daughter, just a factory girl having her weekly night
out at the palais.

She works a 45 hour week and takes home up to £20 per week.

Her lifestyle was the consequence, the article went on to explain, of
the current 'booming business in nylons'. Images of girls and
women came, in the late 1950s and 60s, to occupy a far more central
position in many areas of the youth spectacle: this phenomenon can
itself be interpreted as a reflection of the perception that traditional
gender roles and divisions were also breaking down as a part of the
more general complex of social and cultural changes that were
supposedly transforming post-war Britain.

The Teenager therefore came to the fore in the youth spectacle at
just that period in post-war British history when the supposed
advent of affluence for all and political consensus were widely held
to be eroding the traditional class-based pattern of the division of
the nation as a whole, and when, furthermore, the young were
widely seen as the major beneficiaries or trailblazers of this new,
more fluid and democratic social order. (It is also interesting to note
how much of this period falls in the hiatus between the heyday of
two successive highly visible, problem working-class youth subcultural groups, the Teds and the mods.) The semi-mythical world
inhabited by the Teenager as depicted in the youth spectacle was
precisely a world of new-found affluence and conspicuous consumption, of apolitical quiescence, and of a new, basically middle-class,
classlessness.

We have now come, in later years, to use the word 'teenager' in
the more or less straightforward sense of the mere classification of
those inside the age range thus demarcated. (More than anything
else now perhaps, the term summons up the image of 'conventional
youth'.) The richness of connotation present in the discussion and
representation of Teenagers at around the period of their emergence and rise to prominence has largely disappeared, as indeed has
the sheer volume of what was then a major obsession in the media
and elsewhere throughout society. The term 'Teenager' in the
above discussion, and also in what is to follow, is therefore
capitalized – as with the term Youth Culture – to refer specifically to
the semi-mythical 'new youth' of the period in question. As such it
should be stressed that the Teenager as a social type was primarily

an inhabitant of the youth spectacle, with only a secondary and approximate correspondence to the objective realities of the circumstances, lifestyle, attitudes etc., of the youth of the day.

The Teenager began to emerge in Britain as a distinct social type around the fateful years of 1956 – also the year of the Suez Crisis and the first anti-nuclear demonstrations. As has been noted in the previous chapter, the birth of the Teenager was inextricably bound up with the new (youthful) affluence of the mid to late 1950s, and the consequent creation of an adult-controlled 'youth culture industry' to exploit the emergent consumer market amongst the younger generation. One particular sector of this industry was pivotal to the process of the definition of youth, as it has been in one way or another ever since: that of rock and pop music.[12] There had been mass culture/youth idols before the coming of rock 'n' roll: most notably, in the early post-war years, James Dean and Marlon Brando in the cinema, and Frank Sinatra and Johnny Ray in the world of mainstream white American popular music; what changed now, however, was that for the first time the commercial culture of youth was seen as being distinctively and exclusively the property of the young themselves. As Simon Frith has written:

> If the young always had had idols . . . the novelty of rock 'n' roll was that its performers were 'one of themselves', were the teenagers' own age, came from similar backgrounds, had similar interests. The rise of rock 'n' roll was accompanied by the development of a generation gap in dancing as dance halls advertised rock 'n' roll nights or became exclusively rock 'n' roll venues. . . .   (Frith, 1978a)

In many respects the coming of rock 'n' roll, and its explosion into the youth spectacle, helped further to crystallize, on both sides of the Atlantic, what was increasingly perceived as a generational watershed between old and young, and the sense that had been building throughout the early post-war period that contemporary youth was somehow 'different' and a new phenomenon.

In Britain, however, as had earlier been the case in the USA, the first rock 'n' roll idol/icon of the 'new' post-war youth was not Presley, but the somewhat unlikely personage of Billy Haley, a hitherto small-time American country-style performer, who was already nearing 30 by the time that he eventually achieved notoriety, and chubby and baby-faced into the bargain. Nonetheless it was the music of Haley and his band The Comets, in accompaniment to the film *Blackboard Jungle* (1955), dealing with teenage delinquents in a New York High School, which served first to highlight in the popular imagination the links between rock 'n' roll, youth, and juvenile delinquency.[13]

In Great Britain the initial screenings of Haley's own film *Rock Around the Clock* in September 1956 were accompanied by the first 'rock 'n' roll riots': the young predominantly working-class audience would attempt to dance, thus bringing about the intervention of management, police and 'bouncers', who had been specially brought in in anticipation of trouble, and in the general fracas which followed cinema fittings would be damaged or deliberately vandalized, and bodily injuries incurred. After a while the violence and vandalism associated with screenings of *Rock Around the Clock* – and later with live performances by the 'classic' rock 'n' roll performers – took on the form of a self-fulfilling prophecy and became almost ritual in nature.

The coming of rock 'n' roll to Britain was in fact anticipated as a media event well before the first screenings of *Rock Around the Clock* and the subsequent disturbances and moral panic of September. For example, a *Daily Mirror* feature of 20 July 1956 – appearing perhaps significantly on the same page as a juvenile delinquency story concerning 'Schools where pupils carry knives' – reviewed *Rock Around the Clock* in the following terms:

'THIS WILL ROCK THE TEENAGERS'
It won't surprise me a bit if Mum and Dad describe it as a deluge of discord. But youngsters will really enjoy this hot rhythm-musical about the launching in America of a new style band.

(*The Times* of 23 July 1956 commented rather more soberly that the film 'mirrors American youth finding fulfilment in what seems to be a mingling of primitive dance and ritual'.)

A later *Daily Mirror* piece by the paper's music and show business correspondent Patrick Doncaster on 16 August 1956 made a good deal more explicit the already building connection, at the level of image, between rock 'n' roll and youthful deviance:

'DO WE WANT THIS SHOCKIN ROCKIN?'
Can it happen here – the trouble that goes with Rock 'n' Roll

music in the United States? Over there it has been blamed for starting riots, rape and alcoholism among the youngsters.

Now . . . rock 'n' roll is to make a big bid in Britain.

It is, in some circumstances definitely sexy – and equally it appeals to teenagers.

With such a climate of anticipation already established it is hardly surprising that when *Rock Around the Clock* did go out on general release in British cinemas, trouble soon followed and was eagerly seized upon by the media. Accounts of 'rock 'n' roll disturbances', of the banning of *Rock Around the Clock* in several towns and – somewhat later – letters to the editor and a leading article on this topic, are to be found, enjoying varying degrees of prominence, in the pages of *The Times* throughout September 1956 (and thereafter the topic disappeared from view as suddenly as it had appeared). One relatively understated account from *The Times'* overall reporting of the month's 'rock 'n' roll disturbances' – which reached some kind of crescendo in the paper itself, and presumably in actuality, at around the middle of September – will perhaps convey something of the flavour of them all, as well as giving some indication of what 'really went on' at the disturbances in question:

'POLICE EJECT "ROCK 'N' ROLL" YOUTHS

Police broke up a crowd of youths and girls dancing and jiving in the aisles of the Davis Theatre, Croydon, last night during the showing of the 'Rock 'n' Roll film, *Rock Around the Clock*. The Theatre, which holds 4,000 people, was full.

Trouble started during the last 10 minutes of the first house performance of the film. About a dozen youths ran onto the front of the stage and jived in front of the screen. A number of young people were ejected by the police. After the first house fighting broke out on the pavement outside the cinema. Later, two young men were taken to Croydon police station.

The *Daily Mirror* of the same day was considerably less restrained in its front page story of a rock 'n' roll riot in Manchester:

'1,000 ROCK 'N' ROLL RIOTERS TAKE CITY BY STORM'

A thousand screaming, jiving, rhythm-crazy teenagers surged through a city last night, sweeping aside police cordons and stopping traffic. . . . A police spokesman said 'Nothing like it has ever been seen in this city'.

As well as reporting the month's rock 'n' roll disturbances at some length, the media also set out to analyse and comment upon this strange collective mania that was supposedly afflicting contemporary youth. As early as 1 September the *Daily Mirror* organized a 'rock 'n' roll party' to which it invited an assortment of 'typists, Teddy boys and teenagers' and such concerned professional adults as a psychologist and a vicar: 'Within minutes, feet were tapping, fingers drumming, heads jerking to the jungle beat – except the parson.' The psychologist's judgment was that 'It is a perfectly good outlet for the exuberance of youth. But the impact depends upon the person. A boy liable to smash a cinema seat could be aroused by many circumstances.' The vicar thought the music 'primitive' but basically harmless enough and went on to argue that it was in any case wrong to blame it for the 'bad behaviour of the Teddy boys'. (These moderate remarks contrast strongly with those of a Pentecostal minister, also quoted in the *Daily Mirror* – 27 September 1956 – equating rock 'n' roll with devil worship and seeing the music as likely to promote lawlessness, impair nervous stability and undermine the sanctity of marriage!)

The Times was similarly concerned to comment on *Rock Around the Clock* and its associated disturbances, noting that 'Never has the showing of a film in this country had so impressive an aftermath. . . . Since the beginning of September 60 youths have appeared in court [on charges directly related to the disturbances] . . . and many cities have banned the film' [either entirely or else on Sundays!] (15 September 1956, p. 4). Nonetheless *The Times* itself was on the whole quite measured and level-headed in tone when it came to the analysis of the causes of the current wave of disorders, taking the line that these were probably in the main attributable to the frustration of audience participation coupled with a subsequent 'imitation effect' as the rock 'n' roll riots attracted a high level of media publicity.

The same moderateness of response was not however to be found amongst all of *The Times*'s readers, as exemplified in this letter to the Editor from the Bishop of Woolwich calling for the censorship or banning of *Rock Around the Clock*, published on 13 September 1956:

It was not pleasant to witness the rowdyism during and after the performance at a South London cinema, in spite of the presence of the police. It was still less pleasant on the way home to see a group outside another cinema which could only be dispersed with the aid of police dogs.

There is nothing immoral or violent about the film itself [but it] . . . comes in the wake of a steady growth of jive [sic] and toughs have used the opportunity to cause trouble in several districts. The hypnotic rhythm and the wild gestures have a maddening effect on a rhythm-loving age group and the result is a relaxing of all self control. . . .

The tragedy is that it comes at a time when Teddy boy activity is dying down and the worst of our gang troubles have passed: I have myself confirmed some of their gangleaders in recent years. . . .

In some quarters, then, it seemed as though the potential for deviance of youth in general – and especially post-war youth – had been brought to a head by this new and 'wild' form of music, and this idea contributed in its own right to the new awareness of youth and concern over youth in general that was emerging in the mid-1950s.[14]

What is perhaps of more significance, however, is the way in which the spectacle of rock 'n' roll helped to *create* the Teenager.[15] The early–mid-1950s already had a problem adolescent in the shape of the Ted. The Ted however was from the beginning widely perceived as a minority figure, the product of a specific deprived urban working-class background, and therefore unrepresentative, some of the wilder current flights of fancy notwithstanding, of contemporary British youth as a whole. (The Ted was also in origin a creature of early 1950s' austerity rather than late 1950s' affluence, and as a distinct social type actually pre-dated the arrival of rock 'n' roll – which in its original, 'classic' form has now become the quintessential Teddy boy music – by a number of years.) With the advent of rock 'n' roll and the supposedly new and uniquely youthful popular culture that went with it, it started to appear as though *all* of the young of the current generation were coming to constitute a potentially highly problematic group. The idea of 'teenage rock 'n' roll riots' from 1956 superimposes the images of the Ted and the Teenager and thus casts all of then-contemporary youth in a minority stereotyped role.

As the decade drew to a close, however, these two momentarily superimposed images of youth began in many respects to distance themselves from each other, and as this occurred the Teenager came to be viewed in a far less uniformly unfavourable light. In part, this separation out of Ted and Teenager is reflected in the realities of the cultures of the two 'groups'. The Teds, and their indirect descendants the Rockers, maintained as 1956 receded a largely deviant style and stance *vis à vis* adult society, and with this went a continuing allegiance to the aggressive and rebellious classic rock 'n' roll of Elvis Presley, Little Richard, Jerry Lee Lewis, Chuck Berry, Eddie Cochran, Gene Vincent and others.[16] (Bill Haley was never exactly discarded by this group but he was soon superseded as idol by more authentically 'youthful' and 'rebellious' artists such as Presley.)

The vast majority of British and American 'conventional youth', on the other hand, moved on in their musical tastes from classic rock 'n' roll to more generally acceptable material. By the late 1950s contemporary pop music had replaced rock 'n' roll proper as the new music of the majority of the younger generation, and such more-or-less clean-cut American stars as Pat Boone – the 'good boy' antithesis of the early Presley – Paul Anka and Connie Francis began, with their home-grown British equivalents, to dominate much of the burgeoning British market for single-play 45-rpm pop records, which was now itself largely in the hands of the young.[17] A good deal of the material of such stars can be categorized under the heading 'High School', and it reflected fairly closely the essentially wholesome and conformist climate of the culture documented in James Coleman's *Adolescent Society* (see Cohn, 1970: 52–7). As such, the world it depicted was at some considerable remove from the realities of the British youth scene, but nonetheless it still seems to have contributed towards the formation of the image of the fully fledged British Teenager. On both sides of the Atlantic teenage pop music dealt with the 'problems of adolescence' as its major theme, but largely in terms of the individual psychological and emotional difficulties of this stage of life.

Coupled with this trend towards the domination of the pop music scene and market by clean-cut stars performing clean-cut material was the tendency, perhaps especially pronounced in Britain, for the initially deviant and rebellious image of many of the early rock 'n' roll performers to be fairly rapidly watered down into something more conventional, generally acceptable and thus commercially viable. This process can be clearly discerned in the progress of the 'post army' Elvis Presley and can also be traced, in this country, in the careers of such early youth idols and icons as Tommy Steele and Cliff Richard. By the late 1950s the *Daily Mirror*'s Donald Zec was able to conclude a full-page interview with Cliff thus '. . . and I am thinking Cliff Richard is a very nice kid indeed . . . trembling lips, wiggle and all' (6 April 1959).

By 1960, then, the 'dangerous' and deviant image of youth that had been associated with the emergence – seemingly out of nowhere – of rock 'n' roll had been replaced by the relative safety and conformity of the current image of the Teenager. Pop music, in so far as it both directly and indirectly now formed a central part of the youth spectacle, played an essential part in the reflection and reinforcement of this shift of images. The news media presented adult society with images of the Teenager, and the entertainment media moved in to exploit commercially the new Teenage market. To be more accurate about this process, the entertainment media, and indeed the whole flourishing Youth Culture industry, served simultaneously to *create the Teenager* and thus to *exploit the young*. With the coming of rock 'n' roll and later contemporary pop music, the sales of the newly introduced pop 45 single boomed – a total UK production of 4,587,000 in 1955 rose to 51,811,000 in 1960 and 61,342,000 in 1963 (Frith, 1978a: p. 102, table 10). By the late 1950s a survey showed that nine-tenths of adolescents were spending at least some of their leisure time listening to pop records (Workers' Educational Association, 1960).

At the same time the *content* of pop records and the – again semi-mythical – personae projected by the various pop star idol/icons served to define the Teenager and his or her world. The widespread currency at this time of these images, conveyed by records and radio and also by TV, films, newspapers and magazines, spread elements of the new Teenage style to the young almost everywhere throughout the Western world and beyond, and brought the cult of youth to a particularly high pitch. Early singles by the Coasters ('Yakety-Yak'), Chuck Berry ('You Never Can Tell', 'School Days', 'Sweet Little Sixteen . . .'), Paul Anka ('Diana'), Eddie Cochran ('Summertime Blues'), Dion and the Belmonts ('Teenager in Love') and many others provide a comprehensive picture of the concerns, limitations and problems of (American) Teenage life. Similarly the stances of Elvis Presley,

Eddie Cochran, Pat Boone, Connie Francis, Tommy Steele and the rest embraced and projected the various possibilities, some deviant but most largely conventional, inherent in the general notion of 'being a teenager'.[18]

Rock 'n' roll music – and later pop – helped to provide a model, or a range of models, for the various self-images of 'the Teenage generation' and did much to bring the Teenager, as a new and fascinating and perplexing being, to the attention of adult society. Pop or rock music in all of its post rock 'n' roll forms, both directly as entertainment and also indirectly as news, sometimes coupled with film and TV, has sinced 1956 formed a central part of the youth spectacle in general, but perhaps at no time has this been so important as at the period of the emergence of the Teenager.

In the cinema *Rock Around the Clock* was followed rapidly by many other films for the newly discovered teenage market. *Love Me Tender* (1956), the first Elvis Presley film, is thought to be the only film in the history of the cinema to have recouped its entire production costs within its first three days of release. This tells us a lot about the shoestring budget on which the early rock 'n' roll films were made and also about the volume of demand that existed for such representations of the new and exclusively Teenage culture. By 1957 over twenty-five major films devoted to rock 'n' roll were featuring in the cinema. *The Girl Can't Help It* (1956) was the first 'high gloss' Teenage film – the studios were now coming to realize just how much money was to be made in this field – and showcased the talents of many rock 'n' roll artists. The floodgates were now open to films aimed exclusively at the new and increasingly significant youth market (see Jenkinson and Warner, 1974: 13–60). (It should be remembered here that the 1950s and 60s were a period of marked decline in the general level of cinema attendance amongst the population as a whole, but that this trend was particularly pronounced amongst the adult, i.e. 24 plus, age group.)[19]

As the decade progressed – in part in line with the process of the cleaning up of the image of the Teenager in pop music described above – the original rock 'n' roll vehicle films gave way to a whole range of 'teen exploitation' films 'featuring such widely differing subjects as surfing, lycanthropy [!], stock car racing, teenage science fiction and puppy love' (Jenkinson and Warner, 1974: 16). Such films were to continue well into the 1960s, perhaps going into decline towards the end of the decade as the image of youth itself became more complicated and 'serious'. From the mid-1970s on, the genre has made a comeback in a modified form, coupled with a continuing vogue for 1950s and 60s nostalgia.

Television was not slow to jump on to the Teenage bandwagon either. From 1956 onwards Jack Good's '6.5 Special' and 'Oh Boy' presented the latest pop stars – generally the home-grown British variety in the form of Tommy Steele, Cliff Richard, Marty Wilde, Billy Fury, Adam Faith *et al.* – performing their latest hits. These shows endeavoured to create and reflect an authentically Teenage ambiance through their 'coffee bar' type setting, their informal and, for the time, lively presentation and production, and the presence of a 'live' audience of carefully groomed token Teenagers (Melly, 1972: 163–4). The practice of providing exclusively youth-oriented TV programmes, based largely on current pop music, and depicting with greater or lesser degrees of success aspects of the current youth scene was to reach a high point with ITV's 'Ready Steady Go' in the mid-1960s. In the debased form of 'Top of the Pops' and in other more recent and 'serious' youth-oriented programmes, it has of course been a central aspect of the TV youth spectacle down until the present day.

The emergence of the Teenager in the mass media of the mid-1950s was also, finally, accompanied by the emergence of a number of popular publications aimed specifically at this age group. The period 1955–57 saw the publication of three new magazines, *Romeo*, *Mirabelle* and *Valentine*, all aimed at teenage girls, and containing almost exclusively a diet of pop and teenage romance. Together with films and TV programmes – and to a far lesser extent at this period radio programmes – these magazines served simultaneously to define the female Teenager as a new and distinctive social type while exploiting teenage girls as a market.

By no means all responses to the newly emergent commercial Youth Culture were favourable. Initially at least, negative images in this area continued to feed into negative evaluations of the state of the nation in the time-honoured pattern of conservative social criticism. This was particularly the case with reference to the idea of the 'Americanization' of popular culture and its accompanying fear for the decline of solid, traditional *English* (working-class) values as developed in Richard Hoggart's *The Uses of Literacy* (1957). Here Hoggart painted a grim picture of 'juke-box boys . . . who spend their evening listening in harshly lighted milk bars to the "nickel-odeons" . . . with drape suits, picture ties and an American slouch' (Hoggart, 1968: 247–8; see also Hall and Jefferson, 1976: 19).

As the 1950s turned into the 1960s, however, and 'affluence' and its related parcel of real and supposed social changes and shifts in attitude became more manifest, so too the dominant tone to be found in the representation of youth and especially of the Teenager changed to something far more ambivalent. At times, indeed, it now came to take on a note of almost unmitigated admiration that can be viewed as one of the peaks of the entire post-war cult of youth.[20]

The trend for the popular media to report, at least half-admiringly, on all things Teenage, explaining the peculiar dress, argot, dances, customs, etc., that were manifestations of this apparent social revolution to an adult readership was perhaps initiated by the *Daily Mirror* in the mid-1950s.[21] By 1960 such a practice had spread throughout nearly all the popular press and was to be found in such diverse and now defunct papers as the *Daily Herald* and *Sunday Graphic*.

From the start much of the media's new-found obsession with the Teenager was centred around the – themselves interrelated – topics of the 'greater maturity' and the relative affluence of post-war youth, and indeed the supposed affluence of contemporary British society in general, as in this comment from the father of a precocious 13-year-old girl in the *Daily Mirror*'s 'Beanstalk Generation' series (see above):

I am fully convinced that there are two factors responsible for children growing up quicker – better food and more money to spend. . . . There is no problem about it, I just think that boys and girls of today are a better lot all round than we were. (17 September 1958)

The new teenage spending power of the period and its perceived implications was the object of a good deal of popular media attention in its own right:

'BEANSTALKERS ARE BIG BUSINESS'
. . . spending a large slice of the £225 million a year teenagers lay out on clothes, shoes, make up, foundation garments and hairstyles.

The bulletin today is that the beanstalkers have won their fight hands down. They have won over the parents and teachers. Now industry is on their side.   (*Daily Mirror*, 4 November 1959)

(See also the case of the Leicester hosiery girls above.)

One of the major areas where the coming of Teenage culture was seen as presaging a more fundamental transformation of British society was held to be on the London social scene. As early as 1955 (pre-rock 'n' roll and pre-'Swinging London') the *Mirror* was beginning to anticipate this theme with pieces on the 'new [young] nightclubbers': 'Shop girls and students are the new nightclubbers of Mamboland. . . . It's breathtakingly ALIVE . . . and that's what counts with the youngsters who pack Soho's Mambo dens until midnight'.

As with the entertainment media the popular news media now also began – in the name at least – to *cater directly* for the Teenager as well as merely depicting him or her to a largely adult readership. Thus in the late 1950s the *Daily Mirror* ran at weekly intervals a 'Teen Page' 'for the young of all ages' which, in the now largely abandoned tradition of *vox pop* journalism of that paper, aimed to be both *about* and also in part *by* Teenagers. As well as featuring the usual articles by staff reporters on aspects of the Teenage scene, it therefore invited its young readers to write in each week in answer to such questions as 'do you like being called a teenager?' (the ratio in favour was five to one), 'what do you do with your pocket money?' and 'what do you think of boys/girls/parents?' At the turn of the decade, the Teen Page sponsored a 'Great Teenage Ball', with competitions to decide who should be the lucky youngsters to attend, and very considerable prominence was then given to this piece of manufactured news in the issue of 1 January 1960.

It was also during this period that the popular press first started to treat the doings of pop stars as news – sometimes front-page news. To take but one example of this tendency, again from the period of the turn of the decade, the front-page headline of the *Mirror* of 2 December 1959 was 'Marty Wilde Marries Vernons Girl'. This was accompanied inside the paper with a full-page 'poor boy makes good' story: Marty, 20-years-old, formerly a five pounds per week timberyard worker, had been swept to fame and fortune on the back of the Teenage boom and was now, to crown it all, wedded to the beautiful member of an all-girl pop group. The next day the *Mirror* featured front-page wedding pictures with the headline '3,000 Fans Yell as Marty Weds'. (Such media attention and mass adulation was of course the direct continuation of the adulation which had previously been accorded, on a broader generational base, to the Hollywood film stars.)

This treatment of Marty Wilde's wedding again exemplifies the obsession with all things Teenage that was widely current at this time but it also illustrates much of the *ambivalence* that was present in contemporary attitudes towards Teenagers, and therefore perhaps towards the way in which society was perceived to be 'going'. There was no doubting Marty's popularity, the articles seemed to be saying, nor the fact that he was basically an ordinary decent lad – although others probably took a different view on this – but was it somehow right that he should become so rich and famous through doing so little?[22] Such images and their possible variations – which range from the favourable through the ambivalent to the highly negative and unfavourable – have been a perennial feature of the youth spectacle in the popular media ever since. From Marty Wilde, Cliff and the rest in the late 1950s through the Beatles and the Rolling Stones in the 1960s (often cast as good and bad boys respectively) to David Bowie and later the Sex Pistols in the 1970s, the range of images of pop and rock stars has been inextricably bound up with broader images of contemporary youth and ultimately therefore with generalized perceptions of change in contemporary society.

The classic statement from the mid-1950s of the Teenager as a fully-fledged and semi-mythical being is, however, to be found not in the popular press but in the journalism, essays and fiction of Colin MacInnes.[23] It was MacInnes, writing in a number of 'quality' periodicals such as *Encounter*, *Twentieth Century* and *Queen*, who first brought the topic of the Teenager to the attention of the intelligentsia and the more 'progressive' elements of the middle classes, and who thus foreshadowed the way in which aspects of youth culture – e.g. pop music and all things 'pop' – were to become increasingly fashionable and deserving of serious attention in the 1960s. After MacInnes the positive cult of the Teenager, and indeed the whole subsequent cult of youth, ceased merely to be a phenomenon of the popular mass media but became for a time rather a feature of élite culture.

In a piece written for *Twentieth Century* in February 1958

MacInnes attempted, well before these things were either fashionable or acceptable as the topic of serious adult attention – except
perhaps in a highly condescending manner – to explain 'Pop Songs
and Teenagers':

> The teenager is a key figure for understanding the 1950s [he
> wrote] . . . in this decade we witness the second Children's
> Crusade, armed with strength and booty, against all 'squares', all
> adult nay-sayers. An international movement, be it noted, that
> blithely penetrates the political curtains draped by senile seniors,
> as yet unconscious of the might of this new classless class.
> (MacInnes, 1961: 45–7)[24]

Later in the same piece MacInnes summarized his impressions of
the contemporary Teenager and pronounced him or her to be
classless, indifferent to the establishment, *not* Americanized
(Tommy Steele was cited as a quintessentially English idol/icon),
internationally minded (the Bomb was seen as an important factor
here), more mature than previous younger generations, cleaner and
less interested in alcoholic drink. 'Never before', MacInnes concluded, 'has the younger generation been so different from its
elders' (ibid.).

The image of the Teenager as the epitome of all things that were
new – and in this case overwhelmingly favourably so – in the society
and culture of the late 1950s was perhaps best summed up in
MacInnes's novel, *Absolute Beginners* (1959). This first-person
account of the adventures of an 18-year-old London Teenage
hustler, in his way yet another fictional adolescent knowing
innocent, provided a comprehensive gallery of current youthful
types as well as elaborating upon most of the more generalized
social themes and concerns that were coming to be associated with
the concept of the Teenager. This is MacInnes's hero's description
of the impact of the *affluent teenage consumer* upon the London
scene:

> Even here in this Soho, the headquarters of the adult mafia, you
> could everywhere see the signs of the un-silent teenage revol-
> ution. The disc shops with those lovely sleeves set in their
> windows, the most original thing to come out in our lifetime, and
> the kids inside them purchasing the Top Twenty. The shirt-stores

and bra-stores with cine star photos in the window selling all the exclusive teenage drag I've been describing. The hair style salons where they inflict the blow-wave torture on the kids for hours on end. The cosmetic shops – to make girls of seventeen, fifteen, even thirteen, look like pale rinsed-out sophisticates. Scooters and bubble cars driven madly down the road by kids who, a few years ago, were pushing toy ones on the pavement. (MacInnes, 1972: 32)

The supposed *uniqueness and newness* of the Teenager was similarly summed up in the hero's description of his older half-brother, Vernon, in his mid-20s:

The trouble about Vernon, really as I've said is that he's one of the last of the generations that grew up before teenagers existed. . . . Even today, of course, there are some like him, i.e. kids of the right age, between fifteen or so and twenty, that I wouldn't myself describe as teenagers. . . . But in poor Vernon's era . . . there just weren't any . . . In those days it seems you were just an over-grown boy, or else an under-grown man.   (Ibid., p. 33)

The imputed *classlessness* and consequent *apolitical stance* of the Teenager is illustrated in this exchange with Vernon:

'You poor old prehistoric monster', I exclaimed, 'I do *not* reject the working classes, and I do not belong to the upper classes, for one and the same simple reason, namely that none of them interest me in the slightest, never have done, never will do.'   (Ibid., p. 35)

By MacInnes's admission – and this point seems frequently to have been overlooked – the account of the Teenage scene to be found in *Absolute Beginners* was somewhat idealized rather than strictly documentary or naturalistic in its approach (MacInnes, 1961: 147). Such semi-mythical depictions of the new Teenage scene were nonetheless to be found in the guise of 'straight' reporting in at least the popular press, as in this piece by Tony Miles and Patrick Doncaster from the *Daily Mail* of 1 April 1957 that closely parallels – and pre-dates – MacInnes's description above of the 'transformation' of Soho under the impact of Teenage culture:

'THE TEENAGERS OF SOHO – THEY BRING A BREATH OF FRESH AIR
TO THE STREETS OF GANGLAND'

In the past few weeks a new world has sprung up in the sleazy back streets. A new world of young people set in the network of skiffle parlours, jazz joints, rock 'n' roll basements. . . . These new after dark citizens of Soho are typists, nurses, factory workers. They are students, dreamers, bank clerks. . . .

This is a young people's world with its own self-made heroes.

MacInnes's own observations on the Teenager also extended into more or less factual journalism. Thus a glossy article in *Queen* of December 1959 introduced Alex and Jean, a pair of 'real Teen-agers' and, in MacInnes' view, 'typical of their age and time' and 'fairly typical of the "sharper" kind of London teenager'. Alex did clerical work and earnt £8 per week, of which he gave £2 to his mother and saved £2, the rest being spent on clothes, records and going out with Jean. Jean earnt £5 10s per week working in a shop, of which she gave £1 10s to her mother, the rest again being used for Teenage consumption. MacInnes found these two 'responsible young people, quite adequately filial and respectful'; he was also anxious to distinguish the Teenager from the Ted: 'to be a Teddy boy and a teenager is a contradiction in terms since each fervently despises the other.' Here, then, the pendulum is at the other extreme of its swing: in opposition to the highly negative and unfavourable images and evaluations of the Teddy boys and sometimes of 1950s youth in general it is possible to discern a kind of 'inverse minority stereotyping': 'English teenagers are remarkably attractive by their self-reliance, their manifest joy in life, and their easy freedom from sterile inhibition.'

MacInnes's Teenagers embody an almost entirely favourable range of characteristics and thus point the way to a vision of the brighter, new and revitalized Britain of the 1960s.

8

The cult of youth II: Angries, hippies and the 'Swinging Sixties'

Alongside the Teddy boy moral panic and the emergence of the Teenager the late 1950s also witnessed the arrival in the arena of the youth spectacle of what were to prove to be a number of other highly significant elements for the establishment of the cult of youth. As well as being the year of rock 'n' roll 1956 was also that of the 'Angry Young Man', who represented yet another social type to be added to the rapidly expanding gallery provided by the youth spectacle of the day.[1] The event which finally brought the Angry Young Man into the full glare of public attention was the opening of John Osborne's play *Look Back in Anger* at the Royal Court Theatre in London in the spring of 1956. The immediate impact of this play and the sensation that soon surrounded it undoubtedly owed a good deal to the somewhat safe, dry and academic tone that had come to dominate serious British drama and literature in the early 1950s. Nonetheless, the diatribes of Osborne's aggressive working-class, university drop-out hero Jimmy Porter against all things respectable and bourgeois were interpreted by many as the battle cry of an emergent *déclassé* and uniquely alienated younger generation. It was Kenneth Tynan who expressed this view in its most extreme form when he wrote that the play showed:

> . . . post-war youth as it really is, the instinctive leftishness, the surrealist sense of humour . . . the casual promiscuity, the sense of lacking a cause worth fighting for . . . the Porters of our time deplore the tyranny of good taste . . . they are classless. (Booker, 1970: 111)

Even less ecstatic reviews of *Look Back in Anger* still tended to see the significance of this work – which along with the other 'youth sensations' of the 1950s now seems remarkably conventional – in terms of its exemplification of the perceived generational disjuncture of post-war British society: as with the *Daily Express*'s comment that it was 'intense, angry, feverish, undisciplined . . . even crazy . . . but it is young, young, young'. Or in *The Times'* review of 9 May 1956:

> The piece consists largely of angry tirades. The hero regards himself and clearly is regarded by the author as the spokesman for the younger, post-war generation which looks round the world and finds nothing right with it.   (p. 3)

A later *Times* editorial article on the stir caused by *Look Back in Anger* (26 May 1956, 'Wrath at the Helm?') concluded however that contemporary (middle-class) young adults were on the whole far from 'angry' – or frivolous – in reality, 'a Cinderella spirit quite alien to the pre-war generation is abroad'. If anything this group was too serious and sober in spirit, being prone to 'visiting prisons and reading Kierkegaard' (!)

The highly critical tone of *Look Back in Anger*, seemingly deriving from a new worldview amongst the rising generation of the intelligentsia, and directed against the staid conformity of the dominant middle-aged culture was not an isolated phenomenon, any more than was the current stance of John Osborne – now strikingly modified! – or the character of Jimmy Porter himself. Beginning with John Wain's novel *Hurry on Down* in 1953 and passing, amongst other works, through Kingsley Amis's *Lucky Jim* (1954), John Braine's *Room at the Top* (1957), and Alan Sillitoe's *Saturday Night and Sunday Morning* (1958), post-war English literature produced a rash of first novels dealing with the frustrations and aspirations of previously largely unnoticed sectors of the younger generation. The two major themes to be found in the body of new British fiction as typified by the above works were broadly 'dissaffected middle-class youth' (e.g. *Hurry on Down* and *Lucky Jim*) and 'working-class youth on the make' (e.g. *Room at the Top* and *Saturday Night and Sunday Morning*). The term 'youth' here is employed in both instances in its extended post-adolescent, post-teenage sense. The protagonists of these novels were all, along with Jimmy Porter, in their 20s; they were all, however, pre-adult in the vital sense of refusing to conform to the demands of 'adult society'.

Beyond this basic division between middle-class and proletarian novels the alienated anti-heroes of all these books shared, along with their authors to greater or lesser extents, the characteristic of being products, in one way or another, of the post-war expansion of educational opportunity and the consequent *possibility* – if not large scale reality – of social mobility thus engendered.[2] The theme of the imputed shift to meritocracy in the post-war British social order engendered by the Butler Education Act, and of the consequent social and cultural 'transformations' that were beginning to emerge from the late 1950s onwards as the 'post-Butler' generation reached its teens and twenties was to be an increasingly prominent feature of the youth question and spectacle from now on.

In the later years of the decade and through into the early 1960s many of the key works of the new British fiction were turned into motion pictures – *Look Back in Anger* (1958), *Room at the Top* (1959), *Saturday Night and Sunday Morning* (1960) – by such 'concerned' young British film makers as Tony Richardson, Karel Reisz and Lindsay Anderson. In this manner the image of the new breed of disaffected post-war British youth came to be further disseminated and to enter more generally into the popular imagination.

If Osborne's *Look Back in Anger* crystallized the concept of the Angry Young Man, it was perhaps the personage of the pop philosopher Colin Wilson who seemed most directly to exemplify the concept in the mass media. Wilson's book *The Outsider*, a convoluted examination of the lives and works of such diverse 'outsiders' as Blake, Van Gogh, Nijinsky, Dostoyevsky, Kafka, Eliot *et al.*, and an attack on the 'metaphysical sickness' of contemporary society, burst upon the literary and intellectual scene in 1956, only two weeks after the opening of *Look Back in Anger*, and when Colin Wilson himself was only twenty-five. The critics reacted with almost universal adulation with, for example, Edith Sitwell referring to it as 'this astonishing book', the *Daily Mail* proclaiming that it had received 'the most rapturous reception of any book since the war' and Philip Toynbee in the *Observer* acclaiming it as 'an exhaustive and luminously intelligent study of a representative theme of our time'.[3] Five thousand copies were sold on the day of publication and a further twenty thousand in the following six months.

What made this adulation and overnight success all the more

remarkable in one sense, although this may also serve as their partial explanation, was the fact that Wilson was not merely young but also provincial – he hailed from Leicester – working-class, and an auto-didact, having left his secondary modern school at 16. For the next eighteen months until the critical disaster of his next offering, *Religion and the Rebel*, Wilson was never far from the public eye and the attention of the media, the seeming walking embodiment of all that was most distinctive about intellectual post-war youth and indeed of many aspects of the wider post-war 'youth revolution'. Thus the *Daily Mirror* feature on 'The Teenagers of Soho' quoted in Chapter 7 (above) had also described the scene in the 'Two I's' coffee bar in the following terms:

> In the basement a young man with glasses and a beard sat and talked and listened and wrote. Name of Colin Wilson – author of the best seller for highbrows, *The Outsider*.

It should be borne in mind however that part of the popular image of alienated and disaffected youth (again in the *extended* sense of this term) at this time derived from external, non-British sources. Much of the style and stance of what was, in the Great Britain of the late 1950s, coming to be a small but growing and increasingly visible group of dissident middle-class youth derived not only from the Angry Young Men, but also from the – themselves cross-pollinating – cultures and images of post-war French existentialism and the American Beat Generation.[4] Mass media representations of disaffected middle-class youth also drew on these foreign sources and applied them, often in a fairly 'unrealistic' fashion, to the contemporary British scene. The youthful oppositional style pioneered and mythologized in the USA of the late 1940s and early 1950s by such largely middle-class bohemian types as Allen Ginsberg, Jack Kerouac, Neal Cassady, William Burroughs and Norman Mailer,[5] with its idolization of all things negro, its use of drugs, its involvement with modern jazz, the artistic avant-garde and Eastern mysticism, and its commitment to living in the existential present, first began to make its impact on the imaginations of old and young alike in the Great Britain of the late 1950s.

Around this time bohemian middle-class youth with a manifestly 'beat' style appeared periodically in the youth spectacle via a number of well-publicized prosecutions for drug offences and petty theft of members of the so-called 'Chelsea set', as in the following story from the *Daily Mirror* of 8 April 1959:

'A "CHELSEA SET" GIRL ROBBED METER'
Solicitor's daughter Suzanne Roper-Piesse wore a duffle coat, jeans and sandals when she faced theft charges in court today.

The story went on to describe how her father agreed with the JP's remarks at the conclusion of the hearing – Suzanne was conditionally discharged – and quoted him as saying that her behaviour was 'perfectly disgraceful . . . she does it for publicity . . . she has evidently got herself into a Chelsea set – and followed their habits'. Or again in the *Mirror* of 12 November of the same year:

'BAREFOOT ANNA (OF THE CHELSEA SET) IN A MYSTERY'
Ex public schoolgirl Anna Redburn – the girl the Chelsea Set call 'Barefoot Anna' – was last night unconscious in hospital believed to be suffering from an overdose of drugs.

By the early 1960s this same image of deviant middle-class youth had come to be focused in the semi-mythical social type of the Beatnik, as in a *Daily Mirror* story of 12 November 1963 on the 'Beatnik heiress' who refused to go home after her mother's collapse – occasioned by seeing her daughter's current lifestyle portrayed in a 'late night magazine programme' on television:

'HEIRESS CAROLE STAYS A BEATNIK'
Beatnik heiress Carole Humphries . . . left home two months ago to live with a crowd of other beatniks in a house in . . . Edgbaston.

Throughout the 1960s, indeed until it came to be superseded by images of the Counter Culture, the term 'Beatnik' was applied in an indiscriminate and often quite erroneous fashion to all of the disparate elements of the growing and well-publicized minority of unconventional and radical middle-class youth. In particular the minority stereotypical image of the Beatnik was centred on the issue of *drugs*. As late as the 'Summer of Love' of 1967 the *Daily Mirror* was quoting a spokesman from the National Gallery as complaining that 'it [the Gallery] has become a place of congregation for beatniks' and that there was 'obvious taking of drugs' ('Drugged Beatniks Among the Old Masters', 7 July).

It should perhaps be re-emphasized at this point that the then-current images of the Beatnik and the Beat Generation bore, as with that of the Angry Young Man, an only marginal and indirect relation to the realities of the situation and attitudes of the majority of British middle-class youth over the period in question. There were beatnik types to be found in the bohemian enclaves of Chelsea and Soho and also in the major art colleges, and somewhat earlier the so-called 'movement' of the Angry Young Men had influenced the style and stance of a small minority of the disaffected young. Nonetheless, throughout the large part of the 1950s, the majority of middle-class youth remained generally in accord with the dominant culture of adult society and its norms, values and goals. In effect the phenomenon of oppositional middle-class youth – and therefore the idea of the separation out of extended youth as a possibly autonomous age grade and Counter Culture – had yet to make its appearance on anything approaching a mass scale.

In particular the university students of the early to mid-1950s seem to have been on the whole remarkable for their conformism and acceptance of the status quo. Oxbridge types were generally keen to pursue the 'glittering prizes' while the upwardly mobile grammar school boys of the expanding Redbricks were generally content with their prospective careers in teaching and middle management.[6] Ferdynand Zweig mounted a study at around this time into the problems of the student in an 'age of anxiety' which examined the university scenes at Oxford and Manchester and found its subjects to be on the whole 'honest, sincere young men taking their studies very seriously', who were moreover generally 'self-disciplined', 'altruistic' and even 'religious' (Zweig, 1963: xiii). This study lamented the fact that university students were perhaps *too* serious, hardworking, content with their lot, etc., a far cry indeed from the dominant image of the student that was to emerge in the late 1960s.

In the USA of the 1950s the story was much the same, although with a greater emphasis on the apathy, alienation and apolitical stance of the current student population (see, e.g., Keniston, 1960). Here the argument was widely advanced that the perceived apathy of the middle-class young was rooted in the then-current 'chronic' rate of technological and socio-cultural change, and the consequent 'end of ideology' which had in turn brought about an 'end of identification' amongst youth and an opening up of an almost unbridgeable generation gap. As Kenneth Keniston wrote, stating what seems to have been the dominant 1950s view of students and middle-class American youth in general:

> With no exemplars, no objects of identification and an obdurate refusal to accept them, the result is often that perplexity, self fragmentation and confusion that we see in many alienated young men. (Keniston, 1960: 233)

In Britain and America, then, the dominant images associated at this time with middle-class, student youth seem only to have spanned the range from quiescent and apolitical alienation through to passive acceptance of the status quo and conformism.

This was to begin to change at around the end of the 1950s with, in America, the coming of the Civil Rights Movement, SDS and the folk music revival, and in Britain the coming of the Campaign for Nuclear Disarmament.[7] CND, together with the then-current boom in more or less authentically recreated 'trad' jazz, was at this time coming to form the focus for what was arguably the first major subculture – if, as often in the middle-class case, a somewhat diffuse one – of post-war middle-class British youth.[8] The style of this subculture was described thus by George Melly in a contemporary account of an 'all nighter' at the Alexandra Palace in 1962:

> The audience were dressed almost without exception in 'rave gear'. As the essence of 'rave gear' is a stylized shabbiness, the general effect was of a crowd scene from a biblical epic. To describe an individual couple, the boy was wearing a top hat with 'Acker' printed on it, a shift made out of a sugar sack with a CND symbol painted on the back, jeans and no shoes. The girl, a bowler hat with a CND symbol on it, a man's shirt worn outside her black woollen tights. 'Trad' dancing in the contemporary sense is deliberately anti-dancing. (Melly, 1972: 65)

This British Trad/CND subculture – whose members were sometimes referred to generically and somewhat misleadingly as 'beatniks' – is of special significance from the point of view of the post-war youth spectacle in as far as it was widely seen as a mass phenomenon amongst the middle-class young of an explicitly political and oppositional nature. In the late 1950s and early 1960s the annual Eastertime CND Aldermaston March began, as its numbers swelled, also to attract a great deal of media attention, and thus to disseminate the idea that, for the first time since the 1930s, a sizeable minority of British youth was being attracted in its politics and culture to an activist/radical-left position.

It should be noted, however, that empirical research into the political attitudes, affiliation and voting behaviour amongst British youth carried out by Abrams and Little in the mid-1960s (the period immediately after the collapse of original CND and the manifest failure of its attempt to re-define British politics through a youth movement centred upon one moral issue) revealed the young, once again, as being remarkably 'conventional': this time in the area of politics (Abrams and Little, 1965a: 315–32; 1965b: 95–110). 'Young voters' as a whole were found to be 'realistic' in their political judgements and to be largely following paths already established by their parents in their political involvement (or more likely lack of it), voting intentions and assessment of political leaders (Abrams and Little, 1965a: 324, 1965b: 102–8). 'Young activists' (Young Socialists, Young Liberals and Young Conservatives) were found either willingly or else under duress to conform to the adult party line and were indeed themselves often 'activist' by virtue of family succession. A 'youth breakthrough' in British politics was seen as being beyond the structural possibilities of the nation's political system (the recent failure of CND was taken as one clear indicator of this) and radical and non-radical youth alike was, if anything, seen as becoming increasingly disengaged from politics (Abrams and Little, 1965a: 325–30).

The overall conclusion to emerge from Abrams and Little's research was that *de facto* intergenerational political continuity was such that there was 'no need to invoke the concept of generation' – despite the attempts of all three major parties to win the support of youth – in the analysis of contemporary British politics: 'British youth has no collective political self-consciousness. There has been no breakthrough and there is little prospect of one' (ibid., p. 331). What is of most significance about this work from the point of view of the present study is precisely the indication that it provides of the currency in the mid-1960s of the (inappropriate) concept of political generation, and the related idea that contemporary events such as the coming of the Bomb and the Suez Crisis could form intergenerational political watersheds. Such then-prevalent ideas – brought into question by the whole thrust of Abrams and Little's research – can clearly be seen as another aspect of the post-war period's cult of youth and of its use of the concept of youth in a projective or metaphorical fashion.

The *image* of radical middle-class youth in the late 1950s was all the more striking against the background of the earlier images of the political apathy of middle-class youth and the classless conservatism of the Teenager. Despite being led by such 'old faithfuls' of the Left as Canon Collins, Bertrand Russell, Michael Foot and the Revd Donald Soper, the Aldermaston marches of the period were clearly a youth phenomenon (in 1962 a *Guardian* reporter estimated that not more than one in twenty of the marchers was over 21) almost as institutionalized and ritualized as the days and traditions of misrule of previous eras.

Initially, and even as numbers began to swell in each successive year (approximately 5,000 at Aldermaston in 1958 to around 100,000 in Trafalgar Square in 1960) the media portrayal of this annual event was predominantly benign:

'TWENTY THOUSAND ON THE H TREK'
. . . half a dozen jazz bands played all the way. Teenagers jived and sang.
. . . woollen cloak, speckled sweater, jeans and boots – that was the garb for this girl marcher.   (*Daily Mirror*, 18 April 1960)

And again in the *Mirror* two days later:

'ONE HUNDRED THOUSAND JAM TRAFALGAR SQUARE'
. . . when the first weary marchers reached the Square many cooled their aching feet in the fountains, like the young people in the picture, right.   (centre spread, 20 April 1960)

'A FANTASTIC END TO THE H MARCH'
. . . Said a senior policeman, 'It is unbelievable. It is bigger than the VE or VJ night celebrations'.

'WHAT THE *MIRROR* SAYS'
'Well done, marchers'.

By 1963, however, in conjunction with the breakaway from CND of the radical 'Committee of 100' and the policy of mass civil disobedience of this group (the number of arrests in political demonstrations and clashes in the Metropolitan Police District rose from less than 25 in 1959 to an all-time peak of 1,600 in 1962: Gurr *et al.*, 1977: 178, fig. 11.4.12) the Easter march had become a less peaceable affair and its image had shifted accordingly. 'End of the Road: Ban the Bomb marchers reach London . . . then came scuffles and arrests. . . .' (*Daily Mirror*, 13 April 1963).

In the early 1960s CND and its associated subculture served to bring into the public eye for the first time on a significant scale the 'deviant' and, more importantly, ideologically oppositional potential that was inherent in the image – and reality – of *middle-class* youth. This was the image that was to culminate in the youth spectacle of the late 1960s and early 1970s in the themes of Student Radicalism and Counter Culture.[9]

By the early 1960s, then, the process of the separation out of adolescence/youth as a universal and distinct age grade had by and large been completed. The major objective, social-structural, economic and social-institutional changes that were to provide the parameters for this process were either complete or else well on the way to completion (see Chapters 5 and 6, above). At the same time almost the full array of subjective *images* and *meanings* that have been associated with youth, in one way or another, from this time onwards, had been formed in outline, with reference to a range of contemporary semi-mythical youthful social types and youth-related phenomena. The youth spectacle from the early 1960s onwards has in fact presented a range of variations, and in some cases developments, on themes that had then already begun to emerge, as youth itself had been emerging, ever more clearly as a highly visible and particularly 'problematic' age grade.

The entire period of the 1960s (and to a lesser extent the early 1970s) was one that was characterized by an almost bewildering range of events and phenomena at all levels of the youth spectacle. At the level of youth subcultures and movements, both working-class and middle-class, the 1960s witnessed the explosion on to the stage of the youth spectacle of the mods and rockers, the hippies, student activists, and the skinheads. At the level of generic images of youth, the first part of the decade saw a continuation, in a heightened and increasingly 'unrealistic' form, of the cult of the

Teenager. Finally, and at the most general level, the 1960s was also the decade of the full emergence into the youth spectacle of such interconnected youth-related sociocultural images as the 'Permissive Society', 'Drug Culture', 'Swinging London', and 'Counter Culture' and, in association with these, of the idea of *youthfulness* itself as partially divorced from its original point of reference of youth-as-age-grade.

The popular preoccupation with the Teenager as a new and semi-mythical social type persisted well into the 1960s, as did the general tendency to view the Teenager in a largely favourable light as the embodiment of a coming bright new future. The Teenager increasingly became, in effect, a creature to be closely studied for the light which his or her habits and opinions could shed, amongst other things, upon the way in which British society might be expected to develop. One example of this tendency, taken from the then-burgeoning field of the pop sociology of youth, was provided by Charles Hamblett and Jane Deverson's *Generation X*, a collection of interviews with 'today's generation talking about itself' and also about 'education, marriage, money, pop, politics, parents, drugs, drink, God, sex, class, colour, kinks and living for kicks'.[10]

Pop and rock stars such as Adam Faith early in the decade and Mick Jagger later on were sometimes singled out as representatives and spokesmen for 'the Teenagers', 'the kids' or 'the younger generation' *en masse*, and their views on weighty issues publicly sought – if not actually heeded – by the powerful and important. This widespread idea of the Teenager as a new force to be reckoned with in the social order (or at least of the Teenager as a new group to be courted by business and political interests) and of the Teenager as representative of the future, was expressed in a particularly heightened form in an article which appeared in an issue of the glossy periodical *Town* specially devoted to youth in 1962, under the heading of 'Bulge Takes Over':

> We know that they'll [the new Teenage generation] be bigger than us. . . . The new generation will demand more than ninety-odd miles of modern motorway. . . .
>
> They will be cleverer than us . . . they're going to be classless. Their clothes already are. So are the things and places they like most – Wimpy Bars, bowling alleys, the M1: all too new to have any connotation of upper or lower, in-group or out-group. When

they come to furnish homes they'll pick 'contemporary' design with none of the connotations antiques carry of a bygone aristocratic taste. . . .

The cult of the Teenager in the early to mid-1960s seems in fact to have been just as pronounced, if not more so, in glossy, 'quality', often otherwise conservative publications as in the popular press (and the latest youth style or subculture has of course remained basic colour-supplement fodder right down until the present). The *Weekend Telegraph Supplement* for example, of 28 May 1965, devoted itself to an examination of 'Youth '65', and the question of 'Are Teenagers People?' In the 'Comment' section of this issue the current obsession with all things Teenage was in fact bemoaned under the headline 'I don't WANT to worship adolescents'. In the view of the author of this piece, pundits of all kinds, including, *par excellence*, sociologists, were far too much given to asking teenagers' opinions:

> The question of what does *the* teenager think, the assumption being that one selected at random will speak for all. . . .
> The assumption is all too often justified since an essential feature of Teenagery is its togetherness and mass mindedness. . . .
> Once upon a time it was considered normal for adolescents to want to be adults, now the world seems full of adults wanting to be adolescents.

However, by the mid-1960s the image of the Teenager had become a highly complicated and ambiguous one, in part as a response to its blurring into other current aspects and levels of the youth spectacle, and in part as the general response to the 'new Britain' of the time became more contradictory and double-edged. The *Weekend Telegraph* issue of 1965, cited above, noted elsewhere that 'teenagers like cowboys are divided into goodies and baddies', thus furnishing in passing another example of the way in which the perennial theme of 'most of them are fine but some – a small minority – are not' can, through its subdivision of the totality of 'contemporary youth', be used to overcome any contradictions that may be manifest in the latter's overall stereotypical image. As exemplifying the 'goodies', an account was provided of British

Teenagers doing VSO in Nigeria. The 'baddies' were represented by a piece on London's rockers as 'transport café cowboys'. By the time of this *Weekend Telegraph* article the working-class youth subculture of the rockers had, together with that of the mods, come to be *the* central focus for the entire youth spectacle, through the seaside Bank Holiday clashes of what were widely perceived as these two rival 'super gangs'. The idea of the rivalry between the mods (or 'moderns' as they were initially called) and the rockers had in fact begun to appear in the youth spectacle *before* the famous seaside riots of the mid-1960s, as in this piece from the *Daily Mirror* of 13 March 1963:

'WHEN A MODERN MEETS A ROCKER'

Gang rivalry between the 'Moderns' and the 'Rockers' was mentioned in a court yesterday.

The 'moderns' it was said wear Italian style suits, and chisel toe shoes and have 'college boy' haircuts.

The 'rockers' wear long coats or black leather jackets, tight jeans and suede boots. They have 'Tony Curtis' haircuts.

After the case a Modern said 'Trouble is always flaring up between us and the Rockers. They don't like our smart dress – and we don't like their appearance either'.

It was, however, the first 'mods and rockers riot' in Clacton in the Easter of 1964 (followed by similar events over the next two years) that set in motion a spiral of media-conveyed and amplified moral panic, whereby these two subcultural groupings were widely cast in the role of folk devils – minority stereotypes for the expression of all manner of anxieties in the parent society and culture (S. Cohen, 1980).

As with earlier images of post-war juvenile delinquency and the rock 'n' roll/Teddy boy riots of the 1950s, the mods and rockers riots were also viewed as a manifestation of a new 'mindless' group orientation and a supposedly unprecedented violence amongst certain sectors of contemporary youth:

'"WILD ONES" INVADE SEASIDE'

The Wild Ones invaded a seaside town yesterday. 1,000 fighting, drinking, roaring, rampaging teenagers on scooters and motor-cycles. (*Daily Mirror*, 30 March 1964)

The mods as folk devils and the disturbances themselves were again seen as somehow the product of post-war affluence, as in the remarks of Marcus Lipton, Labour MP for Brixton, calling for jail sentences for the Clacton offenders: 'They earn big money and just laugh at the fine. It means nothing to them' (Quoted in the *Daily Mirror*, 1 April 1964, front page: 'Jail These "Wild Ones" Call by MPs').[11]

The career of the mods and rockers moral panic has been charted in detail by Cohen, as has the image of the Bank Holiday disturbances presented in the youth spectacle, the latter being largely a matter of the transposition into another key of the minority stereotypical aspect of the portrayal of working-class subcultural post-war youth which was already well developed by the late 1950s. There are, however, a number of points that might still be noted here. Firstly it should be made clear that even at the time of the eruption of these two supposedly fundamentally opposed groups into the arena of the youth spectacle it was primarily the mods who were viewed as the 'new' and significant sociocultural phenomenon. The so-called rockers seem always to have been considerably outnumbered by their rivals in the ritualized Bank Holiday confrontations, but more than this they appeared in contrast old fashioned, even – or perhaps especially – in the period of the early to mid-1960s (S. Cohen, 1980: 185–91). In Jeff Nuttall's telling phrase, the rocker, with his motorcycle, leather and denim and straight-forward machismo, now already seemed 'almost endearingly butch' (Nuttall, 1970: 35). His image could be equated fairly unambiguously with the juvenile delinquent/motorcycle gang/Teddy boy/rock 'n' roll image constellation that was by this time already well established. The mods, however, as well as being numerically speaking the period's dominant youth subcultural phenomenon, were also much more ambiguous in image. They were clean, short-haired, well dressed in what seemed at first a fairly conventional manner, and perhaps in part because of their fondness for amphetamines (the *image* of the mods as 'purple heart kids' certainly figured prominently in the media accounts of the Bank Holiday riots), apparently 'bright' and 'alert'. On the basis of a superficial and uninformed examination they were also far more difficult for most adults to locate in terms of their social class background.

Cohen's *Folk Devils and Moral Panics* has dissected the processes through which the mod, through his growing association with 'mob violence', and the official (over-)reaction to this image, came to be cast in the role of contemporary folk devil – the walking embodiment of much that was seen as going wrong with the affluent society. The idea of the mod as folk devil and the centre for a moral panic has, however, perhaps been over-emphasized at the expense of noting that, in more general terms, he or she evoked a rather more contradictory response. As has been pointed out, the mod was more or less simultaneously depicted in the youth spectacle as the folk devil in the magistrate's court and as the trendsetter of the new Britain in the colour supplements.[12] The latter, positive image of the mods, as well as the contrast that was sometimes drawn between this and that of the rockers, was exemplified in an early *Daily Mail* feature on 'Mods and Rockers' (11 November 1963):

> Teenagers with an urge to group identification are likely to join the MODS or ROCKERS . . . the two 'in' cults . . . [there is] West Side Story rivalry between them. . . . Here's how to spot them. . . .

The piece then went on to describe the mods as clean, against fighting, ambitious, 'with it', etc., whereas the rockers were presented as traditional, even regressive, motorcycle delinquents.

In many respects then the mod, with his or her imputed qualities of modernity, brightness and classlessness can be and was seen as the direct descendant of the idealized Teenager as described above. As with the image of the Teenager, this largely positive image of the mod reflected a more or less 'progressive' view: the future of British society, as exemplified by the younger generation, was towards greater affluence, classlessness, dynamism, mobility, etc. In reality the mod style itself grew out of the earlier sharp Teenage style as chronicled by Colin MacInnes, and by the period of the mid-1960s a modified and commercialized version of this had come to predominate amongst working-class British youth. At this time, then, the (semi-mythical) social types of Teenager and mod had come in some considerable measure to *overlap*. Most working-class teenagers were by the same token now seen as 'Mod', if not mods.[13] This overlapping of images and categories is, together with the ambivalence of the period's overall response to social change itself, responsible for much that was contradictory in the image of 'the Mod'.

The contradictory nature of the image of and social response to *the mods* as a highly visible working-class youth subculture was further compounded by the fact that the more general concept of 'Mod' at this time was coming to stand as a kind of shorthand for almost anything that was seen as a manifestation of the youthful, progressive and classless 'new Britain' of the 1960s. In short, the idea of 'Mod' signified a range of youthful values – spontaneity, creativity, opposition, etc. – at a period when these were much emphasized in the overall social spectacle.[14]

The standard-bearers of the image of the 'new Britain' of the early 1960s were the Beatles.[15] It has been noted above how by the early 1960s the bulge of post-war British youth had money to spend on 'distinctive teenage products' and how this spending power was being tapped by the relatively new youth-oriented pop music industry. However, whereas say 1956 was a year of excitement and innovation in this field, by 1962 most pop music had become largely a matter of formula, as well as still being essentially American in origin, and therefore reflecting only the fairly alien American youth scene. All of this was to change dramatically in 1963 when the Beatles and their British adaptation and synthesis of pre-existing if somewhat obscure American popular music forms precipitated a 'British Beat Boom' that surpassed in every way the earlier impact of rock 'n' roll.

The phenomenon of the Beatles first began to register in the popular imagination at large and in the youth spectacle in the late summer of 1963. By the end of the same year with the smash hits of 'From Me to You', 'She Loves You' and 'I Want to Hold Your Hand' behind them and the advent of 'Beatlemania', the group had become nothing short of a major national obsession – the focus for a quite inordinate amount of popular *and* 'serious' mass media attention (see Melly, 1972: 68–72). Something of the flavour of the initial, largely highly favourable, media response can be gained from the following excerpts from two major feature articles that appeared in the *Daily Mirror* and the *Sunday Times* respectively in September 1963:

> 'THE BIG BEAT CRAZE! FOUR FRENZIED LITTLE LORD
> FAUNTLEROYS WHO ARE MAKING £5,000 EVERY WEEK'
> Four cheeky looking kids with stone-age hair styles, Chelsea boots, three electric guitars, and one set of drums, who know

their amps and ohms if not their Beethoven. They are the Beatles, the smash hit, refuse all imitation, Number One group in the sensational Beat Craze now devastating, if not deafening, the British Isles.

Who are the Beatles? . . . They are pleasing to look at, friendly of manner . . . [they favour] tea and cakes rather than Dry Martini with a twist of lemon [a reference to the preferred drink of that other hero of the sixties, James Bond]. (Donald Zec, *Daily Mirror* 10 September 1963)

and

'THE BEATLES BEAT THE LOT'

By night they flood out into that raw mistral that rips in from Liverpool Bay; over 200 quartets, trios and fivesomes on Merseyside trailing their electric guitars, drums, voices and amplifiers.

[the Beatles are] . . . individualists within a well established mainstream of younger generation cult and fashion which began in the Fifties when the mass producers of clothes, coiffures and canned music began to court the multi-million teenage market.

The Beatles are products of their generation, not its pacesetters . . . one genuine novelty however may make the sociologists twitter. Their talk reveals them as very much a part of that questing, confident, cool, sharp and unshockable stream that has come out of the grammar schools in the last decade. (Derek Jewell, *Sunday Times*, 15 September 1963)

One of the early highspots of Beatlemania in Britain occurred in November 1963 when the group performed in the otherwise staid and 'safe' Royal Variety Performance:

'NIGHT OF TRIUMPH FOR FOUR YOUNG MEN AT THE ROYAL VARIETY SHOW'

Last night Everybody loved the Beatles – Yeah! Yeah! Yeah! (*Daily Mirror*, 5 November 1963)

'WHAT THE MIRROR SAYS'

You have to be a real square not to love the nutty, noisy, happy Beatles. . . . How refreshing it is to see these rumbustious young

Beatles take a middle aged Royal Variety Performance audience by the scruff of their necks and have them Beatling like teenagers.   (6 November)

Even here however there was the occasional dissenting voice to be heard in the midst of the general adulation. In terms remarkably similar to those of the denunciation of rock 'n' roll current some seven years earlier, Henry Price MP (Conservative) addressed a conference of Tory women as follows:

It is useless decrying it . . . we must offer teenagers something they will like better [than Beatlemania]. . . . It has a hypnotic effect on them . . . their eyes become glazed and their mouths gape, their hands wobble loosely and their legs wobble just as loosely at the knees . . . this is known as 'being sent'. It doesn't send me but it sends them. (Quoted in *Daily Mirror*, 5 December 1963)

The Royal Variety appearance was also the occasion for yet more 'serious' analysis of the Beatles phenomenon, as in the following remarks from a psychiatrist, published in a *Sunday Times* piece on the 'Anatomy of Beatlemania', which also nicely reflects much of the period's new-found awareness and fascination with adolescence and youth:

In a sense . . . the open hero worship of the group is an indication of how fully emancipated adolescents have become, a sign that adolescence is now a proud experience rather than a shameful phase. Instinctively they turn to heroes with whom they can positively identify.   (3 November 1963)

In 1964 the Beatles went from strength to strength, taking the American pop music world by storm – at one time occupying the first five places in the US charts – and thus becoming a truly international pop phenomenon. In the summer of this year the Beatles' film *A Hard Day's Night* was also predictably a major hit, and established a new look as well as a new claim to adult attention for the pop genre. Finally in 1965 the Beatles were awarded MBEs in the honours list of the recently elected Wilson Labour Government, perhaps partially out of a somewhat ill-founded belief that this gesture could woo the support of youth as a whole.

In the wake of the Beatles' runaway success, a full-scale 'British Beat Boom' ensued, both at home and abroad, catapulting first other Liverpool groups, then British rhythm and blues groups such as the Rolling Stones, to success. In contrast with the pop charts of 1962 those of 1964 and 1965 were almost entirely dominated by new British groups. As was the case with the emergence of rock 'n' roll, the British Beat Boom also generated considerable spin-offs in other mass media: new teen magazines were launched: *Jackie*, *Rave*, *Fab 208*; pirate radio appeared, first in the form of Radio Caroline at Easter 1964; and the TV programme 'Ready, Steady, Go, did much to define and diffuse the general mod style (see Melly, 1972: 170–2).

The changes in British mass culture ushered in by the advent of the Beatles – but not in any fundamental sense 'caused' by this event, it should be stressed – were therefore wide ranging. In contrast to what had gone immediately before, the Beatles' music and its impact undoubtedly seemed at the time to be quite revolutionary; what is of even more importance from the point of view of the present study, however, is the fact that the group themselves were in image uncompromisingly *working class, provincial* and *British*. At the height of Beatlemania the universally known figures of John, Paul, George and Ringo seemed to define in one way or another most of the positive qualities of the supposed new youth of the late 1950s and early 1960s: energy, wit, lack of time for hypocrisy and pomposity, refusal to bow before the worn-out conventions of class society, etc. In this respect the early image of, and national obsession with, the Beatles can in fact be regarded as an extension of the cult of the Teenager discussed above. (The later, 'mature' Beatles in their counter-cultural phase presented a far less unambiguously positive image, and probably a far more disturbing one from an adult point of view, as did such more explicitly 'deviant' groups as the Rolling Stones and The Who right from the outset.)

More than this, however, the Beatles marked the extension of the market base for pop music in terms of age and social class and its claims to be taken seriously by post-adolescents.[16] The Beatles inspired a rash of critical pieces on their music in the quality press, as in the now famous article by *The Times'* music critic William

Mann, claiming for John Lennon and Paul McCartney the title of the 'outstanding English composers of 1963' and discussing their music in terms of 'its distinctly indigenous character . . . chains of pandiatonic clusters . . . major tonic sevenths and ninths . . . flat submediant key switches' and the 'Aeolonian cadence at the end of 'Not a Second Time' (the chord progression which ends Mahler's 'Song of the Earth')' ('What Songs the Beatles Sing', *The Times*, 27 December 1963, p. 4). The most extreme of such statements was undoubtedly that of Richard Buckle in the *Sunday Times* of 29 December 1963 who went so far as to suggest that the Beatles were in fact the 'greatest composers since Beethoven'! In these ways the Beatles heralded a number of important developments in the emergence of the cult of youth in its fullest sense: one notable trend of the 1960s was the way in which teenage culture came to be superseded for a while by extended Youth Culture and the latter in turn came to constitute a central element of the period's commercial mass culture in general.

By the mid-1960s the Beatles, having moved to the capital and become far more complicated and sophisticated figures than the Liverpool lads of yore, were well installed in the youth spectacle, along with the other major figures of the pop world, as leaders of the 'new aristocracy' of 'Swinging London'. The Britain of the early 1960s was widely perceived as undergoing a number of revolutionary shifts in the arts, culture, and morality. It was the myth and image of 'Swinging London', populated by the youthful trailblazers of these supposed shifts – the 'New Aristocracy' – that served most directly at this time to crystallize the notion of sociocultural 'revolution' in the popular imagination.

The classic statement of the image of 'Swinging London' is to be found in the feature 'London: The Most Exciting City' by John Crosby, a journalist on the staff of the *New York Herald Tribune*, which appeared, somewhat belatedly, in the *Weekend Telegraph* supplement of 16 April 1965. This piece is quite remarkable – amongst other things – for its constant reiteration of the terms 'young', 'youth', 'youthful' and 'youthfulness'; indeed a shorthand in this instance for the full range of sociocultural changes that were then apparently transforming the face – if not, as it later turned out, the underlying reality – of contemporary British society. Crosby described the scene at the Ad Lib Club, the headquarters of the New Aristocracy, thus:

In Soho the hottest and swingingest spot in town, the noise is deafening; the beat group is pounding out 'I Just Don't Know What to Do With Myself'; on the floor under the red and green and blue lights, a frenzy of the prettiest legs in the whole world belonging to models, au pair girls or just ordinary English girls, a gleam of pure joy on their pretty faces, dancing with the young bloods, the scruffy very hotshot photographers like David Bailey or Terry Donovan, or a new pop singer – all vibrating with youth.

This 'swinging' nightlife was in its turn seen as a symptom of a 'deeper turbulence' emerging in British society over the period 1958–60 when 'youth captured this ancient island and took command in a country where youth had always before kept properly in its place'. The same 'deeper social turmoil that [was] transforming England especially among the young' was also manifesting itself in fashion. In the case of male styles for example:

English men's clothes were once almost a uniform: staid, sober and above all, correct, advertising your precise rung on the social ladder and even your bank account. Today the working class boys – many of them fresh out of the Army or Navy and in full revolt against conformity of dress – their pockets full of money, are splurging on suede jackets, skin-like tweed trousers . . . etc.

Finally this was all associated with what *appeared* like nothing short of the collapse of the power of social-class origins to define and determine life chances and lifestyle, and the replacement of the dimension of class by that of age as the prime determinant of the major contours of society and culture. The young at both extremes of the social spectrum were (seen as) combining together to combat the 'middle ground' occupied by the 'old' and the middle classes, thus forming in embryo a society ruled by youthful values:

The caste system, in short, is breaking down at both ends. The working-class young are bursting out of the lower depths and invading fields where they can make more money and the upper class is breaking down walls to get into the lower levels where they can have more fun.

In the world of women's fashion Mary Quant's mini skirt and its accompanying 'dolly bird' look was sweeping all before it, itself a symbol of the supposed new climate of youthful and *female* emancipation.[17] The belief that the 'Sixties Revolution' was having a particularly pronounced effect upon the lives of the new generation of girls and young women – which was itself in turn part of the vanguard of this (imputed) revolution – was to be found frequently in discussions of contemporary youth in the popular press of the early–mid-1960s, as in the following *Daily Mirror* centre-page spread of 1964 by Marjorie Proops:

'FOR THESE GIRLS IT'S ALL HAPPENING'

This is the strange new younger generation with new ideas about life and living. . . . These zestful girls found at all levels of society. From the Prime Minister's daughter to the beat girls of the Liverpool cellars.

Examples of this new species of young woman were actresses such as Julie Christie and novelists such as Sheena Makay, Proops continued:

They are prototypes of a whole new race . . . [they are] ambitious, zany, non-conformist, bright, intelligent, and resourceful.   (5 March)

The Quant-led style of the early 1960s *was indeed* revolutionary in a limited sense in as far as it reversed the direction in which fashion had traditionally flowed across age and social-class boundaries, a phenomenon much remarked upon in its own time (see Lewis, 1978: 205).

'THE NEW ADVENTURERS'

These youngsters are turning our High Streets into fashion parades. I have been on a safari in the fashion jungle . . . tracking down the young adventurers who have recently put a bomb under all the old ideas about clothes . . . meeting the brilliant boys and girls who are pushing the exciting new fashions in every High Street.

[They are] a brand new race of artist . . . all in their twenties, and they all came from grammar schools.

'Fashion today is coming up from the High Street instead of down from the palace' [said Janey Ironside, Professor of Design at the Royal College of Art].

Everywhere you look in the full speed ahead world of fashion, youngsters from the RCA are bursting to the top . . . they all know each other and swap ideas.

They are the new people who design the sort of clothes that fit the new homes, the new cars, the new ideas.

Anyone who is still trying to say that Britain is on the skids because our youth is not good should remember that most of these world-trendsetting kids come from ordinary homes. (Noel Whitcombe, *Daily Mirror*, 5 November 1963)

As with rock music the 'Quant breakthrough' represented another example of the 1960s phenomenon of 'youth culturization' of mainstream adult culture: from this time onwards the youth sector came to play a leading role in many aspects of mass cultural development, commercial and otherwise.

At the same time, but even more fleetingly and ephemerally, the British cinema was booming with such films as *The Knack*, *Help*, *The Bed Sitting Room*, and later *Darling*, *Alfie* and *Blow Up*, all dealing with and further disseminating 'swinging' themes. This was also the period of the Theatre of Cruelty, Pop and later Op Art, the satire boom and 'That Was the Week That Was' on television, and the emergence of James Bond and the cult of the spy. Young working-class actors such as Michael Caine and Terence Stamp, photographers such as David Bailey and model girls such as Twiggy were lionized by the media (see above) and seemingly joined effortlessly with certain fashionable members of the youth of the upper classes in the revolt of the New Aristocracy against all things old and *petit bourgeois* (Melly, 1972: 167–77).

In the political life of the nation the loss of confidence in the old guard Conservative ruling élite that had begun with Suez and the dismantling of the British Empire was further fuelled in the early 1960s by the Vassal affair and the seemingly ever-ramifying Profumo scandal. These and other aspects of what amounted to a crisis of traditional authority bore fruit in October of 1964, with the election on a majority of four of the first Labour Government in thirteen years, brought to office on the promise of a new start for the nation with an end to economic stop – go policies and the instigation of a 'white hot technological revolution'. As noted above, the theme of youth-as-national-asset and the idea that the latter was currently being under-exploited or wasted under modern 'techno-logical' conditions formed in one way or another an important part of the political rhetoric of *all* the major parties throughout the late 1950s and early 1960s. As early as 1955 Sir David Eccles, then Conservative Minister of Education, was proclaiming in the House 'The first job of those who believe in the scientific revolution and Britain's contribution to a dramatic rise in world standards is to communicate to young people this spectacular dream they alone can make come true' (reported in *The Times*, 22 July 1955).

The most skilful exponent of this theme in the period's political discourse, however, was undoubtedly Harold Wilson, as in the following excerpts from a speech delivered as part of the run-up to the 1964 election on the topic of 'The New Britain':

> This is the time for a breakthrough to an exciting and wonderful period in our history, in which all can and must take part. Our young men and women, especially, have in their hands the power to change the world. We want the youth of Britain to storm the new frontiers of knowledge, to bring back to Britain that surge in adventurous self-confidence and sturdy self-respect which the Tories have almost submerged with their apathy and cynicism.
>
> We believe that Britain's future depends on the thrusting ability and even iconoclasm of millions of products of our grammar schools, comprehensive schools, technical schools and colleges, secondary moderns, and the rest, who are today held down not only within the Government Party but over a wide sector of industry. . . .
>
> This is what 1964 can mean. A chance for change. . . . (Wilson, 1964: 10)[18]

The period before the 1964 election was also a time in which all of the major parties attempted directly to woo the youth vote itself, a constituency which was widely (if perhaps erroneously, in the light of the research of Abrams and Little as discussed above) believed to be 'up for grabs' at this time. Much of the Labour Party's official rhetoric, as exemplified above, was clearly pointed in this direction, but it should be noted that the Liberals were also issuing a 'Charter for Youth' at this time, demanding that the vote be given to 18-year-olds and arguing that 'the earlier maturity and self-sufficiency of young people today are powerful indicators of youth's readiness for responsibility' (quoted in *The Times*, 26 September 1963). Not to be outdone, the Conservatives too made much of the theme of youth, and an appeal to young voters is clear from the following account from the *Sunday Times* of 1963 of Sir Alec Douglas Home's final speech in his Kinross and West Perthshire by-election campaign:

'SIR ALEC GIVES YOUTH A PLEDGE: "ONLY THE BEST"'
The Prime Minister tonight linked his leadership with the demands of the rising generation. . . .
It is significant that he devoted nearly all of his speech to the theme of youth at this final stage of his by-election campaign. . . .
'The key to the future lies in Britain's schools, technical colleges and universities' [he said]. 'At a time when our country must earn its living in increasingly competitive markets British youth deserves and needs and – if I have anything to do with it is going to get – the best education in the world'.   (3 November)

The 1960s idea of 'youth revolution' was to reach what was perhaps its logical conclusion with the emergence of the hippies, student radicalism and the concept of the 'Counter Culture'. In Britain, as throughout the Western world, the largely middle-class and more or less explicitly ideological strands of 'youthful opposition' thus variously designated, came for a time to dominate the entire youth spectacle with a range of accompanying images and meanings from the most positive to the most negative. In their representation in the mass media and their general hold over the popular imagination at this time, these diverse but loosely interrelated phenomena of oppositional/extended Youth Culture marked what can be regarded as a second high spot for the cult of youth that had been ushered in with the appearance of the Teenager.
Initial images of the hippies from the 'Summer of Love' of 1967 – a time when this new and startling phenomenon was seldom out of the headlines of at least the popular press – were far from

overwhelmingly negative overall, tending in the main rather towards a tone of amused condescension, with perhaps just the suggestion that something important might be occurring:

'MARCH OF THE FLOWER (POT) MEN'

Even the regulars down at Speakers' Corner who are well versed in eccentrics had to admit that yesterday was quite something.

Hundreds of young 'Hippies' wandered into London's Hyde Park to spread their love thy neighbour beliefs. And, in passing, they advocated that the smoking of 'pot' – marijuana – be legalized.

With bells on their toes, flowers in their hair and carrying 'Flower Power' banners they recited poetry, sang and danced.

In true Hippie tradition they showered police and bystanders with flowers.   (*Daily Mirror*, 17 July 1967)

A Franklin cartoon printed in the *Mirror* on the following day depicted a number of hirsute, flower- and bead-bedecked hippies in a doctor's waiting room: Doctor to Nurse: 'Nothing much, one sprained ankle and three with greenfly!'

What was initially characterized as the 'underground culture' of the second half of the 1960s developed alongside of and in central relation to the 'new seriousness' of rock music that was also now emerging. Again the Beatles led the way, at least as far as the youth spectacle was concerned. Under the influence of Bob Dylan, himself a latter-day representative of the American radical-bohemian tradition, and of LSD, they began in the mid-1960s to abandon their previous nice-boy personae, falling all the while from generalized public favour, and to produce increasingly complex and 'meaningful' work. The latter process in turn involved concentrating upon long-playing records rather than singles, and can be seen exemplified in their musical development from the 'Rubber Soul' album in 1965, through 'Revolver' in 1966, to the climactic 'Sergeant Pepper' at the height of the flower power era in 1967 (see Melly, 1972: 78–82).

By this time the Beatles had lost much of their 'respectable' adult support, but they had gained the imputed if not self-claimed status of spokesmen and leaders of the new counter-cultural generation, setting trends in such fashionable areas as drug use, mysticism and meditation that were widely publicized and perhaps emulated the world over. Following the Beatles' lead, and responding to the general mood of the times, most of the British 'rock aristocracy' also became 'artistically serious', 'mystical' – later 'political' – and heavily committed to illegal drugs and all things underground.

The Rolling Stones in particular became victims of the building 1967 British 'panic' about drug use that had been given considerable extra impetus by the emergence of the hippies, as the story of the prosecution and brief imprisonment of Mick Jagger and Keith Richards for minor drug offences – following a police raid on a party at Richards's home – provided the popular media with a great deal of highly titillatory copy throughout the summer of that year.[19] In the late 1960s the image of the (hippy/rock star) drug-taker came for a while to be close to occupying the youthful folk devil role which had usually been reserved for high visibility working-class subcultural types such as the Teddy boy or the mods and rockers (see Young, 1972). This highly negative minority stereotyping of the hippy/drugtaker was in some ways further reinforced in the late 1960s when the wave of youthful – largely student – activism and demonstrations of the period blurred this image with that of Revolutionary Youth in general, and that of the Revolutionary Student in particular: social types which themselves enjoyed considerable elements of folk devil status. Such minority stereotyping of radical youth began to set in in Britain as a major theme of the contemporary youth spectacle in the summer following the 'Summer of Love', as protests against the Vietnam war grew larger and more directly confrontational in their nature. The following account from the *Daily Mirror* of 1968 of the first Grosvenor Square peace demonstration of that year is fairly representative:

'HOOLIGANS ON RAMPAGE AT BIG PEACE RALLY'
Hooligans turned a Vietnam peace rally into one of London's worst riots . . . a 1,000 strong mob broke away from the rally and went on a five-mile rampage of terror and destruction through the West End.
. . . outside the Royal Academy in Piccadilly, youths tore down Union Jacks and trampled on them. . . . (22 July)

This is only one half of the picture, however. The totality of images and meanings that came to be associated with the phenomenon of the Counter Culture as a whole – employing the term here in a catch-all sense – was in fact extremely wide in its range along the continuum of positive and negative evaluations, and embodied many contradictions. This may in part have been due to the essentially middle-class membership of the Counter Culture as a whole – well-educated sons and daughters of the middle and ruling classes are much less readily typed unambiguously in the role of folk devils. It was also certainly due in part to the diverse and diffuse strands of youthful protest that went to make up the counter-cultural milieu in its entirety.[20] To make the obvious crude division, the original hippies with their naive creed of anti-materialism and 'love and peace' were often favourably received by popular and serious adult opinion – even their drug-taking was by no means universally condemned – whereas the later 'violent' student radicals were the subject of a generally more adverse reaction, both in the media and also on the receiving end of police truncheons. Even in the latter case, however, the reaction was far from totally negative, if one considers the more 'progressive' and radical elements within adult opinion as a whole.

These considerations point to the conclusion that more than any other aspect of the youth spectacle before or since, the image of Counter-Cultural Youth, with its apparently transcendent or revolutionary goals, provided the opportunity for social commentators and analysts to make a wide range of displaced and projective points about the ills of current society and the likely or desirable features of the future – in this case widely interpreted in terms of nothing short of the *future of humanity*. Early images of 'Counter Culture' from the late 1960s are often in fact quite positive in tone.

The hippies were of course initially and perhaps essentially an American phenomenon – the latest in a line of native bohemianisms – emerging most notably in San Francisco in the mid-1960s and first exploding into the youth spectacle in the USA and Great Britain during the 'Summer of Love' of 1967.[21] Amongst the initial pieces of journalism which precipitated the rise of the hippy phenomenon to its eventual status as the focus of world-wide media attention, and which undoubtedly itself did much to swell the 'movement' was the *Time* cover story of that summer, which began thus:

Whatever their meaning and wherever they may be headed, the hippies have emerged on the US scene as a wholly new sub-culture, a bizarre permutation of the middle class American ethos from which it evolved. Hippies preach altruism and mysticism, honesty, joy and non-violence. They find an almost childlike fascination in beads, blossoms and bells, blinding strobe lights and ear shattering music, exotic clothing and erotic slogans. Their professed aim is nothing less than the subversion of Western society by 'flower power' and force of example.[22]

The same article also set the tone for much of the subsequent commentary on the topic of the hippies and Counter Culture in general in its concluding remarks:

It could be argued that in their independence of material possessions and their emphasis on peacefulness and honesty, hippies lead considerably more meaningful lives than the great majority of their fellow citizens . . . [this] helps explain why so many people in authority treat them gently and with a measure of respect. In the end it may be that the hippies have not so much dropped out of American society as given it something to think about. (Brown, 1967: 13)

What this 'something to think about' often turned out to be was the fairly widely promoted notion that the hippies could be understood as a kind of revolt against their parent society's materialism, and a rehearsal for a future, post-industrial society where affluence and technological change would render the work ethic redundant, thus making the way clear for the development of previously suppressed potentialities within 'Western man'. Another contemporary American commentator elaborated thus upon these themes in connection with the hippies' use of LSD:

I think therefore that the use of psychedelic drugs by large numbers of our young people may well have cultural significance of immense scope, resulting in a new – for us – definition of what man is and his place in the universe should be. We may in a very real sense become like primitive or Eastern man, not, indeed, abjuring the progress we have made as a civilization, but going no further except, perhaps, to perfect the automation that will allow us to function in a society without working 'by the sweat of our brows'. (Earisman, 1968: 98)

As the hippy phenomenon and its accompanying media attention spread, so too these themes were taken up by social commentators elsewhere. In Britain for example the *Observer* of 28 September 1969 carried a feature by Rudolph Klein relating to the recent wave of 'hippy' squattings in unoccupied buildings in central London – which predictably enough had received a thoroughly bad press at the level of news – on 'Why the Hippies Matter'. Here the connection between the concepts of youth and affluence that had been building throughout the 1960s was taken to its extreme: the hippies, 'the portents of what is to come' were seen as a youthful reaction against the age of affluence which – somewhat paradoxically – was made possible *through affluence*. The feature assumed that British society would continue to become more and more affluent, and because of technological changes, less dominated by the necessity for adults to be engaged in full-time work. In this context the hippies could be seen, the piece argued, as the possible 'beginning of a larger movement' representing the future of humanity as a whole:

> What we may be seeing is nothing less than the beginning of the collapse of the whole Puritan ethos which has dominated the advanced industrial societies of the West for the past 150 years. Just as the pill has completed the destruction of the Puritan ethos of sex, so affluence is beginning to undermine the Puritan ethos of work. Here is a group which challenges the entire assumption on which the wealth of industrial countries has been built. . . .[23]

This view of the hippies as the vanguard of post-industrial society and the embodiment of the post-industrial human being was in fact central to conceptions of the Counter Culture as a whole. In one form or another it crops up in the views of serious and sympathetic adult commentators of the time and also in the self-perceptions of the 'movement' itself, on both its cultural and political wings.[24] It represents a culmination of the cult of youth in the further highly significant sense that here the age grade of youth is seen as extending upwards through and enveloping what had previously been seen and defined as adulthood. The hippies and members of the Counter Culture in general were not merely chronologically and socially post-adolescent and pre-adult in their dropping out from 'the system', it was argued. They were seen as actively engaged in a refusal to *ever* 'grow up' and indeed in a subversion of the previously linear structuring of the human life-cycle.

In their practical denial of the existential centrality of work, of the work ethic and of the quest for material possessions, the hippies were seen as denying a core component of the conventional, contemporary Western definition of adulthood and maturity. In a post-industrial society, the argument ran, adult *work* in the accepted sense would no longer be necessary, and *play*, previously the more or less exclusive property of the pre-adult, would become the dominant social activity and goal. In such a society therefore no one would ever need to 'grow up' and youthful values would predominate; such an ideal had yet to be realized, but meanwhile the Counter Culture was actively exploring the full range of post-industrial possibilities (Neville, 1971).

Notwithstanding such arguments, the positive aspects of the image of the Counter Culture as represented by the original hippies became increasingly tempered by more negative evaluations as intergenerational conflict became more pronounced – in image and reality – in the late 1960s and early 1970s. In Britain and elsewhere a backlash was setting in against the currents of liberalization that had been at work in society earlier in the decade, and this was in many respects brought to a head – thereby further politicizing aspects of the Counter Culture and further polarizing its antagonism to 'straight' society – in the response of society's control agents to the perceived threat posed by Revolutionary Youth.[25] The year 1968 was the year of world-wide student insurrection – notably 'May 68' in France – and specifically in Britain of the increasingly heavily policed and consequently violent second and third Grosvenor Square demonstrations and of the first 'troubles' at the London School of Economics, Essex University, Hornsey Art College and Hull University.[26] At the level of news – if not always of analysis – much of the youth spectacle as both internally and externally (largely American but seemingly also 'globally') derived, now came to centre on demonstrations, police 'busts' of Counter-Culture institutions, and sit-ins, and on the mainly negative images of Youth Revolution in general and Revolutionary Students in particular.

Although in many respects the fruit of seeds of radicalism which had been sown earlier in the decade – SDS in America, CND in Britain – and which were now fertilized perhaps above all else by the Vietnam war, the wave of student activism of the late 1960s seems to have taken most commentators by surprise in both its quantitative and qualitative extents. 'The Uncommitted' of the early 1960s had seemingly become *en masse* 'Young Radicals'.[27]

The concept of Youth Revolution not only received a great deal of (unfavourable) mass media attention at this time, it also became very quickly the focus for a great deal of academic theorizing.[28] Starting from the common, undoubtedly real, phenomenon of student unrest, social analysts of all ideological persuasions were caught up in a rush to explain what was then widely considered as 'society's number one problem'. Conservative explanations ranged from Freudian formulations concerning 'Oedipal hatred' to the equation of student radicals with juvenile delinquents. Liberal or radical interpretations both from outsiders and from within the 'movement' itself, on the other hand, all tended to stress in one way or another the idea that it was now the 'class' of youth that represented the major hope or even promise for the long overdue (revolutionary) transformation of society.[29]

This latter idea – now patently naive and unrealistic – represented the final working-through of the notion of the primacy of the dimension of generation over the other divisions of society, and the final component of the climax of the cult of youth.

Conclusion: Into the 1990s: 'Plus ça Change . . .'

The preceding chapters have explored the historical processes of the conceptualization, institutionalization and universalization of adolescence/youth as a distinct age grade (processes which had their roots in the mid-nineteenth century if not before, but which were to culminate finally post Second World War) and the ways in which over the same period this stage of the life-cycle also began to take on a special subjective sociocultural significance by virtue of its metaphorical or projective utility to the project of *making sense* of a seemingly rapidly and fundamentally changing social order. By the late Victorian and Edwardian period the youth question – and in particular the question of working-class youth – had already come to be identified with the broader questions of the future of Britain and of the nation's peculiar strengths and weaknesses. The prominent youth question discourse of this time can therefore not only be seen as embodying demands that youth itself be increasingly formally *contained* (especially in the face of concern over rising juvenile delinquency) and *trained*; it can also in part be read as a reflection – even sometimes a displacement – of wider and more fundamental social concerns and anxieties. Thus statements ostensibly 'about youth' from this period evince at a deeper level fears concerning the decline of the British Empire, the possibility of ever-deepening class conflict and the impact of urbanization, to name the three perhaps most salient and basic themes.

The inter-war period, in contrast to the one which had immediately preceded it, was a time when initially at least the youth question enjoyed a more limited prominence, and in which negative or hostile images of working-class youth in particular were relatively little to the fore. (The period's low recorded levels of juvenile delinquency are clearly of significance here.) However, as the Great Depression of the 1930s set in and rates of delinquency began once more to rise, so also the youth question debate began to reflect a concern over the likely psycho-social impact of unemployment on the current younger generation and over the projected long-term consequences of this for the future of the nation as a whole. Here it is possible to see an early expression of the idea of *youth as national asset* – not to be squandered but rather in urgent need of 'proper' development – that was also emerging in the period's official educational and social policy statements and that was to form so central a component of the post-war youth question. The inter-war period also saw the establishment, initially with reference to the image of disaffected middle-class youth, of 'generational' modes of social thought that were once again to culminate post-war in the – for a time prevalent – belief that it was *age* rather than class that was coming to constitute the major structural principle of society, and that it was *youth* – for better or worse – that was becoming the major dynamic force in a 'new' social order.

This 'cult of youth' really took off, however, in the 1950s, fuelled by social structural and institutional shifts that served as never before to single out adolescence/youth as a distinct and 'special' age grade (increased educational and recreational provision and the rise of the teenage consumer were the two most significant – if by no means always mutually reinforcing – factors here) and given further impetus through the ever-multiplying images of the youth spectacle as manifest in the mass media. (It is worth noting again here that in this era of more or less full employment the young were also much in demand simply as a source of labour.) In a period whose overall social, economic and political discourse was so permeated by the – largely mythical – ideas of affluence, consensus and embour-geoisement, the idealized image of the Teenager reflected and symbolized all that was seen as 'newest' and most 'different' about contemporary society. The idea of youth as a new, unified and progressive culture – an emergent 'classless' class indeed – the product of post-war, post-industrial affluence, and the equation of youth with a 'bright new future' was raised to a higher power and reached its peak in the transcendent images of Youth Revolution and Counter Culture of the late 1960s.

The equation of youth with the national future also reached a high point in the 1950s and 60s in a range of official and unofficial youth question statements embodying variations on the well-established theme of youth as a national asset, themselves produced in direct or indirect response to the underlying realities of Britain's loss of empire and status abroad, and continuing class conflict, slow economic growth and lagging technological innovation at home. In this case, while the analysis of the national future advanced was predominantly bleak, unlike that implicit in the myth of affluence, the image of youth presented remained basically *positive*: youth was the great national resource which if correctly and sufficiently utilized could still provide the way out of the nation's troubles.

At the same time, however, it should be stressed once more that the period's overall preoccupation with youth was from the start an essentially *ambivalent* phenomenon. It was clearly possible to view the advent of the Teenager – and later the Counter Culture – as some did, as a portent of *worse* things to come rather than better. More fundamentally, the rising juvenile delinquency statistics of the 1950s and the appearance of first the Teddy boys, and then a whole range of youthful minority stereotypes and folk devils in the youth spectacle, marked the beginning of a response to youth that was essentially negative, hostile or even fearful in nature. Here negative and often highly unrepresentative and overdrawn images of specific sectors of youth came to stand in the classic, projective, minority stereotypical relationship to more diffuse yet fundamental anxieties about national decline, both internally and externally. The dark side of the positive cult of the Teenager was the more generalized minority stereotypical process in evidence from the 1950s onwards whereby the threatening image of deviant working-class youth 'spilled over' into the image of *youth as a whole*: at the same time as he or she was seen as the trailblazer of the new order, the Teenager was also feared as a new and particularly threatening problem of social control. Such anxieties were considerably heightened from the mid-1960s onwards by the appearance in the youth spectacle of specifically *middle-class* forms of youthful deviance of a seemingly quantitatively and qualitatively different order from anything previously encountered. The image and moment of Youth Revolution from the late 1960s and early 1970s, as well as marking the high point of the cult of youth, also saw the beginning of its dissolution.

There was a kind of cumulative internal logic involved in the progression of youth-associated images and meanings from the emergence of the Teenager in the late 1950s, through 'Swinging London' in the mid-1960s, to the Counter Culture in the late 1960s and early 1970s. At each step in this progression the positive cult of youth can be said to have become further advanced, while the concept and category of youth itself took on an ever-widening, and also less objectively realistic, frame of reference. Thus the Teenager as a semi-mythical social type may have been 'classless' but he or she was also definitely *adolescent* chronologically and socially, and (merely) the youthful harbinger of an affluent consumer society. In the mythical complex of 'Swinging London', on the other hand, the idea of extended youth and *youthfulness* began to detach itself from its original anchorage in the adolescent age group. The mythical 'New Aristocracy' was young by virtue of its qualities, culture and life-style, which were in turn attuned to the 'revolutionary' mood and requirements of the 'new Britain' of the early to mid-1960s. This image of youth therefore cast the quasi-group thus identified in an *active* role in the processes of social transformation that were then widely regarded as being under way.

The vision of social transformation of this period was still, however, couched in terms of ever-expanding consumerism within an overall social and political consensus, and as such youth was seen as revitalizing, but not fundamentally changing, the existing order. In the closing years of the decade, however, this vision began to shatter, and one of the most basic signs – and 'causes' – of this was the dramatic rise of the Counter Culture and student activism. In one sense these phenomena represented a culmination for the cult of youth. Middle-class adolescents and post-adolescents *en masse* were now seen as ushering in the revolution of a post-industrial, post-affluent, post-rational society where *no-one* would ever 'grow up'.

At the same time, however, such images of youth were simply becoming too contradictory, both internally and also in aspects of their 'fit' with wider social realities. The blanket term 'Counter Culture' itself embraced a diverse and diffuse range of phenomena, some of which from the outset were more capable of being favourably interpreted in adult opinion than others. More than this the image and concept of Counter-Cultural Youth also embodied a number of contradictions at a more general level. This phenomenon as a whole was widely regarded as a luxury of an affluent, materially bounteous, late industrial social order, and yet at the same time it also seemed to represent a retreat from and rejection of material plenty. Similarly the Counter Culture was seen as a utopian movement, a necessary and desirable pilot study in post-industrial living and the potentialities of human liberation, and yet at the same time hippies and student militants alike were increasingly coming to be cast in the role of highly dangerous and subversive folk devils, whose ascendency could only lead to dystopia, chaos and anarchy. The Counter-Cultural promise and ideal implied never growing up, and yet in a whole range of ways people continued to do so. These and other contradictions interacted with the tightening economic, political and ideological circumstances of the early 1970s in such a way as to bring to a halt, and then fairly rapidly reverse, the building idea of social transformation through youth.

The climax reached specifically by the *cult* of youth in the late 1960s and early 1970s has therefore remained unsurpassed, and is unlikely to be so in the foreseeable future. By the same token, the idea of social regeneration through youth and the 'inverse minority stereotyping' of the whole or part of the younger generation have also now largely ceased to be of significance. What has remained has been almost entirely a matter of moral panics and minority stereotyping.

The youth spectacle has continued as a prominent feature of the overall social spectacle down until the present day, and has in many respects itself come to be institutionalized through the attentions of the media and the market. The specifics change, subcultures, styles, problem adolescents and youth problems come and go, but the spectacle itself remains, as does the close linkage between images of youth and diagnoses of the condition of England. Youth still possesses a power to fascinate if not to incite adult admiration and emulation. Since the demise of the cult of youth proper, the *range* of such images has similarly come to be locked into a restricted and largely negative cycle. Thus from the 1970s onwards the youth spectacle has been dominated by images of working-class and/or ethnic minority problem adolescents or young people, often cast as folk devils in relation to some semi-mythical form of deviance and all set against a backdrop of generalized youth unemployment.

The first signs of this reversal were in fact to be fairly clearly read in the late 1960s. Urban working-class youth is, as a group, particularly vulnerable to economic recession and generalized material decline. It is in the context of the rising youth un-employment and inner-city decay of the latter part of the 1960s that the emergence of the working-class youth subculture of the skinheads must be located. The style and culture of this group – the boots, cropped hair and braces, exaggerated machismo and intense territoriality – has been taken as an expression of the 'downwardly socially mobile option' (see P. Cohen, 1972). It seems likely, however, that 'option' is the wrong term here for a group that was responding directly, albeit within limits creatively, to an increasingly stringent and limiting set of objective material circumstances. This was what essentially differentiated the skinheads from the mods, since the latter subculture may well have been not merely symbolically exploring the 'upward option' but also, in the expansionist climate of the early 1960s, was actually faced with at least some small possibility for *real* mobility and material advancement. The essentially middle-class Counter-Cultural hippies and students of the late 1960s were even further removed from a directly constraining set of material circumstances, and thus even 'freer' to elaborate creative, complex and potentially progressive sociocultural forms. The appearance of the skinheads in the arena of the youth spectacle proclaimed a major break in this progression.

At the subjective level of image and meaning – which in this case does not seem to have been too far removed from objective reality – the skinheads, with their violent antipathy towards those perceived as 'hippies' and minority groups in general, and their caricatured lumpen proletarian style and stance, represented a return to the unambiguously deviant male working-class position last occupied by the Teds.[1] As such, the skinheads marked a very considerable regression from the positive cult of youth that was at this time still flourishing in other areas of the youth spectacle, and pointed the way for much of what was to follow. Nearly all shades of serious opinion, including much of that of the Counter Culture and the New Left, saw the skinheads as 'reactionary', a problem and even a threat.

The downward trend in the image of youth signalled by the appearance of the skinheads was to continue throughout the 1970s and 1980s. From the outset the skinheads had been associated, in reality and image, with what was seen as the 'new' social problem of football hooliganism.[2] As the 1970s wore on, the Football Hooligan was to be elevated to one of the major positions in the gallery of working-class deviant youthful types that was increasingly to form the focus for the youth spectacle. The Football Hooligan, shorn of his earlier skinhead guise, and now made over in a newly 'casual' and 'affluent' style, has continued to haunt the youth question of the 1980s accompanied – more recently – by his close relations the Lager Lout and the Rural Rowdy.[3] As the 1970s have been succeeded by the 1980s the perceived threat of deviant working-class youth has been further compounded with the fraught issue of race as the image of the Black Mugger has been succeeded by that of the Inner City Rioter.[4]

In terms of the succession of highly visible working-class youth subcultures the line of development from the skinheads onwards was to remain for some years unclear with a range of part-commercial, part-original styles and groupings – Crombies, Bowie-ites *et al.* – at various times enjoying fairly widespread allegiance, but never fully taking off at the level of spectacle.[5] Finally, in 1977, following the media outrages perpetrated by the Sex Pistols, punk was to emerge as the major deviant and problem youth subculture of the decade.[6] It is highly debatable as to what extent punk can be seen, even in the first instance, as 'dole queue rock', the symbolic and creative response of sectors of youth itself to the bleak economic circumstances of the late 1970s. One thing is certain though, in common with other predominantly working-class youth subcultural manifestations, its representation in the youth spectacle was in the main yet another variation on the by now well-established theme of minority stereotyping. Punk may for a while have also been an object of serious adult scrutiny and analysis, and certainly as a commodity – an area where the power of youth is still a force to be reckoned with – it enjoyed great success from the most exalted to the humblest level of the cultural market-place.

In the early 1980s the image of punk was largely superseded by that of the relatively 'safe' New Romantics, but in 1989 yet another youth-centred moral panic would appear to be building around the (possibly predominantly middle-class) subculture of 'Acid House'.[7] A return to a more positive evaluation of youth culture and subculture, whether working class or otherwise, still seems un-likely. In the meantime it has certainly fallen largely to working-class youth to bear the brunt of the economic recession whilst at the same time providing the raw material for the manufacture of new minority stereotypical folk devils, and therefore the justification for the ever more overt mobilization of the forces of social control.

Compared to the heyday of the Counter Culture and student radicalism, middle-class youth has reverted over the same period to an essentially quiescent position, and youthful qualities and values have ceased to be widely held up as of special social significance.[8] (It is of course questionable whether in reality they were ever otherwise.) Images of middle-class youth from other facets of the youth spectacle, whilst not entirely negative, have continued to reflect a deep ambivalence over the condition and direction of Britain in the 1980s. Thus the semi-mythical figures of the Sloane Ranger and – especially – the Yuppie have been widely viewed as the embodiment of the culture of Thatcherism, generally in a far from approving manner. It is interesting to note the proliferation of 'Yuppies get their come-uppance' media items that followed in the wake of the Stock Market crash of 1987.

Throughout the 1980s the climate of economic recession and constricting material circumstances has been too harsh to support the continuance of any large-scale positive cult of youth. Youth unemployment has persisted as perhaps the central issue of the youth question. At the same time youth subcultures and groupings have themselves become too fragmentary – and too commercial, too deviant or too alienated in image – to sustain the idea of youth as a ('progressive') class. For the present the youth spectacle would seem to be locked into the more or less routine and institutionalized portrayal of the latest youth fashions and fads, of the latest youthful deviants and sometime folk devils, and of ever-multiplying youth-centred social problems. Beneath the continuance of such images the true potential of all of youth as indeed the nation's major asset still goes largely unrealized, the continuing rhetoric of youth training and educational reform notwithstanding.

Nonetheless as we move towards the twenty-first century there is a gleam on the horizon in terms of the *prospect* for the whole of youth in the shape of the radically changing demographic profile of British society. Since a peak in 1964, the birth rate has been falling dramatically, with the likely consequence that between 1985 and 2025 the number of 15–24-year-olds will drop by just over 2 million; between 1985 and 1996 alone the number of 15–19-year-olds is set to decline by over one million (Wicks, 1988). Significantly fewer young people in absolute terms and an expansion of the proportion of this group in education and training should combine to produce a 23 per cent reduction of 16–19-year-olds in the British workforce, from 2.5 million to 1.9 million, over the period 1988–95 (Penycate, 1988). (The current target for the proportion of young people in higher education by the turn of the century is 18.5 per cent as against 13.5 per cent in 1985, although this proportional increase will still mean a decline in students under 21 in absolute terms) (ibid.).

The implications of this imminent scarcity of youth – the 'baby bust' as it has imaginatively been termed – are considerable, not only for the young themselves but also for such other potential sources of labour as women currently not engaged in full-time work outside of the home, and are only now being grasped by employers, social policy-makers and social analysts alike. At the very least, while the high birth rate of the mid-1960s underpinned the high youth unemployment of the early 1980s, the falling birth rate of the 1970s and 80s will undoubtedly lead to a situation in which *appropriately qualified* young people will be very much at a premium, and courted accordingly by potential employers in Britain as indeed throughout Europe, where similar or even greater demographic shifts are likewise in process. One image of youth for the 1990s has already been encapsulated in a Department of Employment poster depicting a pigtailed teenage schoolgirl as a mounted big game hunter's trophy! Certainly many major employers are already setting out to capture and retain their required quota of the species through such inducements as cheap mortgages, course sponsorships, and non-contributory pension schemes.

The force of sheer demographic necessity then may well lead to a situation when at long last the idea of youth as a national asset or resource, to be properly and fully developed, will need to be taken seriously. Similarly, on demographic grounds alone, the idea of youth *en masse* as an urgent problem of social control would seem set to recede. Whether these projections will apply across the board to *the whole* of the younger generation is of course another matter. While British society remains as unequal as it is at present, and while the educational system serves in some large measure to reproduce that inequality, a more pessimistic but perhaps more probable scenario would envisage persistent youth unemployment for a significant unqualified minority and, in the face of increased youthful affluence in many social strata and sectors, the deepening of youth-centred social problems. It remains to be seen whether the youthful beneficiaries of the 'new demographics' also come to constitute a real or imagined 'problem group'; they may well do so in one way or another, but given their likely indebtedness to the status quo in the form of student loans, mortgages, etc., a re-run of

1960s radicalism and of the image of youth as an active force for social change would seem unlikely. Images of youth in the 1990s and beyond are set to remain as contradictory and polarized as ever, but in all probability the alienated and disadvantaged young will continue to occupy centre stage. The extent to which this prediction proves untrue will be a measure of the extent to which our society succeeds in moving finally beyond the *rhetoric* of 'youth as national asset' to the provision of *real* opportunities for all young people.

What then, finally, does a detailed focus upon youth, or more precisely upon *social responses to youth*, have to tell us in relation to the broader question of the extent of conflict and change in twentieth-century British society?

At the level specifically of the much-vaunted idea of intergenerational conflict, the present work has sought to argue that, whilst this has been a real enough phenomenon with respect to certain individuals and groups in certain specific social and historical contexts, there has nonetheless existed – and continues to exist – a strong tendency for the case to be overstated. The image of individual adolescents, of 'problem' youth subcultures and phenomena, and at times of youth as a whole has, with certain exceptions associated with the 'cult of youth' in the post-war period proper, tended to focus on conflict and social dysfunction when conformity and at least potential eufunction have been the norm. As has been argued, the persistence and power of the *myth* of pronounced and extensive intergenerational conflict derives in part from the currency of certain social scientific theories around adolescence and youth (storm and stress, role moratorium, subcultural theory, generationalism, etc.) which were themselves developed in tandem with – and thus helped to construct – the emergence of adolescence/youth as a distinct age grade. Beyond this, however, it has also been further argued that this socially problematic and conflict-ridden view of youth has had particular resonances in a period which has seemingly been characterized by rapid and all-pervasive social change. In this context, as has now been explored at length, images of youth, often of an unwarrantedly heightened and negative nature, have indeed come to stand in a kind of projective relationship to the formulation of diagnoses of the nature and implications of social change itself.

That considerable change has occurred at social-structural and institutional levels in twentieth-century British society would seem to be beyond dispute.[9] (And indeed one aspect of this has been the changing situation of youth itself as charted above.) Externally, furthermore, Britain's position in the international order has clearly undergone a marked decline over the same period and such a decline has undoubtedly played its part in the persistence of a generalized and acute sense of anxiety over the state of the nation (such anxieties are certainly there to be read in the discourse surrounding the youth question). It is probably also reasonable to assume – although here the case becomes less directly tangible and the question of *continuity* within apparent change becomes ever more pressing – that the present century has seen considerable shifts in the realms of culture, beliefs and values.

What is more questionable, however, is whether such changes as have occurred in twentieth-century British society – and in the period since 1945 in particular – have been significantly 'greater' in either quantitative or qualitative terms, or 'faster' than at any other time in the modern era. The reality of rapid social change, and perhaps even more significantly the *sense* of rapid social change, would seem to be fundamental to the modern condition. It is now generally accepted that the origins of sociology itself are closely bound up with an attempt to come to terms at both theoretical and practical levels with the newly emergent urban-industrial-capitalist social order of the late eighteenth and early nineteenth centuries.[10] It is also arguable, however, that all of the classical sociologists produced theories which in one way or another foreshortened the timing and overestimated the speed and extensiveness of the undoubtedly momentous processes of social transformation to which they bore witness.[11] From its inception right down until the present day, sociological theory has indeed tended to conceptualize social change in terms of more or less clear-cut breaks of a fundamental nature (pre-industrial/industrial/post-industrial; traditional/modern/ [and currently particularly fashionable] post-modern) whereas the trend of change, whilst extensive and rapid enough in many senses, has nonetheless been essentially uneven, embodying leads, lags and even continuities.

If each generation of professional theorists of social change has considered itself as astride some major historical watershed, such a tendency has been even more pronounced in *popular* analyses of the condition and direction of British society. The recent preoccupation with youth as documented in the foregoing chapters provides a major case in point. We have seen how time and time again the projective relationship between images of youth and diagnoses of the state of the nation tends, through its evocation of the idea of generational disjuncture, towards the vision of the opening up of a fundamental break, for worse *or* for better, between 'now' and the 'then' of not so long ago. Rapid social change must always put the youth question on the public agenda, but there would seem to be a particular affinity between the perception of social change as punctuated by a succession of epocal breaks and the prevalence of unduly heightened images of youth. This was perhaps especially so in the period from 1945 until roughly 1975 (the 'post-war period': the very terminology is loaded towards the idea of a new era) when the equally distorted images of youth as a new and particularly threatening social problem and youth as an active force for social regeneration flourished in uneasy coexistence.

Notes

Chapter 1

1.   The pages of *New Society*, from its inception in 1962 until its demise in 1988, provide an excellent overview both of this 'explosion' of youth subcultures, styles, etc., and also of the period's *interest in and concern about* youth. See also the anthology edited by T. Raison, *Youth in New Society* (1966) for the period 1962–65.

2.   The classic British study in this respect must by now be S. Cohen, *Folk Devils and Moral Panics* (1980). See also S. Hall *et al.*, *Policing the Crisis* (1978) on the 'mugging panic' of the mid-1970s.

3.   See J. C. Coleman, *The Nature of Adolescence* (1980), pp. 2–11 for further discussion of the *theoretical* view of adolescence that has come to be developed in academic psychology, psychoanalysis and sociology. One intention of Coleman in this study is to highlight the discrepancies between this theoretical (or 'classical') picture of adolescence with that which emerges from empirical research.

4.   In this case the context being the American 'end of ideology' debate of the 1950s and early 1960s. It is interesting to note in this respect how Douvan and Adelson ultimately sought to connect their own empirical findings with the arguments of one of the period's influential speculative-social critical commentators on youth, Edgar Z. Friedenberg (of whom more later): 'These rather dismal conclusions', they write, 'are akin to those stated by Edgar Friedenberg in his brilliant book *The Vanishing Adolescent*. Adolescence, he says, is disappearing as the period in which the individual can achieve a decisive articulation of the self . . . the passions, the restlessness, the vivacity of adolescence are partly strangled, and partly drained off, in the mixed childishness and false adulthood of the adolescent teen culture' (p. 354).

5.   The Eppels' sample for their survey of adolescent values was made up of 250 male and female working-class 15–18-year-olds in London who had left school and were attending day-release classes. Musgrove administered his various projective tests and questionnaires to a total of approximately 775 boys and girls aged 9–15 in six Midlands schools; the bulk of his analyses

however rest on a smaller sub-sample within this group (see ch. 5, pp. 85–105, 'Inter-Generational Attitudes'). The Eppels's analysis of adult attitudes towards youth was based upon the sampling of a small number of London magistrates, probation officers and youth leaders, with only a 20 per cent response rate, while Musgrove's survey of adult attitudes in two Midlands towns fared little better in this respect, with a response rate of approximately 33 per cent.

6.   J. Nicholson, *Seven Ages* (1980). Note also the London Weekend Television series of the same title. Nicholson and his team interviewed 600 men, women and children, on the topic of the experience of ageing, in Colchester in the winter of 1979–80. Further in-depth interviews were carried out with a sub-sample of 80 individuals in the 19–60 age range. The general thrust of Nicholson's findings is towards a refutation of the conceptualization of the human life-cycle as a sequence of distinct and unique psychological stages, and especially of the view, popularized by Gail Sheehy and others, that the adult life-cycle can be seen as punctuated by a series of 'predictable crises' (see Sheehy, *Passages* (1977)).

7.   Here the working chronological definition of adolescence is the 11–17 age range: see Nicholson, *Seven Ages*, ch. 2, pp. 58–97. On the 'post adolescent' years (roughly 18–25) see *ibid.*, ch. 3, pp. 98–122.

8.   Chapter by chapter Coleman examines adolescent physical development (pp. 12–24); thinking and reasoning (pp. 25–52); self concept and development (pp. 43–63); the role of parents and other adults (pp. 64–95); friendship and the peer group (pp. 96–120); sexuality (pp. 121–46); and turmoil and treatment (pp. 147–76). In each case theoretically derived hypotheses are found to be out of accord with empirically derived research findings. Note, however, the critique of Coleman's own 'focal theory' of adolescence as advanced in Coffield *et al.*, *Growing up at the Margins*, pp. 211–12.

9.   The term 'hooligan' now tends to conjure up one stereotypical image above all others – that of the 'football hooligan'. For an 'inside' account of football hooliganism as meaningful and ordered behaviour for its participants, and therefore for a rejection of the common external attribution of this behaviour as meaningless and irrational, see Marsh, Rosser and Harre, *The Rules of Disorder* (1978). For a history of 'hooliganism' – and the social anxieties that have accompanied it – in a wider sense, see Geoffrey Pearson, *Hooligan* (1983).

10.   Here I am following the loose classificatory terminology employed by Stan Cohen in his discussion and critique of recent developments in the British sociology of youth in the introduction to *Folk Devils and Moral Panics* (1980 edn). The major works subsumed under this rubric are S. Hall and T. Jefferson (eds), *Resistance Through Rituals* (1976); D. Robbins and P. Cohen, *Knuckle Sandwich* (1978); G. Mungham and G. Pearson (eds) *Working Class Youth Culture* (1976); D. Hebdige, *Subculture: The*

Meaning of Style (1979); P. Willis, *Learning to Labour* (1978); and Corrigan, *Schooling the Smash Street Kids* (1979). The acknowledged theoretical starting point for the 'new subcultural theory' is to be found in Phil Cohen's seminal paper 'Subcultural Conflict and Working Class Community', *University of Birmingham Working Papers in Cultural Studies* no. 2 (1972). The classic text of what might now be termed as the 'old subcultural theory' is A. K. Cohen, *Delinquent Boys* (1955), of which more later.

Perhaps the most distinctive and central feature of the work of this group as a whole is in fact summed up by the phrase 'resistance through rituals': the working-class youth subcultures of post-war Britain – whether they be spectacular leisure-based subcultures such as the mods or skinheads or the delinquent subcultures of the classroom or shop floor – are analysed in terms of the (generally 'symbolic' or 'misplaced') *resistance* that they are variously seen as proffering to ruling-class or capitalist hegemony.

For the application of this approach to the analysis of the 'disaffection from school work, classroom disobedience, school strikes, larking about, social crime, street-gang violence, rebellious sexual behaviour, absenteeism and acts of industrial sabotage' (p. 1) of working-class children and young people in the period 1889–1939, see S. Humphries, *Hooligans or Rebels?* (1981).

11.   For a discussion of the range of specific stances and formulations of the various new subcultural theorists on this central question of the symbolic (etc.) nature of youth subcultural resistance see S. Cohen, *Folk Devils and Moral Panics*, pp. x–xiv.

12.   Corrigan, *Schooling the Smash Street Kids*; Willis, *Learning to Labour*; and Humphries, *Hooligans or Rebels*, all in one way or another deal centrally with this theme. A poignant and revealing moment in Willis's *Learning to Labour* study is recorded in an edited transcript of a discussion between the author and some of 'the lads' whose resistance to schooling he had previously studied, and who had now in turn read parts of his account and analysis of this (appendix, pp. 194–9). The lads' major reactions were perhaps predictably those of hostility and incomprehension.

13.   For a general discussion of this idea in the context of mid-1960s America see E. Friedenberg, 'Adolescence as a Social Problem', in H. S. Becker (ed.), *Social Problems: A Modern Approach* (1966), pp. 35–75.

14.   For a theoretical statement of the transactional – and relativized – approach to the study of social problems in general see Becker (ed.), *Social Problems*, pp. 1–35. S. Cohen, *Folk Devils and Moral Panics*, can be seen as exemplifying the application of such a perspective to the study of aspects of the youth question in post-war Britain – in this case the mods and rockers moral panic of the mid-1960s.

15.   For further discussion of this point see S. Cohen, *Folk Devils and Moral Panics*, pp. xxi–xxiv.

16.   For a discussion of the concept of metaphor from the point of view of

literary and linguistic theory see T. Hawkes, *Metaphor* (1972). According to Hawkes this concept 'refers to a particular set of linguistic processes whereby aspects of one object are "carried over" or transferred to another object, so that the second object is spoken of as if it were the first' (p. 1). Note however that the metaphorical aspect inherent in discussion of youth is often not consciously perceived by social commentators or analysts.

17.   Re-cast in more properly sociological and historically specific form, such arguments are central to Geoffrey Pearson's *Hooligan*. In this work Pearson demonstrates how in British society each successive historical era has been characterized by anxieties concerning youthful deviance and lawlessness, which are always assumed moreover to be essentially *new* phenomena. In this way a sharp contrast between a highly imperfect present and a mythical (safe and law-abiding) 'golden age' is drawn, and diagnoses of the state of contemporary youth once again come to stand as a metaphor for national decline. The present study, whilst sharing this concern for images of deviant working-class youth, seeks also to broaden out the discussion to the *totality* of images of youth (working-class, middle-class; deviant, conventional; negative, positive . . .) in modern British society and to the *range* of metaphorical or projective relationships in which such images have stood to wider perceptions of social change.

18.   It is also possible for radical social criticism to invoke the image – and perhaps also the reality – of contemporary youth as conformist, quiescent, apathetic, etc., to point the way towards what is regarded as a potentially *worse* future.

This in particular was a theme of the (adult) protestors against conformity, 'greyness', alienation, etc., of middle-class American society in the 1950s and early 1960s. The work of Friedenberg as discussed above can be viewed in this light: Friedenberg saw the (classical) adolescent as a kind of noble savage who was *vanishing* because his qualities of courage, honesty, ardour, etc. were no longer required in an increasingly regimented mass society.

In a similar vein Paul Goodman, writing at the start of the 1960s, saw the 'disaffection of the growing generation' – manifested in widespread working-class juvenile delinquency and middle-class apathy – as the consequence of the absence of a worthwhile world *to grow up into*. Hence for Goodman American youth at this time was merely 'growing up absurd': 'Our abundant society is at present simply deficient in many of the most elementary objective opportunities and worthwhile goals that could make growing up possible' (*Growing Up Absurd* (1970), p. 22).

19.   An excellent example of this is provided by the contradictory nature of the overall media presentation of mod subculture in the mid-1960s. The mods gained considerable media coverage at this time not only as folk devils in connection with Bank Holiday mods v. rockers riots and the subsequent court cases, but also as trendsetters in the 'New Britain' of the

1960s. The latter positive image is exemplified in the *Sunday Times* colour magazine of 2 August 1964 with its adulatory article on, and front page picture of, Denzil the Mod: see Dick Hebdige, 'The Meaning of Mod', in Hall and Jefferson (eds), *Resistance Through Rituals*, pp. 87–96.
20.   On the history of the period 1945–75 see H. Hopkins, *The New Look* (1963); B. Levin, *The Pendulum Years* (1970); P. Lewis, *The Fifties* (1978); P. Calvocoressi, *The British Experience 1945–1975* (1979).

Chapter 2

1.   For overviews see S. N. Eisenstadt, *From Generation to Generation* (1956); F. Henderson-Stewart, *Fundamentals of Age-Group Systems* (1977).
2.   Clearly in societies such as our own the major lines of social division must be regarded as being drawn along the dimensions of class, gender and ethnicity. However, the anthropological literature reveals instances where age grading would appear to occupy a considerably more fundamental position in the overall structuring and stratification of the social order. See e.g. A. C. Hollis, *The Nandi* (1909); E. E. Evans-Pritchard, *The Neur* (1940); M. Wilson, *Good Company: A Study of Nyakyusa Age Villages* (1970).
3.   For the history of education see S. J. Curtis, *History of Education in Great Britain* (1968). On the rise of universal elementary education see N. Middleton and S. Weitzman, *A Place for Everyone* (1976).
4.   Note how Aries stresses that the lack of an *idea* of childhood need not imply a lack of *affection* for children. However, a number of influential family historians have recently argued that up until the dawning of our 'progressive' modern era of child-rearing, indifference and brutality were the common lot of the child (see L. de Mause (ed.), *The History of Childhood* (1974); E. Shorter, *The Making of the Modern Family* (1977); L. Stone, *The Family, Sex and Marriage in England 1500–1800* (1977)). Such arguments should be met with a good deal of scepticism: in the absence of 'direct' evidence (unrepresentative literary sources aside) concerning the *reality* of parent–child relations in past times, all three authors are forced to *infer* levels of sentiment and modes of behaviour on the basis of social structural and demographic data. Thus, in particular, the high infant mortality rate of the medieval and early modern periods is taken as the basis for an imputed situation whereby parents could not afford to 'invest' any significant degree of emotional attachment in the younger generation. Hence the supposedly widespread neglect of children and often their outright abuse. However, we cannot simply *assume* across a wide range of historical societies that neglect and abuse are the necessary and

invariant concomitants of a high mortality rate. An alternative and equally plausible scenario would indeed have children all the more cherished simply because they were so likely to die. For further discussion see E. P. Thompson, 'Happy Families', *New Society*, 8 Sept. 1977, pp. 499–501; J. Davis, *The Favourite Age: The Origins and Rise to Prominence of the Concepts of Adolescence and Youth with Special Reference to the 'Cult of Youth' in Post-War British Society* (PhD thesis, University of Essex, 1982), ch. 2. The latter work is the primary source for the present study as a whole.

5.   See especially L. A. Pollock, *Forgotten Children* (1983). (This work is also highly critical of the 'neglect and abuse' school of the history of childhood as discussed above.) For a sympathetic reassessment of the work of Aries as an important contribution to debates within sociology concerning the genesis and interdependence of our contemporary institutions of childhood, the family and education see C. C. Harris, 'The Changing Relation between Family and Societal Form in Western Society', in M. Anderson (ed.), *Sociology of the Family* (2nd edn, 1980).

6.   The question of the terminological distinction – if such can be made – between 'adolescence' and 'youth' is a notoriously difficult one, with various authors in this field adopting a range of usages and conventions. (On the lack of any one agreed term for *young people* – itself a reflection of the anomalous position of this group in Western societies – see Coffield *et al.*, *Growing up at the Margins*, p. 3). The present study has generally followed the common usage in employing the two terms interchangeably, although at points indicated in the text 'youth' has been employed of choice to refer to the continuation of 'pre-adulthood' beyond the early–mid-teens that has come to characterize contemporary society, and 'adolescence' to denote a specifically biological and psychological frame of reference.

7.   For the argument for adolescence as a 'modern' (i.e. nineteenth-century) phenomenon see J. and V. Demos, 'Adolescence in Historical Perspective', *Journal of Marriage and the Family*, 31 (Nov. 1969), pp. 632–8, and J. F. Kett, 'Adolescence and Youth in Nineteenth Century America', *Journal of Interdisciplinary History*, 2, no. 2 (Autumn 1971), pp. 284–98. On the debate between early modern and modern historians concerning the period of the emergence of adolescence see J. Springhall, *Coming of Age* (1986), pp. 8–37.

8.   See Stone, *The Family, Sex and Marriage in Britain*, pp. 68–72. These rates would of course have fluctuated to a degree over time, and also they probably varied to a degree by social class. Nonetheless 'it was not until about 1750 in England that the level of infant and child mortality began to fall, and the expectation of life at birth began to rise' (ibid., p. 72). Furthermore it was not until the end of the nineteenth century that infant and child mortality and life expectancy began to attain their contemporary

levels across society as a whole. It is for these reasons that the figures cited here can be taken as broadly representative for all of the period under discussion.

9.   For a review of the various practices of the *charivari* throughout traditional and early modern 'Atlantic society' see Shorter, *The Making of the Modern Family*, pp. 216–24. See also Pearson, *Hooligan*, pp. 197–202.

10.   In England this tendency seems to have become more pronounced in the early stages of industrialization. See Gillis, *Youth and History*, p. 42. Also E. Hobsbawm and N. Rudé, *Captain Swing* (1972).

11.   On carnival in general in traditional and early modern society see P. Burke, *Popular Culture in Early Modern Europe* (1978), pp. 178–204.

12.   See also Shorter, *The Making of the Modern Family*, pp. 35–7, for further discussion of the system of 'fostering out' and its implications.

13.   For a detailed discussion of the 'youth abbeys' of the early modern French villages and how the members of these 'played *certain* functions that we attribute to adolescence' see N. Z. Davis, 'The Reasons of Misrule: Youth Groups and Charivaris in Sixteenth Century France', *Past and Present*, 50 (Feb. 1971), pp. 41–75.

14.   A similar line of argument is advanced in Musgrove, *Youth and the Social Order*, p. 127: 'When the young are segregated from the adult world, held in low esteem, and delayed in their entry into adult life they are likely to constitute a potentially deviant population; but when they are segregated from the adult society in a position of high status and power (for instance in warrior groups) a conservative society is the probable result.'

15.   In contradistinction to the concept of age grade, an *age set* was defined by Radcliffe-Brown as 'A recognised and sometimes organised group consisting of persons (often male persons only) who are of the same age'.

16.   On the origins, from the late-sixteenth century onwards, of the aristocratic practice of sending sons on the Grand Tour as a final part of their education see L. Stone, *The Crisis of the Aristocracy* (1967) pp. 313–17. For the end of this practice in the eighteenth and early nineteenth centuries see Stone, *The Family, Sex and Marriage in England 1500–1800*, pp. 451–2.

17.   For a structural-functionalist analysis of this phenomenon see S. N. Eisenstadt, 'Archetypal Patterns of Youth' in E. H. Erikson (ed.), *Youth Change and Challenge* (1963), pp. 24–42.

18.   For the exemplification of these now widely taken-for-granted typifications, see the work of E. Erikson, especially *Identity: Youth and Crisis* (1974).

19.   However, Kett argues that in America the recognition of adolescence proper did not come until the nineteenth century and the 'Second Great Awakening' of religious enthusiasm with its great emphasis on teenage conversion. New England Puritan writers and preachers were certainly much concerned with the dispensing of 'advice to youth' (although Kett

argues that the latter category was used in a highly imprecise fashion) but against this must be balanced the fact that this society was relatively *stable* and largely *agrarian*, and did not therefore present the same possibilities for intergenerational discontinuity and conflict as did a great city such as London.

20.   S. R. Smith, 'Religion and the Conception of Youth in Seventeenth Century England', *History of Childhood Quarterly*, 2 (1975), parts 3–4, pp. 493–516. Here Smith argues counter to the position of Kett, 'Adolescence and Youth'; Pinchbeck and Hewitt, *Children and English Society*; Demos and Demos, 'Adolescence in Historical Perspective'; and others when they assert that any awareness of adolescence as a concept or social reality was lacking until the late nineteenth century.

21.   Kett also points out that medical literature in both Europe and America from the mid-eighteenth century onwards paralleled Rousseau's insistence on the significance of the changes in all spheres of development ushered in by puberty. One indication of this was the emergence of a scientific literature in the late eighteenth and early nineteenth centuries concerning 'masturbatory insanity' – and how to avoid it – that was marked by Samuel A. Tissot's *Onania or a Treatise upon the Disorders Produced by Masturbation* (Lausanne, 1758). This literature was popularized in early nineteenth-century America in a proliferation of books and pamphlets offering 'candid talks with youth'.

22.   It is worth noting at this point that the late eighteenth and early nineteenth centuries were also witness to other historical developments that have proved influential in the formulation of the modern conceptions of adolescence, and which may specifically be considered as further antecedents of *youth* in its extended, middle-class sense. The first of these was the Romantic movement whose ideology and lifestyle can be taken as foreshadowing that of twentieth-century middle-class bohemianisms, especially the hippies (see F. Musgrove, *Ecstacy and Holiness* (1974), ch. 4). The second was the wave of public-school rebellion of the same period which arguably provided a foretaste of the potential for more directly activist forms of radicalism amongst middle-class youth as manifested, par excellence, in the student unrest of the 1960s. (See D. Matza, 'Subterranean Traditions of Youth', *Annals*, 338 (Nov. 1961), pp. 103–18; Curtis, *History of Education in Great Britain*, pp. 126–945; Gillis, *Youth and History*, p. 74).

Chapter 3

1.   On the establishment of universal elementary education in the late nineteenth and early twentieth centuries see Middleton and Weitzman, *A Place for Everyone*, pp. 71–4.

2.   Minutes of the Council of Education 1850–1, p. 119, quoted in Johnson, 'Educational Policy and Social Control'.

3.   For a detailed account of the urban working-class youth subculture(s) and street gangs of the period see Humphries, *Hooligans or Rebels*, pp. 174–208. According to Humphries's extensive oral history-based evidence, the gangfights themselves were generally far more ritualized and less dangerous affairs than has commonly been assumed. Humphries also differentiates between a majority of territorially based and only intermittently (or 'semi') delinquent 'informal' gangs and a minority of delinquent gangs proper which actually constituted a real and abiding threat to property and public safety. See ibid., especially pp. 176–80.

4.   P. Thompson, 'The War With Adults', p. 29. Original quote from Sally Alexander, 'St Giles's Fair', *History Workshop Pamphlet*, 2 (1970) p. 12.

5.   On the expansion of leisure time for working-class youth in this period (and the intervention of the various newly founded youth organizations into this 'gap') see J. Springhall, *Youth, Empire and Society* (1977), esp. introduction and conclusion. On the commercial exploitation of youth through the music hall and the public house see Gillis, *Youth and History*. On the cinema as a focus for early twentieth-century anxiety about youthful immorality see P. Thompson, 'The War With Adults', p. 35 and *The Edwardians*, p. 75. On the history of commercially provided leisure pursuits for adolescents (music hall, football, cinema, 'Penny Dreadfuls') from the 1860s until the early twentieth century, and the adult middle-class anxieties and interventions provoked by each of these see Springhall, *Coming of Age*, ch. 4.

6.   The identification of this newly-emergent problem of the discipline of the post-school age group should not, however, by any means be taken as indicating that the problem of discipline amongst working-class schoolchildren had actually been 'solved'. See Humphries, *Hooligans or Rebels?*, pp. 28–130 for the varied and extensive resistance of working-class children to state schooling over the period 1889–1939.

7.   It is unclear to what extent this account of London low life at around the turn of the century should be seen as a straight documentary account or as fiction. See the introduction to the 1979 edition by Benny Green, pp. vii–xx. The 'typical hooligan' according to Rook, was 'a boy who, growing up in the area bounded by the Albert Embankment, the Lambeth Road, the Kennington Road, and the streets about the Oval, takes to tea leafing as a Grimsby lad takes to the sea' (p. 15). Portions of Rook's account of the career of Young Alf, the Hooligan of *Hooligan Nights*, first appeared in the *Daily Chronicle* of 1899 where they aroused considerable public outcry (see Rook's introduction to the 1899 edition, pp. xxi–xxii). On the 'original Hooligans' and the hooliganism moral panic of the late nineteenth century see also Pearson *Hooligan*, ch. 5, pp. 74–116.

8.   Note also bibliography to 1973 edition, p. xliii, for a select list of polemical pamphlets, tracts and articles occasioned by the Boer War.
9.   For the nineteenth-century antecedents of the boy-labour problem see R. H. Tawney, 'The Economics of Boy Labour', *Economic Journal*, 19 (1909), pp. 517–37. For an outline of the problem of youth unemployment in the twentieth century see M. Casson, *Youth Unemployment* (1979), ch. 2.
10.   For discussion of the boy-labour problem in the last quarter of the nineteenth century see G. Stedman-Jones, *Outcast London* (1971), pp. 69–73. On the boy-labour problem as *the* youth problem of the 1890s and 1900s see Springhall, *Coming of Age*, pp. 95–108.
11.   For a bibliography of the extensive late nineteenth- and early twentieth-century literature see A. Freeman, *Boy, Life and Labour* (1914). For a contemporary discussion see especially Tawney, 'The Economics of Boy Labour' and W. H. Beveridge, *Unemployment: A Problem of Industry* (1909), pp. 125–31 and p. 384.
12.   Quoted in A. M. Carr-Saunders *et al.*, *Young Offenders* (1942), p. 7. (Note the explicit emphasis on class subordination and control in this quotation.) Chapter 1 of this work, 'Previous Investigations' by H. Mannheim, pp. 1–32, provides a useful guide to British studies of juvenile delinquency up until the Second World War.
13.   For discussion of Morrison's *Juvenile Offenders*, see Carr-Saunders *et al.*, *Young Offenders*, pp. 9–12. For the legal construction of juvenile delinquency over the period 1850–1910 see Springhall, *Coming of Age*, pp. 164–75.
14.   See T. R. Gurr *et al.*, *The Politics of Crime and Conflict* (1977), pp. 11–115. Gurr *et al.* argue that this downturn in the various criminal statistics over the period in question represented a *real* decline in actual levels of criminality. Their reasons for this assertion are twofold: firstly because the downturn is to be discerned in all of the major statistical indicators, and secondly because the period 1870–1920 was one of *increased efficiency* in policing and the administration of justice when, other things being equal, one would expect an overall *rise* in criminal statistics (see p. 115).
15.   Figures estimated from Fig. II.3.1., Gurr *et al.*, *The Politics of Crime and Conflict*, p. 111: 'All indictable offences known to police per 100,000 London (MPD) and England and Wales, 1869–1931'.
16.   Figures from Table II.3.1. ibid., p. 114: 'Percentage Decline in Crime Indicators in London, 1869–70 to the late 1920s'.
17.   On the parallel case of the rise of the juvenile court system in the USA see A. M. Platt, *The Child Savers* (2nd edn, 1977). For a stringent critique of the Marxist framework within which Platt ultimately seeks to locate his account of the child-saving movements see J. Hagan and J. Leon, 'Rediscovering Delinquency: Social History, Political Ideology and the Sociology of Law', *American Sociological Review*, 42 (1977), pp. 587–98.

18.   For practical examples of the resistance of working-class youth to this attempted imposition see Humphries, *Hooligans or Rebels?*, pp. 130–6.

19.   For inside accounts of the harsh and repressive nature of reformatory life in the early part of this century see Humphries, *Hooligans or Rebels?*, pp. 209–39.

20.   For a discussion of the Scouts see Springhall, *Youth, Empire and Society*, ch. 3, pp. 53–70. Also for a table of comparative strengths of the various major British youth movements 1900–41 see ibid., appendix V, pp. 138–9.

21.   See B. Simon, *Education and the Labour Movement, 1870–1920* (1974), pp. 61–71. C. F. G. Masterman and several of the other contributors to *The Heart of the Empire* were at this time closely involved with the university settlement programme in London. See introduction to the 1973 edition by Bentley B. Gilbert.

22.   This work is an invaluable guide to Hall's life, work and times. See also Springhall, *Coming of Age*, pp. 28–37.

23.   For an outline of Hall's developmental psychology see R. E. Muuss, *Theories of Adolescence* (1966), pp. 13–17.

24.   There is a close parallel with the ideas of Freud here, see for example *Civilization and its Discontents* (1929).

25.   From G. S. Hall, 'The Moral and Religious Training of Children', *Princetown Review* (Jan. 1882), pp. 26–48, quoted in Demos and Demos, 'Adolescence in Historical Perspective', p. 635.

26.   For reactions to Hall's *Adolescence* see Ross, *G. Stanley Hall*, pp. 336–7.

27.   For a British example of the psychoanalytical approach to adolescent problems see M. Laufer, *Adolescent Disturbance and Breakdown* (1975).

28.   For a summary of Piaget's mature thought see B. Inhelder and J. Piaget, *The Growth of Logical Thinking from Childhood to Adolescence* (1968).

29.   See N. Kiell, *The Adolescence Through Fiction* (1959), esp. pp. 56–9. For critical discussion of the novel of adolescence from the eighteenth century onwards see also P. M. Spacks, *The Adolescent Idea* (1983).

30.   See W. Tasker Witham, *The Adolescent in the American Novel 1920–1960* (1964), p. 25. Modern English literature has been on the whole much less preoccupied with the probing of adolescent psychology, but nonetheless the period from around the turn of the century onwards has certainly seen a considerable outpouring of popular literature *for* adolescents. The writings for boys of such figures as Kipling and G. A. Henty can be located fairly directly in the cults of Empire and 'muscular Christianity' discussed above, and in the first decade of the twentieth century the public school stories of Frank Richards and his imitators seem to have enjoyed a wide and avid readership amongst youth in general. Writing of his childhood and youth in early-twentieth-century Salford

Robert Roberts has claimed that: '. . . the public school ethos, distorted into myth and sold among us weekly in penny numbers, for good or ill, set ideals and standards. This our own tutors, religious and secular, had signally failed to do. In the final estimate, it may well be found that Frank Richards during the first quarter of the twentieth century had more influence on the mind and outlook of young working-class England than any other single person, not excluding Baden-Powell. . . .'   (R. Roberts, *The Classic Slum*, p. 161).

Chapter 4

1.   (Excerpt from) Board of Education, *Final Report of the Departmental Committee on Juvenile Education After the War*, vol. 1 cd. 8512, 1917, in Van Der Eyken, *Education, the Child and Society*, p. 211.

2.   See Van Der Eyken, *Education, the Child and Society*, pp. 306–7 for an outline of proposals and overview and more especially J. S. Maclure (ed.), *Educational Documents: England and Wales 1816–1963* (1965), pp. 179–87.

3.   The aftermath and implications of the 1944 Act are discussed in many places, see e.g. Middleton and Weitzman, *A Place for Everyone*, pp. 312–85.

4.   On the high level of concern over increasing juvenile delinquency during the First World War see also Springhall, *Coming of Age*, p. 179.

5.   Figures from Springhall, *Coming of Age*, p. 45, table 'Persons under 16 charged in Juvenile Courts with Indictable Offences'.

6.   Figures from A. H. Halsey, *Trends in British Society*, pp. 527–8, table 15.1 'Judicial Statistics for Selected Years 1900–1968, England and Wales'.

7.   The overall rate of indictable offences known to the police, especially in London, but also in England and Wales as a whole has risen rapidly from around 1930 onwards, doubling between the early 1930s and 1946, and then climbing even more steeply between 1955 and 1975 (Gurr *et al.*, *The Politics of Crime and Conflict*, fig. 11.4.1., p. 159). Figures from Carr-Saunders *et al.*, *Young Offenders*, p. 45.

8.   Note, however, that the Children and Young Persons Act of 1933 raised the age ceiling of the juvenile offender category from16 to 17 years, thereby inflating the latter (1938) figures. Nonetheless separate statistics for the conviction of under-16-year-olds also reveal a very sharp increase over the same period: in the 10–14 age range the number of boys found guilty of indictable offences rose from 7,196 to 14,724 between 1931 and 1938 and in the 14–16 age range from 4,592 to 7,629 (Carr-Saunders, *et al.*, *Young Offenders*, p. 47). All in all the rapid increase in the levels of juvenile delinquency from the 1930s onwards may in some large measure

reflect an increased willingness to charge young offenders engendered by the 1933 Act itself.

9. For outline and discussion see Carr-Saunders *et al.*, *Young Offenders*, pp. 18–23. For further selective discussion see Humphries, *Hooligans or Rebels?*, pp. 150–2.

10. For an overview of studies of youth unemployment in the Depression see Casson, *Youth Unemployment*, pp. 13–18. For a contemporary analysis of youth employment (and unemployment) and for bibliography see J. Gollan, *Youth in British Industry* (1937).

11. Approximate figures calculated from Gollan, *Youth in British Industry*, p. 159, table.

12. For an outline of the findings as such of Cameron *et al.* see Casson, *Youth Unemployment*, pp. 14–16.

13. On the continuing influence of the experience of active service in the First World War on its veterans see Ronald Blythe, *The View in Winter* (1981), pp. 153–96. See also ibid. for the cult of 'lost youth' of the 1920s.

14. On the English literary-artistic 'generation' of the 1920s and 30s, see also M. Green, *Children of the Sun* (1977).

15. In post-First-World-War Britain the phenomenon of generationalism was not so much social-theoretical as literary-artistic in nature, being exemplified chiefly in the highly successful and influential output of the war poets – Sassoon, Owen *et al.* – and later the war writers – Graves, Williamson, Brittain *et al.* See Wohl, *The Generation of 1914*, pp. 105–10.

16. Note that the equation of 'youth' with 'cultural renewal' was particularly strong in early twentieth-century German social and political thought (Wohl, *The Generation of 1914*, p. 42). In the 1920s and 30s this idea was of course put to particularly effective use as a part of National Socialist ideology. In so far as it attempts to 'cut across' class divisions 'generationalism' (i.e. the tendency to analyse society in terms of generations) always contains within itself dangerously totalitarian elements. In so far as it offers a critique of mass society (the other major strand of twentieth-century generational thought) it can also be dangerously élitist. Wohl portrays the 'generationalists' (those inclined to theorize in terms of generation) of the first part of the twentieth century as chiefly urban, middle-class intellectuals with a view of themselves as representatives of the future residing in the present, and a deep sense of anxiety concerning the nature of their relation to the masses.

17. For one first-person account of the British working-class youth culture of the 1920s and the purported 'loosening' of conduct which accompanied this see R. Roberts, *The Classic Slum*, pp. 222–36.

18. For a critique of Mead's study as *anthropology* see D. Freeman, *Margaret Mead and Samoa* (1983).

19. See also W. Waller, 'The Rating and Dating Complex', *American Sociological Review* (1937), pp. 727–34.

20.   For the initial analysis of the essentially social-class differentiated nature of American High School adolescent subcultures, see A. B. Hollingshead, *Elmtown's Youth* (1961), first published in 1949.

21.   For the history of this (mis)conception in sociology and an attempt at the explanation of its roots see G. Murdock and R. McCron, 'Youth and Class: The Career of a Confusion', in G. Mungham and G. Pearson (eds) *Working Class Youth Culture* (1976), pp. 10–26.

Chapter 5

1.   But note that the response to the initial programme of evacuation was far less pronounced elsewhere: 'The Black Country sent only a quarter of its school children. Only 8% left Rotherham and only 15% went from Sheffield' (Calder, 1971: 43). For an overview of the period of mass evacuation of September 1939 to April 1940 see ibid., pp. 40–58. The major primary sources here is R. M. Titmuss, *Problems of Social Policy* (1950), one volume of the official British history of the Second World War.

2.   This line of argument was taken to what is perhaps its extreme conclusion in Jeff Nuttall, *Bomb Culture* (1970), where it was suggested that the coming of the atomic bomb had so fundamentally altered the human condition that there could be little understanding between 'pre-atomic' and 'post-atomic' generations. According to this thesis, which now seems very much the product of 1950s Cold War preoccupations and conceptions, post-war youth/pop culture was therefore at its most basic level, *bomb culture*.

3.   For a thorough contemporary critique of Wilkins see G. Prys Williams, *Patterns of Teenage Delinquency: England and Wales 1946–61* (1962). Prys Williams points out that: (*i*) for technical reasons Wilkins' statistical inferences are invalid; (*ii*) his predictions fail since delinquency did not rise in higher age groups in later years and fall in the same age group as his 'delinquency-prone' age cohort got older; (*iii*) he fails to take into account variations of delinquency rate across *type* of offence and fails to consider non-indictable offences at all; and (*iv*) childhood conditioning hypotheses neglect the social context of crime and justice, in particular the significance of cultural and 'opportunity' variables.

4.   It should be noted here that it was only the *juvenile* delinquency figures that registered a rise during the war. Such statistics as are extant in the field of adult criminality suggest falling rates. See Titmuss, *Problems of Social Policy*, pp. 340–1.

5.   A. E. Morgan, *Young Citizen* (1943), p. 7. This work is itself a summary and updating of a survey of youth commissioned in the immediate pre-war era by the King George's Jubilee Trust (A. E. Morgan, *The Needs*

of Youth (1938)). It is interesting to note in it the continuation of the essentially pre-war anxiety about youth unemployment: 'it is essential above all that boys and girls should not be allowed to fall into idleness which is the condition most apt to produce carelessness and irresponsibility, or anxiety or disappointment' (p. 32), a danger which could in part be averted through improved and expanded educational and recreational provision.

6.   The two major reports on the youth service, both of which sketch its previous history, are: Report of the Albermarle Committee (The Albermarle Report), *The Youth Service in England and Wales* (1960), and Report of the Youth Service Development Council (YSDC), *Youth and Community in the Seventies* (1969).

7.   Note however that *housing* was at this time the number one priority in the overall programme of national reconstruction, and that there were in any case severe economic constraints operative upon the proposed level and rate of educational expansion. See Middleton and Weitzman, *A Place for Everyone*, p. 320.

8.   Figures from M. Pinto-Duschinsky, 'Bread and Circuses? The Conservatives in Office 1951–1964', in V. Bogdanor and R. Skidelsky (eds), *The Age of Affluence 1951–1964* (1970), pp. 55–77.

9.   On the 'economic grounds for the raising of the school leaving age' see Ministry of Education, 1959: ch. 12, pp. 117–34.

10.   The report's terms of reference were 'to consider the education between the ages of thirteen and sixteen of pupils of average or less than average ability who are or will be following full-time courses either at schools or in establishments of further education. The term education shall be understood to include extra-curricular activities' (p. xv).

11.   Speech reported in *The Times*, 19 October 1963, p. 6.

12.   Speech made at the Town Hall, Birmingham, on 19 Jan. 1964, 'The New Britain'. Published in *The New Britain: Labour's Plan Outlined by Harold Wilson, Selected Speeches 1964* (1964), pp. 16–17.

13.   See, respectively, Report by a Subcommittee of the National Joint Advisory Council (The Carr Report), *Training for Skill: Recruitment and Training of Young Workers in Industry* (1958); Gertrude (Lady) Williams, *Recruitment to Skilled Trades* (1957); Kate Liepmann, *Apprenticeship: An Enquiry into its Adequacy under Modern Conditions* (1960); Report of the National Advisory Committee on Art and Education (The Coldstream Report) (1960); Report by the Advisory Committee on Further Education and Commerce (The McMeeking Report) (1959); *The Supply and Training of Teachers for Technical Colleges* (The Jackson Report) (1957); Report of the Committee Appointed by the Central Council for Physical Education, (The Wolfenden Report) *Sport and the Community* (1960); and Ministry of Education, *The Youth Service in England and Wales* (The Albermarle Report) (1960).

14.   See *Carr Report* (see Note 13); G. Williams, *Apprenticeship in Europe* (1963).
15.   For an early statement see Ministry of Education, Report of the Central Advisory Council for Education (England) (The Clarke Report) *School and Life: A first enquiry into the transition from school to independent life* (1947). For the 1950s and early 1960s see M. Carter, *Into Work* (1966).
16.   On the projected problem of the shortage of juvenile labour in the immediate post-war period see also Report of the Committee on the Juvenile Employment Service (The Ince Report) (1945). The latter projected a reduction in the supply of workers under eighteen by 50 per cent in the next ten years.
17.   See also G. W. Goetschius and J. M. Tash, *Working with Unattached Youth* (1967) for a similar approach to the 'problem' of unattachment.
18.   For an overview of the recent literature see Casson, *Youth Unemployment*, pp. 24–9.

Chapter 6

1.   These developments were foreshadowed in the United States: here the term 'teenager' and its equation with a distinctive pattern and style of consumption can be traced back to 1945, when Eugene Gilbert set up the Gilbert Teen Age Services marketing agency to advise firms on how best to exploit the potential of the then-burgeoning American youth market. By the mid-1950s this agency had become a multi-million-dollar concern and 'selling to youth had become big business' in the USA. (See Murdock and McCron, 'Youth and Class', in Mungham and Pearson (eds), *Working Class Youth Culture*, p. 15.) When the British youth market began to emerge in the mid-1950s it was initially exploited almost entirely through the sale of already developed American products – fashions, entertainments, soft drinks etc. – backed by American marketing experience in this particular field. (The same probably applies, although to a lesser extent, to the more general process of the exploitation of the 1950s consumer boom as a whole.) There have subsequently been periods when 'home grown' British entrepreneurship and products have been much to the fore in the tapping of the youth market – in the mid-1960s and late 1970s – but nonetheless this area has remained in many respects one that is characterized by American economic and cultural 'imperialism'. The extent to which British youth culture at a general level was, and is, (merely) imported from America has indeed been somewhat underemphasized in much of the recent British sociological literature with its focus on youth *sub*culture, its central theoretical premise of subcultural 'resistance

through rituals' and its stress on the *internal* continuities of indigenous working-class history and culture.

2.   For an overview of empirical studies demonstrating the relatively low level of income and expenditure of teenagers whilst still at school, see G. Murdock and G. Phelps, *Mass Media and the Secondary School* (1973) pp. 79–81: 'The myth of the affluent teenager'.

3.   On 'teenage classlessness' see Murdock and McCron, 'Teenagers: Harbingers of classless consumerism' in Mungham and Pearson (eds), *Working Class Youth Culture*, pp. 15–18. On gender blindness see McRobbie and Garber, 'Girls and Subcultures' in Hall and Jefferson (eds), *Resistance through Rituals*, pp. 209–22.

4.   There was in many respects a second wave in the establishment of the youth market and the commercial exploitation of 'youth' – this time employing the term in its widest sense – associated with the rise of the broadly middle-class student culture and 'Counter Culture' of the late 1960s and early 1970s. In this context the youth market became, both in terms of its age range and also its social-class range, something rather more than and apart from the original and still thriving teenage/adolescent market, and this was reflected in the nature and range of its products. On the rise of a distinctively student market, in this case for records and live music, from the late 1960s onwards, see Frith, *The Sociology of Rock*, pp. 69–71.

5.   For a statement of a similar view of teenage culture as commercially created consumer culture in the American context see J. Barnard, 'Teen-Age Culture: An Overview', *Annals*, 338 (Nov. 1961), pp. 2–12. Much the same line has on occasion been taken from an orthodox Marxist perspective, see e.g. J. Boyd 'Discussion Contribution on Trends in Youth Culture', *Marxism Today* (Dec. 1973).

6.   For a summary of these and other basic tenets of the 'new youth subcultural theory' see J. Clarke, S. Hall, T. Jefferson and B. Roberts, 'Subcultures, Cultures and Class', in Hall and Jefferson, *Resistance Through Rituals*, pp. 9–79.

7.   The concept of 'moment of originality' is advanced in J. Clarke and T. Jefferson, 'Working Class Youth Cultures', in Mungham and Pearson (eds), *Working Class Youth Culture*, pp. 138–58 (p. 148).

8.   A similar line of argument in this respect is advanced by Willis, *Learning to Labour*, pp. 36–9. For an excellent ethnography of the commercial dance-hall see G. Mungham,'Youth in Pursuit of Itself' in Mungham and Pearson (eds), *Working Class Youth Culture*, pp. 82–104.

9.   For an outline of these processes see Hebdige, *Subculture*, pp. 92–9. (The original statement here is G. Melly, *Revolt into Style* (1972)). Hebdige's analysis should nonetheless be treated with a fair measure of caution in that it still stresses heavily the idea of youth subculture and style as spontaneous creation and 'symbolic resistance'.

10.   The case of punk – and of the variable forms of sense made of it by

various social analysts and commentators – is an instructive one in this respect, exemplifying as it does (amongst a number of tangled theoretical and ideological debates) the conflict between the view which sees subculture as spontaneous creation and expression and that which sees it as the product of market and media manipulation. Two articles from *New Society* in 1977 and 1978 – the period of the punk explosion – when considered in conjunction, express this conflict of viewpoint perfectly: the former with the all-revealing title 'Dole Queue Rock' (P. Marsh, *New Society*, 20 Jan. 1977, pp. 112–14) followed the orthodoxy of the 'new subcultural theory' and analysed punk as the 'creative response' on the part of alienated working-class youth to the bleak economic and socio-cultural circumstances of the late 1970s. The latter (S. Frith, 'The Punk Bohemians', *New Society*, 19 March 1978, pp. 535–6), in reply, argued that punk was in fact right from the outset the creation of certain acute 'lumpenintellectual' cultural entrepreneurs.

11.   This essentially hypothetical argument is repeated at several points.

12.   On the 'irresponsible minority' in general see p. 31, paras. 87–9.

13.   The evidence presented below in the main text is summarized ibid., pp. 28–31, paras. 72–86.

14.   Minority Report by G. Howe and J. Stebbings. Howe and Stebbings argued that there was sufficient evidence counter to the majority recommendations (including the majority opinion of the young themselves as revealed by social survey: 'it is hard to see any reason why teenagers should be dragged kicking and screaming into the permissive atmosphere of the twenty-first century if they have no burning desire to come along') for any conclusions drawn to be wide open. They were also concerned about the high rate of break-up in teenage marriages, the rising level of juvenile delinquency and the vulnerability of youth to commercial exploitation (para. 534).

15.   This timeless quality of much of the youth question/spectacle can perhaps in part be explained with reference to Paul Rock's idea of 'news as eternal recurrence': because of the organizational constraints operative within the news media, aspects of the youth question, once established in the youth spectacle as 'news' and the topic for periodic investigation, have tended to take on a self-perpetuating life of their own as categories under which subsequent perceived events and trends in the same broad area can be subsumed for the purposes of reportage and analysis. See P. Rock 'News as Eternal Recurrence' in S. Cohen and J. Young (eds), *The Manufacture of News* (1973), pp. 73–80.

16.   On the initial reaction to the mods and rockers see A. MacGuire, 'Emancipated Reactionaries'; for an empirical study that does much to de-mythologize this topic see P. Barker 'The Margate Offenders: A Survey': both in Raison, *Youth in New Society*, pp. 109–14 and 115–27 respectively.

17. In 1956, shortly after Dean's death at the age of 24 in a car crash, François Truffaut was to write 'In James Dean, today's youth discovers itself. Less for the reasons usually advanced, violence, sadism, hysteria, pessimism, cruelty and filth [sic] than for others, infinitely more simple and commonplace: modesty of feeling, continual fantasy life, moral purity without relation to everyday morality but all the more rigorous, eternal adolescent love of tests and trials, intoxication, pride and regret at feeling oneself 'outside' society, refusal and desire to become integrated and, finally, acceptance or refusal of the world as it is' (quoted in Herndon, *James Dean*, p. 249).

18. On the widespread international hysteria surrounding the star's death and his subsequent 'cult' see Herndon, *James Dean*, pp. 235–59.

19. For critique of Coleman see, e.g., B. Berger, 'Adolescence and Beyond' *Social Problems*, 10 (1963), 394–408.

20. The classic text here is A. K. Cohen, *Delinquent Boys*. The original English application of this approach was Downes, *The Delinquent Solution*.

21. This rediscovery of class in the area of 'youth' can itself also be seen as part of the more general process of the shattering of the interrelated myths of embourgeoisement, affluence and consensus, as the economic boom of the 1950s and early 1960s gave way to the recession of the late 1960s and early 1970s. See Hall and Jefferson (eds), *Resistance Through Rituals*, pp. 21–5.

22. For an academic expression of this view see F. Musgrove, 'The Problems of Youth and the Social Structure of Society in England', *Youth and Society*, 1 (1969), 38–58, esp. 50–3. Musgrove argued that 'intergenerational conflict [in contemporary society] is a cause rather than a consequence of social change' (p. 52).

Chapter 7

1. It has been argued that it was the Teds' extreme 'sensitivity to insult' that was the immediate cause of such violence. See T. Jefferson, 'Cultural responses of the Teds', in Hall and Jefferson (eds), *Resistance Through Rituals*, pp. 81–6. For outlines and analyses – from a variety of perspectives – of the Teds as subculture and of the Teds' style and its 'meanings' see also P. Rock and S. Cohen, 'The Teddy Boy', in Bogdanor and Skidelsky, *The Age of Affluence*, pp. 288–320; Nuttall, *Bomb Culture*, pp. 25–30; Melly, *Revolt Into Style*, pp. 33–9; and Hebdige, *Subculture*, pp. 50–1.

2. For a full account of this incident and the subsequent trial see T. Parker, *The Plough Boy* (1965).

3. Rock and Cohen, 'The Teddy Boy', similarly describe how the Edwardian look was rapidly dropped by its original upper-class wearers in

the early 1950s when it began to be taken up by sectors of working-class youth and to be associated with delinquency.

4.   As Rock and Cohen have written, 'the accuracy of these melodramatic hyperboles [concerning the Teds] is not important, they may be quite unrepresentative, but the fact that they could be expressed and reported at all indicates something in the climate of the time' ('The Teddy Boy', p. 313). See also Pearson, *Hooligan*, ch. 2 and Springhall, *Coming of Age*, ch. 6.

5.   Fyvel, *The Insecure Offenders*, p. 17, table 3: 461 convictions in 1956 rising to 1,416 in 1961 in the 14–17 age group (as against 80 in 1938) and 1,248 rising to 3,005 in the 17–21 age group (as against 163 in 1938).

6.   On the sharp overall upward trend in the crime rate from 1955 onwards see Gurr *et al.*, *The Politics of Crime and Conflict*, pp. 158–9: indictable offences known to the police per 100,000 of population rose from approximately 1,200 to 5,400 over the period 1955–75 in London (MPD) and from approximately 1,000 to 3,200 over 1955–70 in England and Wales as a whole (ibid., fig. II.4.1).

7.   A similar line was being taken at around this time by analysts of juvenile delinquency and street gangs in the USA. See L. Yablonsky, *The Violent Gang* (1967) e.g., p. 21: 'The violent gang is not a new phenomenon. Yet its contemporary form reflects a brand and intensity of violence that differentiates it from earlier gang patterns'; and p. 257: 'The existence of violent gangs as a recurrent social phenomenon in many places must ultimately be related to deeper, more general disruptions in the social fabric itself'.

8.   As a reviewer of contemporary Japanese fiction remarked in *The Times* in 1956, 'Britain has her "Teddy Boys", France her "zazous" and Japan her "Tayozuku"'.

9.   For the history and 'feel' of this particular period see Booker, *The Neophiliacs*, chs 6 and 7, pp. 131–88. This work as a whole, if one disregards its highly conservative tone and curious Jungian theoretical framework, provides an invaluable surface outline of the cultural history of the 1950s and 60s. See also Hopkins, *The New Look*; Bogdanor and Skidelsky, *The Age of Affluence*, introduction, and Pinto-Duschinsky, 'Bread and Circuses?' in ibid. pp. 55–77.

10.   All the work cited in Note 9, above, alludes in one way or another to the prevalence of these key 'myths' at this time. This question is discussed more explicitly and directly however in Hall and Jefferson (eds), *Resistance Through Rituals*, introduction, esp. pp. 21–5. See also A. C. H. Smith *et al.*, *Paper Voices*, ch. 4, for the diffusion and expression of these myths in the popular press. Both texts also provide in passing an account of the way in which these myths have subsequently been 'exploded'.

11.   On the seeming establishment of a (permanent) Conservative consensus at this time see M. Abrams and R. Rose, *Must Labour Lose?* (1960). See esp. ibid. pp. 45–8 for an account of the way in which 'affluence' was

seen as moving young voters (18–24-year-olds) progressively to the Right. Abrams and Rose's survey research revealed this group as being optimistic about the future, satisfied with its jobs and chiefly preoccupied with the maintenance of its own prosperity: for these reasons it was argued that radical socialist policies were becoming ever more 'unattractive' to contemporary youth.

12. On the early history of rock and pop music, its roots and its origins, see N. Cohn, *Awopbopaloobopawopbamboom: Rock from the Beginning* (1970), and C. Gillett, *The Sound of the City* (1971).

13. In many respects the cinema was somewhat slow in capitalizing upon the emergent post-war sense of generational disjuncture and the growing idea that youth was coming to be a separate and particularly problematic age grade. Perhaps the addition of the final elements of the 'youthful energy' and 'sexual aggressiveness' associated with early rock and roll was needed to make these ideas 'gel' on a widespread scale in the popular imagination. Thus, in their perceptive and entertaining pictorial history of rock music in the cinema, Philip Jenkinson and Alan Warner argue that 'Three years were to pass between the release of *The Wild One* [in 1953] which was to set the scene and *Rock Around the Clock* which was to exploit it . . . it wasn't until *The Blackboard Jungle* in 1955 that the cinema established a dynamic link between the music revolution going on outside its own culture and the relevance of that social upheaval to its dramatization of the current scene. Bill Haley and his Comets played 'Rock Around the Clock' over the credit titles of *Blackboard Jungle* and at once the music took on a new dimension. Suddenly it had a dramatic context symbolizing all the frustrated, energetic and deprived kids in the Western world' (*Celluloid Rock* (1974), p. 10).

14. It may also have been the case that the coming of rock 'n' roll marked some kind of watershed in the consciousness and group identification of at least *some* of the younger generation themselves. Reflecting on his own youth at this time – and undoubtedly himself overstating the case – Ray Gosling put it like this: 'When Bill Haley's "Rock Around the Clock" got shown, and the first Elvis and the way Tommy Steele was all soft and stupid from the second disc he cut. It was the start of something. Everyone felt this – with the James Dean pictures and the start of the teenage thing. It was the start of a revolution' (*Sum Total*, 1962, p. 71).

15. As Cohn has written concerning the impact of rock 'n' roll on adult society: 'For the first time the concept of teenager was used as news, as a major selling point, and, in no time, everyone else was up on the bandwagon . . . Churchmen offered spiritual comfort, psychologists explained, magistrates got tough, parents panicked, businessmen got rich and rock exploded into a central issue', *Awopbopaloobopawopbamboom*, pp. 18–19.

16. For an outline of the careers and work of these performers see Cohn, *Awopbopaloobopawopbamboom*, pp. 31–51 and 58–60.

17.   In Britain especially the classic rockers never actually had a particularly pronounced impact *in terms of record sales*. Throughout the 1956–63 period the majority of number one places in the hit parade were occupied by such 'safe' mainstream British and American artists – quite a few from the pre-rock 'n' roll era – as Johnnie Ray, Tab Hunter, Lonnie Donegan, Frankie Vaughan, Perry Como, Russ Conway, The Shadows, Cliff Richard, *et al*. Characteristically the impact made by rock 'n' roll at the level of media event and moral panic was somewhat out of accord with its hold over the market. See P. and A. Fowler, 'The Log of British Hits 1955–69', pp. 148–56; and 'British Chart Toppers 1955–69', in C. Gillett, (ed.), *Rock File One* (1972). For an overview of the 'home-grown', generally second-rate and derivative, pop of the period, see Cohn, *Awopbopaloobopawopbamboom*, pp. 61–74. On the process of the youth market's becoming of central importance to the music business from the mid-1950s onwards see Frith (1978a), pp. 98–105.

18.   For often brilliant pictorial representations of almost the entire gallery of 'rock personae' over the period 1955–73, see G. Peelart and N. Cohn, *Rock Dreams* (1974).

19.   An all-time peak of 1,635 million admissions in 1946 had fallen to 1,101 million in 1956 and only 289 million in 1966. Figures from Halsey, *Trends in British Society*, p. 559, table 16.20: 'Cinema admissions and gross door takings for selected years, 1934–1966, Great Britain'. In 1960–61, 41 per cent of the 16–24 age group attended the cinema 'regularly' – i.e. once a week or more – compared with an 11 per cent overall rate of regular attendance for the entire 16–65+ age range. The comparable figures for 1968 had fallen to 18 per cent regular attendance amongst the 16–24s and only 5 per cent for the 16–65+ age range as a whole. Source: ibid., p. 560, table 16.22: 'Frequency of cinema attendance: by age, sex and social class, 1960–61 and 1968, Great Britain (percentages)'.

20.   For an account of the 1950s' obsession with all things teenage, see also Hopkins, *The New Look*, pp. 423–40.

21.   According to A. C. H. Smith *et al.*, in the *Daily Mirror* in particular the general theme of youth, along with an explicit appeal to a youthful (teenage) readership, came to be a highly prevalent feature from the mid-1950s onwards, as that paper attempted to find an authentic and valid response to the social transformations that were seemingly being wrought by the advent of affluence: 'effectively the *Mirror* conceded that affluence was eroding the old divisions and solidarities, and that society was no longer to be discussed in terms of class inequalities. Instead it increasingly tried to explain social change in terms of those whose style of life appeared most conspicuously decorated by affluence, young people' (*Paper Voices*, p. 241).

22.   The question of the *level* of pop stars' earnings was, in its own right, a much-aired topic at this time, e.g. 'Cliff Richard, the 19 year old rock 'n'

roller who *earns more than the Prime Minister*, was shaking like a jelly as he set off for America last night' (Donald Zec, *Daily Mirror*, 19 Jan. 1960), perhaps because it somehow encapsulated many fundamental perceptions concerning the 'direction' for better or worse of post-war British society.

23.   For biography see T. Gould, *Inside Outsider* (1986).

24.   This volume anthologizes many of MacInnes' articles and essays of the period, including a number dealing with aspects of the phenomenon of the Teenager.

Chapter 8

1.   For an overview see D. E. Cooper, 'Looking Back on Anger', in Bogdanor and Skidelsky, *The Age of Affluence*, pp. 254–87.

2.   For further discussion of this point and for an entertaining and illuminating account of the careers, impact and significance of the major 'Angries', see Lewis, *The Fifties*, pp. 160–9.

3.   Quotes from the back cover of C. Wilson, *The Outsider* (1971) (contains a new semi-autobiographical postscript by the author).

4.   On the Beat Generation on its native American patch, in this case the bohemian area of Venice West in Los Angeles, see L. Lipton, *The Holy Barbarians* (1959). The picture painted by Lipton of the 'beat scene' and of beat ideology pre-figures the major features of the 1960s and 70s Counter Culture in almost every respect.

5.   The best single account of the careers of the members of this group – with the exception of Norman Mailer, the odd-man-out here in terms of personal affiliation and contacts – is A. Charters, *Kerouac* (1974). For key American Beat Generation literary texts see Jack Kerouac's novel *On the Road* (1961) and Norman Mailer's essay 'The White Negro' in *Advertisements for Myself* (1970).

6.   Lewis, *The Fifties*, pp. 169–70 cites Frederic Raphael's novel *The Glittering Prizes* (1978) and Malcolm Bradbury's novel *Eating People is Wrong* (1959) as exemplifying early 1950s student life, at Oxbridge and the Redbricks respectively.

7.   For the history of early CND see Robert Taylor, 'The Campaign for Nuclear Disarmament', in Bogdanor and Skidelsky, *The Age of Affluence*, pp. 221–53.

8.   On the trad boom see Melly, *Revolt Into Style*, pp. 58–62. On the social background of CND's supporters see F. Parkin, *Middle Class Radicalism* (1968).

9.   For an interpretation of CND as a portent of 'things to come' from the historical vantage point of the late 1960s and early 1970s, see Bogdanor and Skidelsky, *The Age of Affluence*, introduction. Here the editors argue that

CND provided a 'foretaste of the new power of [extended] youth to fascinate, alarm and disrupt adult society, as well as being early symptoms of an alienation from the meritocratic, technological goals of the affluent society'. As such, it 'marked the beginning of the end of consensus' (p. 13).

10.   Charles Hamblett and Jane Deverson, *Generation X* (1964). See also Laurie, *The Teenage Revolution*. This tendency was also rife amongst the more academic studies of youth conducted at this time, see e.g. E. M. and M. Eppel, 'Adolescent Values', 'Teenage Values' and 'Teenage Idols' in Raison (ed.), *Youth in* New Society, pp. 15–34 and 45–53.

11.   The idea of the affluence of the 'rioters' and therefore of their supposed indifference to monetary penalties was a widespread myth at this time, as is further borne out by Cohen's account in *Folk Devils and Moral Panics* of the currency of the apocryphal story of the '£50 cheque' that one mod was alleged to have immediately offered upon being fined.

12.   See Hebdige, *Subculture*, p. 90. On the London Carnaby Street/mod scene, see also pieces by Tom Wolfe in the *Pump House Gang* (1969).

13.   See e.g. the description of mid-1960s teenagers in Hamblett and Deverson, *Generation X*, and Laurie, *The Teenage Revolution*.

14.   As Dick Hebdige has written in preface to his analysis of 'the meaning of mod' as youth subculture, 'like most primitive vocabularies, each word of Wolverine, the universal Pop Newspeak, is a prime symbol and serves a dozen or a hundred functions of communication. Thus "mod" came to refer to several distinct styles, being essentially an umbrella term used to cover everything which contributed to the recently launched myth of "swinging London" . . . Thus groups of art-college students following in Mary Quant's footsteps and developing a taste for the outrageous in clothing were technically "mods", and Lord Snowdon earned the epithet when he appeared in a polo necked sweater and was hastily grouped with the "new breed" of "important people" like Bailey and Terence Stamp who showed a "swinging" disregard for certain dying conventions', (p. 87).

15.   On the career of the Beatles see Cohn, *Awopbopaloobopawopbamboom*, pp. 129–46; Gillett (1971), pp. 307–16 and Melly, *Revolt Into Style*, pp. 67–82 and 106–28.

16.   On the expanding market base for pop and rock music in the 1960s and 70s in Britain see Frith, *The Sociology of Rock*, pp. 98–105.

17.   On the career and impact of Mary Quant see Melly, *Revolt Into Style*, pp. 145–8.

18.   See ibid., pp. 9–22 for Labour's proposed programme of 'social reconstruction'.

19.   As Hall *et al.* have remarked, themselves perhaps somewhat hyperbolically, concerning the image presented by Jagger in the media at this time, 'no figure was more designed to fit the stereotype and trigger moral alarm: overtly if androgynously sexual, flamboyant, hedonistic – and guilty', *Policing the Crisis*, p. 240.

20. On the diversity of the Counter Culture and the consequent inadequacy of the term 'subculture' in this respect see Hall and Jefferson (eds), *Resistance Through Rituals*, pp. 57–71. On the eventually fatal conflicts and contradictions within the 'movement' as a whole see J. Young, 'The Hippie Solution', in L. Taylor and I. Taylor (eds), *Politics and Deviance* (1973).

21. For a sociological analysis of the original American hippy phenomenon see Stuart Hall, 'The Hippies: An American "Moment"', in Julian Nagel (ed.), *Student Power* (1969). For ethnography see L. Yablonsky, *The Hippy Trip* (1973).

22. Anthologized, with other pieces of contemporary journalism on the hippies in *Time* in J. D. Brown (ed.), *The Hippies* (1967), pp. 1–13, (p. 1).

23. For restatement and discussion of this then widely advanced line of argument see Young, *The Drugtakers*. The author concludes 'The hippies were ill advised in that they sought change through individual revolution alone, and inaccurate in that they generalized from their upper-middle class world of affluence to the rest of society. They were not unrealistic however in their sensing the imminent potential of advanced societies for providing material abundance and the concomitant changes in social relationships and industrial consciousness which such a change would facilitate' (p. 205).

24. For sympathetic adult commentary see T. Roszak, *The Making of a Counter Culture* (1970) and C. Reich, *The Greening of America* (1970); for a specifically British 'adult' statement of the same view see Musgrove, *Ecstasy and Holiness*. For 'movement' self-perceptions embodying aspects of this view see R. Neville, *Playpower* (1971) (cultural), and R. Blackburn and P. Cockburn (eds), *Student Power* (1969) (new left/political).

25. On the escalating conflict between the Counter Culture and the agents and agencies of social control over the period 1967–72 and on the consequent politicization of the former see Hall *et al.*, *Policing The Crisis*, pp. 238–60 and 291–3.

26. For inside accounts of the 'troubles' at Essex, Hornsey and Hull see T. Fawthrop, Tim Nairn and David Triesman, 'Three Student Risings' in C. Oglesby (ed.), *The New Left Reader* (1969), pp. 274–89. For an account of the LSE 'troubles' of the period from the side of the college administration see H. Kidd, *The Trouble at LSE* (1969).

27. See K. Keniston, *The Young Radicals* (1968), the sequel to the same author's earlier study of *The Uncommitted*.

28. Hall *et al.* suggest that the media-generated moral panic was in this instance itself a part of the social control response.

29. See respectively L. S. Feuer, *The Conflict of Generations* (1969); Bryan Wilson, *The Youth Culture and the Universities* (1970); Musgrove,

'The Problem of Youth'; Blackburn and Cockburn (eds), *Student Power*, and Neville, *Playpower*.

Conclusion

1.   For further analysis of Skinhead style see J. Clarke, 'The Skinheads and the Magical Recovery of Community', and D. Hebdige, 'Reggae, Rastas and Rudies', both in Hall and Jefferson, *Resistance Through Rituals*, pp. 99–102; 135–54.

2.   On the genesis of football hooliganism see I. Taylor, 'Soccer Consciousness and Soccer Hooliganism' in S. Cohen (ed.), *Images of Deviance* (1979), pp. 134–64; Chas Critcher, 'Football Since the War', in J. Clarke, C. Critcher and R. Johnson (eds), *Working Class Culture* (1980), pp. 161–84. For ethnography see Marsh *et al.*, *The Rules of Disorder*.

3.   On the changing face of the football hooligan see Steve Redhead and Eugene McLaughlin, 'Soccer's Style Wars', *New Society*, 16 August 1985.

4.   On the elevation of the 'black mugger' to folk devil status see Hall, *et al.*, *Policing the Crisis*. On the media image of the 'inner city rioter' and its associated racism see David Rose, 'I was there in Fleet Street's Tribal Bloodbath', *Guardian*, 16 September 1985.

5.   For post-skinhead working-class youth groupings see P. Cohen, 'Subcultural Conflict' and Ian Taylor and David Wall, 'Beyond the Skinheads', in Mungham and Pearson, *Working Class Youth Culture*, pp. 105–23.

6.   On the 'media events' accompanying the emergence of punk and the Sex Pistols and subsequent media responses, see Hebdige, *Subculture*, p. 93.

7.   For contemporary analysis of 'Acid House' see e.g. Marek Kohn, 'Musical Peace and Love Under Clouds of Dry Ice', *The Independent*, 7 November 1988. For the gathering control response see 'Police Arrest 56 in "Acid House" Raids' ibid.

8.   On the mood of students in the 1980s see Sarah F. Green, 'Where Have All the Sit-ins Gone?', *Guardian*, 28 November 1984.

9.   For an attempt at an overview see A. H. Halsey, *Changes in British Society* (1986).

10.   See e.g. R. A. Nisbet, *The Sociological Tradition* (1970).

11.   See Krishan Kumar, *Prophecy and Progress* (1978).

Bibliography

Abrams, Mark (1959), *The Teenage Consumer*.

(1961), *Teenage Consumer Spending in 1959*.

Abrams, Mark and Richard Rose (1960), *Must Labour Lose?*.

Abrams, Philip and Alan Little (1965a), 'The Young Activist in British Politics', *British Journal of Sociology*, 16, pp. 315–32.

(1965b), 'The Young Voter in British Politics', *British Journal of Sociology*, 16, pp. 95–110.

Anderson, Michael (1971), *Family Structure in Nineteenth Century Lancashire*.

(ed.) (1980), *Sociology of the Family*, 2nd edn.

Aries, Philippe (1973), *Centuries of Childhood*.

Bagot, J. H. (1941), *Juvenile Delinquency*.

Barnard, Jessie (1961), 'Teenage Culture: An Overview', *Annals*, 338 (Nov.).

Becker, Howard S. (ed.) (1966), *Social Problems: A Modern Approach*.

Berger, Benet (1963), 'Adolescence and Beyond', *Social Problems*, 10, pp. 394–408.

Beveridge, W. H. (1909), *Unemployment: A Problem of Industry*.

Blackburn, R. and P. Cockburn (eds) (1969), *Student Power*.

Bogdanor, Vernon and Robert Skidelsky (eds) (1970), *The Age of Affluence 1951–1964*.

Booker, Christopher (1970), *The Neophiliacs*.

Booth, Charles (1902), *Life and Labour of the People of London*, final volume.

Boyd, J. (1973), 'Discussion Contribution on Trends in Youth Culture', *Marxism Today* (Dec.).

Brown, Joe David (ed.) (1967), *The Hippies*.

Burke, Peter (1978), *Popular Culture in Early Modern Society*.

Burt, Cyril (1925), *The Young Delinquent*.

Calder, Angus (1971), *The People's War*.

Calvocoressi, Peter (1979), *The British Experience 1945–1975*.

Cameron, C., A. Lush and G. Meara (1943), *Disinherited Youth: A Report* on the 18+ *Age Group Enquiry Prepared for the Trustees of the Carnegie United Kingdom Trust*.

Carr-Saunders, A. M., Herbert Mannheim and E. C. Rhodes (1942), *Young Offenders*.

Carter, Michael (1966), *Into Work*.

Casson, Mark (1979), *Youth Uemployment*.

Charters, Ann (1974), *Kerouac*.

Clarke, J., C. Crichter and R. Johnson (eds) (1980), *Working Class Culture*.

Coffield, Frank, Carol Borrill and Sarah Marshall (1986), *Growing up at the Margins*.

Cohen, A. K. (1955), *Delinquent Boys*.

Cohen, P. (1972), 'Subcultural Conflict and Working Class Community', *University of Birmingham Working Papers in Cultural Studies*, 2.

Cohen, Stanley (1980), *Folk Devils and Moral Panics*, first published in 1972.

  (ed.) (1979), *Images of Deviance*.

Cohen, S. and J. Young (eds) (1973), *The Manufacture of News*.

Cohn, Nik (1970), *Awopbopaloobopawopbamboom: Rock from the Beginning*.

Coleman, James S. (1962), *The Adolescent Society*.

Coleman, John C. (1980), *The Nature of Adolescence*.

Committee on the Age of Majority (1967), *Report* (The Latey Report).

Corrigan, Paul (1979), *Schooling the Smash Street Kids*.

CSO (Central Statistical Office), *Annual Abstract of Statistics* (various yearly volumes).

Curtis, S. J. (1968), *History of Education in Great Britain*.

Davis, John (1982), *The Favourite Age: The Origins and Rise to Prominence of the Concepts of Adolescence and Youth with Special Reference to the 'Cult of Youth' in Post-War British Society* (unpublished PhD thesis, University of Essex).

Davis, Kingsley (1935), *Youth in the Depression*.

Davis, Natalie Zemon (1971), 'The Reasons of Misrule: Youth Groups and Charivaris in Sixteenth Century France', *Past and Present*, 50 (Feb.).

deMause, L. (1974), *The History of Childhood*.

Demos, J. and V. Demos (1969), 'Adolescence in Historical Perspective', *Journal of Marriage and the Family*, 31 (Nov.), pp. 632–8.

Douglas, J. W. B. (1964), *The Home and the School*.

Douvan, Elizabeth and Joseph Adelson (1966), *The Adolescent Experience*.

Downes, David (1966), *The Delinquent Solution*.

Earisman, Delbert L. (1968), *Hippies in Our Midst*.

Eisenstadt, S. N. (1956), *From Generation to Generation*.

Encyclopaedia Britannica, 11th edn (1910), anonymous articles on 'Adolescence' and 'Child'.

Eppel, E. M. and M. Eppel (1966), *Adolescents and Morality*.

Erikson, Erik H. (ed.) (1963), *Youth: Change and Challenge*.

(1974), *Identity: Youth and Crisis*.

(1975), *Childhood and Society*, first published in 1950.

Evans-Pritchard, E. E. (1940), *The Nuer*.

Feuer, Lewis S. (1969), *The Conflict of Generations*.

Floud, J., A. H. Halsey and F. M. Martin (1956), *Social Class and Educational Opportunity*.

Fogelman, Ken (ed.) (1976), *Britain's Sixteen-Year-Olds*.

Fowler, Peter and Annie Fowler (1972), 'The Log of British Hits 1955–69' and 'British Chart Toppers 1955–69' in Gillett (ed.) (1972).

Freeman, A. (1914), *Boy, Life and Labour*.

Freeman, D. (1983), *Margaret Mead and Samoa*.

Freud, S. (1929), *Civilization and its Discontents*.

Friedenberg, Edgar Z. (1959), *The Vanishing Adolescent*.

(1963), 'The Image of the Adolescent Minority', *Dissent*, 10, no. 2 (Spring).

Frith, Simon (1978a), *The Sociology of Rock*.

Frith, Simon (1978b), 'The Punk Bohemians', *New Society* (19 March).

Fyvel, T. R. (1963), *The Insecure Offenders*.

Gessel, Arnold, Frances L. Ilg and Louise Bates (1965), *Youth: The Years From Ten to Sixteen*.

Gillett, Charlie (1971), *The Sound of the City*.

(ed.) (1972), *Rock File One*.

Gillis, John R. (1974), *Youth and History*.

(1975), 'The Evolution of Juvenile Delinquency in England 1890–1914', *Past and Present*, 66–9.

Goetschius, George W. and John M. Tash (1967), *Working with Unattached Youth*.

Gollan, John (1937), *Youth in British Industry*.

Goodman, P. (1970), *Growing up Absurd*.

Gosling, Ray (1962), *Sum Total*.

Gould, Tony (1986), *Inside Outsider*.

Green, Martin (1977), *Children of the Sun*.

Gurr, Ted Robert, Peter N. Grabosky and Richard C. Hula (1977), *The Politics of Crime and Conflict*.

Hagan, John H. and J. Leon (1977), 'Rediscovering Delinquency: Social History, Political Ideology and the Sociology of Law', *American Sociological Review*, 42, pp. 587–98.

Hall, G. Stanley (1907), *Adolescence*.

Hall, S. and T. Jefferson (eds) (1976), *Resistance Through Rituals*.

Hall, S., C. Critcher, T. Jefferson, J. Clarke and B. Roberts (1978), *Policing the Crisis*.

Halsey, A. H. (1986), *Change in British Society*.

(ed.) (1972), *Trends in British Society Since 1900*.

Hamblett, Charles and Jane Deverson (1964), *Generation X*.

Hargreaves, David (1967), *Social Relations in a Secondary School*.

Hawkes, Terence (1972), *Metaphor*.

Hebdige, Dick (1979), *Subculture: The Meaning of Style*.

Henderson-Stewart, Frank (1977), *Fundamentals of Age-Group Systems*.

Herndon, V. (1974), *James Dean: A Short Life*.

Hobsbawm, E. and N. Rudé (1972), *Captain Swing*.

Hoggart, Richard (1968), *The Uses of Literacy*.

Hollingshead, August B. (1961), *Elmtown's Youth*, first published in 1949.

Hollis, A. C. (1909), *The Nandi*.

Hopkins, Harry (1963), *The New Look*.

Humphries, Stephen (1981), *Hooligans or Rebels?*.

Hynes, Samuel (1972), *The Auden Generation*.

Inhelder, B. and J. Piaget (1968), *The Growth of Logical Thinking from Childhood to Adolescence*.

Jenkinson, Philip and Alan Warner (1974), *Celluloid Rock*.

Johnson, Richard (1970), 'Educational Policy and Social Control in Early Victorian England', *Past and Present*, 49.

Keniston, Kenneth (1960), *The Uncommitted*.

(1968), *The Young Radicals*.

Kerouac, J. (1961), *On the Road*.

Kett, Joseph (1971), 'Adolescence and Youth in Nineteenth Century America', *Journal of Interdisciplinary History*, 2, no. 2 (Autumn), pp. 284–98.

Kidd, H. (1969), *The Trouble at LSE*.

Kiell, Norman (1959), *The Adolescent Through Fiction*.

Kitwood, Tom (1980), *Disclosures to a Stranger*.

Kumar, K. (1978), *Prophecy and Progress*.

Lacey, Colin (1970), *Hightown Grammar*.

Laufer, Moses (1975), *Adolescent Disturbance and Breakdown*.

Laurie, Peter (1965), *The Teenage Revolution*.

Leeson, Cecil (1917), *The Child and the War*.

Levin, Bernard (1970), *The Pendulum Years*.

Lewis, Peter (1978), *The Fifties*.

Liepmann, Kate (1960), *Apprenticeship: An Enquiry into its Adequacy under Modern Conditions*.

Lipton, Lawrence (1959), *The Holy Barbarians*.

Lucy, Geoffrey (1964), 'The World's Wild Youth', *Reader's Digest* (Nov.), pp. 43–50.

Lynd, Robert and Helen Lynd (1956), *Middletown*.

MacInnes, Colin (1961), *England, Half English*.
  (1972, first publ. 1959), *Absolute Beginners*.
Maclure, J. Stuart (ed.) (1965), *Educational Documents: England and Wales 1816–1963*.
Mailer, Norman (1970), 'The White Negro', in *Advertisements for Myself*.
Mannheim, Karl (1952), 'The Problem of Generations' in *Essays in the Sociology of Knowledge*.
Marsh, Peter (1977), 'Dole Queue Rock', *New Society*, 20 Jan.
Marsh, Peter, Elizabeth Rosser and Rom Harré (1978), *The Rules of Disorder*.
Masterman, C. F. G. (ed.) (1973), *The Heart of Empire*, originally published in 1901.
Matza, David (1961), *'Subterranean Traditions of Youth'*, *Annals*, 338 (Nov.), pp. 103–18.
Mead, Margaret (1973), *Coming of Age in Samoa*.
Melly, George (1972), *Revolt Into Style*.
Middleton, Nigel and Sophia Weitzman (1976), *A Place for Everyone*.
'Miles' (General Sir Frederick Maurice) (1902), 'Where to Get Men', *Contemporary Review*, 81.
Ministry of Education (1947), *School and Life: A first enquiry into the transition from school to independent life* (Clarke Report).
  (1954), *Early Leaving* (Report of Central Advisory Council).
  (1959), *15 to 18* (Crowther Report).
  (1960), *The Youth Service in England and Wales* (Albermarle Report).
  (1963a), *Half Our Future* (Newsom Report).
  (1963b), *Higher Education: Report*, Cd. 2154 (Robbins Report).
Morgan, A. E. (1943), *Young Citizen*.
Morse, Mary (1965), *The Unattached*.
Mungham, Geoff and Geoff Pearson (eds) (1976), *Working Class Youth Culture*.
Murdock, Graham and Robin McCron (1976), 'Youth and Class: The Career of a Confusion' in Mungham and Pearson (eds) (1976).
Murdock, Graham and Guy Phelps (1973), *Mass Media and the Secondary School*.
Musgrove, Frank (1964), *Youth and the Social Order*.
  (1969), 'The Problem of Youth in the Social Structure of England and Wales', *Youth and Society*, 1, pp. 38–58.
  (1974), *Ecstacy and Holiness*.
Muuss, Rolf E. (1966), *Theories of Adolescence*.
Nagel, Julian (ed.) (1969), *Student Power*.
Neville, Richard (1971), *Playpower*.
Nicholson, John (1980), *Seven Ages*.
Nuttall, Jeff (1970), *Bomb Culture*.
Offer, Daniel (1969), *The Psychological World of the Teenager*.

Ogelsby, Carl (1969), *The New Left Reader*.

Ortega y Gasset, José (1959), *Man and Crisis*.

Parker, Howard (1974), *View from the Boys*.

Parker, Tony (1965), *The Ploughboy*.

Parkin, Frank (1968), *Middle Class Radicalism*.

Parsons, Talcott (1954), 'Age and Sex in the Social Structure of the United States', in *Essays in Sociological Theory*.

Pearson, Geoffrey (1983), *Hooligan*.

Peelart, Guy and Nik Cohn (1974), *Rock Dreams*.

Penycate, John (1988), 'The Generation Game', *The Listener*, 8 Dec., pp. 28–9.

Perry, C. C. (1901), 'Our Undisciplined Brains: The War Test', *Nineteenth Century and After* (Dec.).

Pilgrim Trust (1938), *Men Without Work*.

Pinchbeck, Ivy and Margaret Hewitt (1969), (1973), *Children and English Society*, (vol. 1, 1969; vol. 2, 1973).

Pinto-Duschinsky, Michael (1970), 'Bread and Circuses? The Conservatives in Office 1951–1964', in Bogdanor and Skidelsky (eds) (1970).

Platt, Anthony M. (1977), *The Child Savers*, 2nd edn.

Pollock, Linda A. (1983), *Forgotten Children*.

Prys Williams, G. (1962), *Patterns of Teenage Delinquency: England and Wales 1946–61*.

Radcliffe-Brown, A. R. (1929), 'Age Organisation Terminology', *Man*, 12–14 (Jan.).

Raison, T. (ed.) (1966), *Youth in New Society*.

Redhead, Steve and Eugene McLaughlin (1985), 'Soccer's Style Wars', *New Society*, 16 Aug.

Reich, Charles (1970), *The Greening of America*.

Robbins, D. and P. Cohen (1978), *Knuckle Sandwich*.

Roberts, E. (1975), 'Learning and Living: Socialisation Outside the School', *Oral History*, 3 (Autumn).

Roberts, R. (1977), *The Classic Slum*.

Rock, Paul and Stanley Cohen (1970), 'The Teddy Boy' in Bogdanor and Skidelsky (1970).

Rook, Clarence (1979), *The Hooligan Nights*, originally published in 1899.

Roscoe, Sir H. E. (1901), 'The Outlook for British Trade', *Monthly Review* (May).

Ross, Dorothy (1972), *G. Stanley Hall: The Psychologist as Prophet*.

Roszak, Theodor (1970), *The Making of a Counter Culture*.

Rousseau, Jean Jacques (1974), *Émile*, first published 1762.

Russell, C. E. B. (1910), *Young Gaol-Birds*.

    (1932), *Lads' Clubs*, first published 1908.

Sheehy, Gail (1977), *Passages*.

Sherif, Muzafer and Carolyn W. Sherif (eds) (1965), *Problems of Youth*.

Shorter, Edward (1977), *The Making of the Modern Family*.

Simon, Brian (1974), *Education and the Labour Movement 1870–1920*.

Smith, A. C. H., T. Blackwell and E. Immirzi (1975), *Paper Voices*.

Smith, S. R. (1973), 'The London Apprentices as Seventeenth Century Adolescents', *Past and Present*, 61.

(1975), 'Religion and the Conception of Youth in Seventeenth Century England', *History of Childhood Quarterly*, 2, parts 3–4, pp. 493–516.

Spacks, P. M. (1983), *The Adolescent Idea*.

Springhall, John (1977), *Youth, Empire and Society*.

(1986), *Coming of Age: Adolescence in Britain 1860–1960*.

Stedman-Jones, Gareth (1971), *Outcast London*.

Stone, Lawrence (1967), *The Crisis of the Aristocracy 1558–1641*.

(1977), *The Family, Sex and Marriage in England 1500–1800*.

Sugarman, Barry (1967), 'Involvement in Youth Culture, Academic Achievement and Conformity in School', *British Journal of Sociology*, 18, pp. 151–64.

Tanner, J. M. (1962), *Growth at Adolescence*.

Tawney, R. H. (1909), 'The Boy Labour Problem', *Economic Journal*, 19, pp. 517–37.

Taylor, L. and I. Taylor (eds) (1973), *Politics and Deviance*.

Thomas, Michael and Jane Perry (1975), 'National Voluntary Youth Organisations', *PEP Broadsheet*, 41, no. 550.

Thompson, E. P. (1977), 'Happy Families', *New Society*, 8 Sept.

Thompson, Paul (1975), 'The War With Adults', *Oral History*, 3 (Autumn).

(1979), *The Edwardians*.

Thrasher, Frederic (1963), *The Gang*, first published in 1927.

Titmuss, Richard M. (1950), *Problems of Social Policy*.

Van Der Eyken, Willem (ed.) (1973), *Education, the Child and Society*.

Vigne, Thea (1975), 'Parents and Children 1890–1918: Distance and Dependence', *Oral History*, 3 (Autumn).

Waller, Willard (1937), 'The Rating and Dating Complex', *American Sociological Review*, pp. 727–34.

White, Arnold (1972), *Efficiency and Empire*, first published in 1901.

Wicks, Malcolm (1988), 'Demographic Dreams', *New Society and Statesman*, 19 Aug., pp. 26–7.

Wilkins, Leslie T. (1960), *Delinquent Generations*.

Williams, Gertrude (Lady) (1957), *Recruitment to Skilled Trades*.

(1963), *Apprenticeship in Europe*.

Willis, P. (1978), *Learning to Labour*.

Wilson, Bryan (1970), *Youth Culture and the Universities*.

Wilson, Colin (1971), *The Outsider*.

Wilson, Harold (1964), *The New Britain: Labour's Plan Outlined*.

Wilson, Monica (1970), *Good Company: A Study of Nyakyusa Age Villages*, first published 1951.

Witham, W. Tasker (1964), *The Adolescent in the American Novel 1920–1960*.
Wohl, Robert (1979), *The Generation of 1914*.
Wolfe, Tom (1969), *The Pump-House Gang*.
Workers' Educational Association (1960), *The Leisure Activities of School-children*.
Yablonsky, Lewis (1967), *The Violent Gang*.
   (1973), *The Hippy Trip*.
Young, Jock (1972), *The Drugtakers*.
YSCD (Youth Service Development Council) (1969), *Youth and Community Work in the Seventies* (Report).
Zweig, Ferdynand (1963), *The Student in an Age of Anxiety*.

Index